T · H · E
100
BEST STOCKS TO OWN
IN THE
WORLD
GENE WALDEN

Dearborn
Financial Publishing, Inc.

For Richard and Phyllis Blake

Publisher: Kathleen A. Welton
Senior Project Editor: Jack L. Kiburz
Cover Design: Anthony Russo
Photograph Back Cover: Dell Gross and Doug Davis

Published by Dearborn Financial Publishing, Inc.

Printed in the United States of America

91 92 93 10 9 8 7 6 5 4 3 2 1

Library of Congress Cataloging-in-Publication Data

Walden, Gene.
  The 100 best stocks to own in the world / Gene Walden.
    p. cm.
  Includes index.
  ISBN 0-7931-0124-7
  1. Stocks. 2. Investments, Foreign. I. Title. II. Title: One hundred best stocks to own in the world.
HG4661.W315 1990
332.63'22—dc20   90-13886
                                                                        CIP

TABLE OF CONTENTS

ACKNOWLEDGMENTS

This book was made possible only through the help of a long list of people who were willing to share their ideas and insights on the global market.

Three individuals deserve special mention:

Henry Herbring of Wright Investors' Service steered me through many of the technical aspects of the international market, gave me some excellent, ongoing advice on presenting the material in the most pertinent fashion and worked overtime to keep my mailbox filled with the latest research on several hundred of the leading corporations in the world.

Bill Griffis of CompuStat also worked overtime—and a couple of weekends—running financial screens on the CompuStat database to come up with a list of the world's fastest-growing companies. And when I needed to dig out some additional financial data on a couple dozen companies, he worked nights to pull it for me.

Finally, without John Hogan, who came to my aid in the final months of the project as a research assistant, there would be no book. He dug through data sheets and company reports, crunched numbers, sent letters, made calls and kept the whole project alphabetized, organized and up to speed.

A handful of others also deserve special thanks, including Tom Keyes and David Miller, coauthors of *The Global Investor,* who helped steer me in the right direction; Gavin Dobson of Murray Johnstone International and Kathy Soule of Merrill-Lynch, who answered some tough questions down the stretch; and Kathleen Welton, publisher, Dearborn Financial Publishing, who first suggested the idea of a global stock guide.

PREFACE

Listen closely and perhaps you'll hear it: it's the rumble of walls crumbling, the jingle of deutsche marks changing hands, the sizzle of Big Macs on the grill; it's the whirl of satellites, the clatter of voting machines, the deafening roar of human voices speaking freely. What is it? It's the sound of the earth shrinking, compressing, melding into a single global community.

No one could have foreseen the phenomenal pace of change that ushered in the 1990s. But the transformation seems irreversible. A single Germany; a stock exchange in Budapest; an entire Communist-bred culture in Poland, in Czechoslovakia, even in the Union of Soviet Socialist Republics, trudging intrepidly toward a free market economy.

Other changes also loom on the horizon. Europe is set to shed its internal trade barriers by the end of 1992, forming the world's single largest capitalist market. Japan is reluctantly opening its market to a swell of imports. North and South Korea have initiated preliminary talks aimed at a possible reunification. Even Vietnam has hinted that it may be edging toward capitalism.

For years, international investments have offered exceptional growth potential. Today—with new markets opening up from one corner of the globe to the other—that potential is greater than ever. And thanks to a financial services industry that has become increasingly accommodating toward the global investor, opportunities abound for the small investor.

How can you cash in on the global boom? That's the purpose of this book—to help bring the world of investment opportunities to your doorstep. You'll learn how to buy foreign stocks (they're just a phone call away), how to research and track your investments and how to make wise buying and selling decisions. You'll learn about the major foreign markets and the top international mutual funds, and, of course, you'll get a detailed overview of 100 of the world's best stocks. It's all designed to broaden your world of opportunity—even on a planet that's getting smaller by the day.

THE 100 BEST STOCKS
TO OWN IN THE WORLD
(Numerical Ranking)

Company	Rating Points
1. Banco Popular Español (Spain)	24
2. Mayne Nickless (Australia)	24
3. KNP (The Netherlands)	23
4. Brambles (Australia)	23
5. Philip Morris (U.S.)	23
6. Hong Kong & China Gas (Hong Kong)	23
7. BTR Nylex (Australia)	22
8. Irvin & Johnson (South Africa)	22
9. Rothman Holdings (Australia)	22
10. Newell (U.S.)	22
11. Hang Lung Development (Hong Kong)	22
12. Merck (U.S.)	22
13. Bührmann-Tetterode	22
14. Wolseley (U.K.)	22
15. Higgs and Hill (U.K.)	22
16. Glaxo Holdings (U.K.)	22
17. CMB Packaging (France)	21
18. Wm. Wrigley Jr. (U.S.)	21
19. Email (Australia)	21
20. Adelaide Steamship (Australia)	21
21. Wal-Mart Stores (U.S.)	21
22. Reuters (U.K.)	21
23. Jardine Matheson (Hong Kong)	21
24. Tarmac (U.K.)	21
25. Trelleborg (Sweden)	20
26. Shaw Industries (U.S.)	20

Introduction

The woman obviously had her mind made up. "I don't want to hear about it!" She covered her ears and turned her head away. "Don't say another word. Not another word. There is no way I will ever invest a penny in foreign stocks."

"Just two reasons," I begged. "If I can't convince you with two reasons, you can go buy your T-bills or your muni-bonds or whatever your broker puts in front of you. I promise I won't say another word."

"All right," she conceded, "just two reasons. But it won't change my mind."

I gave my reasons—offered my logic—and looked for her reaction.

"Hmmm," she pondered, lightening up, "maybe I'll stick $10,000 into a foreign stock fund."

True story.

What did I tell her? What two reasons could turn even the most skeptical, most conservative investor into an instant convert to the global stock market? The answer: safety and superior performance. What better reasons are there, after all, for selecting any investment?

SAFETY

You might have considered "safety" one reason *not* to invest in foreign stocks. There's a natural apprehension of the unknown, a fear that when you send your money overseas, you may never see it again.

But the fact is that an international portfolio gives you broader diversity and greater safety. If you're an American and your money is invested only in

U.S. stocks, when the market goes down, your entire portfolio drops with it. By spreading your money around the world, when your U.S. stocks are declining, your foreign stocks may be moving up. To wit: through the first six months of 1990, of the nine major stock markets around the world, four markets were up, four were down and one was about even.

PERFORMANCE

As well as the U.S. market has performed in recent years, it continues to rank in the lower half of the world's stock markets in terms of total return to shareholders. Non-U.S. stocks rose, on average, 18 percent per year during the 20-year period through 1988—about 70 percent faster than the 10.8 percent average annual gain of the U.S. stock market. In dollar terms, a $10,000 investment in the U.S. market in 1969 would have grown to $77,000 by 1989. The same investment in the broad world market would have grown to $280,000.

That trend could continue as long as economies elsewhere around the world continue to expand faster than the maturing U.S. economy.

"Not one year since 1960 has the U.S. market been the best performing market in the world," reports Gavin Dobson, president of Murray Johnstone International, which operates the Phoenix International Fund. "In 1970, U.S. companies accounted for nearly 70 percent of the world's total market capitalization (the total dollar value of all publicly traded stocks). Today it accounts for only about 34 percent."

While past performance is no guarantee of future success, the superior long-term performance of the international market makes a strong case for investing at least a portion of your assets abroad.

BEYOND SAFETY AND PERFORMANCE

Safety and performance are probably the best reasons for investing abroad, but they're not the only ones.

Some investors enjoy the educational aspect of global investing: put some money in the Singapore market and you're likely to develop a sudden interest in Singapore. "That adds a lot of fun to investing," says Thomas Keyes, coauthor of *The Global Investor*. "While you're following your stocks, you're also learning more about the countries. I find I'm more alive, more interested in the markets."

Panache is another hook. Watch heads turn at your next cocktail party when you nonchalantly mention that you "picked up a few shares of L'Oreal, some China Light and Power and a block of Yamanouchi Pharmaceutical."

But one of the best dollars-and-cents reasons for investing abroad is that it broadens your options. "The fact is," says Dobson, "if you want to construct a portfolio of the best stocks traded in the world, you have to trade outside the U.S. market. Only about 20 percent of the major blue-chip stocks in the world are U.S. companies."

THE DOWNSIDE TO GLOBAL INVESTING

Just as there are some excellent reasons to put your money in the international market, there are some equally convincing arguments for keeping a close watch on the money you do invest abroad:

- Currency risk. As if investing in stocks isn't precarious enough, foreign stocks add one more twist to the equation. With foreign stocks, there are three good ways to lose money: if the stock market goes down (pulling your stocks down with it), if your company has an off-year and if the currency of the country where your stock is issued takes a beating relative to the dollar.

    The flip side, of course, is that there are also three good ways for your stocks to go up: if the market moves up, if your stocks continue to show good earnings growth and if the country's currency goes up relative to the dollar. The long-term trend has been a weakening of the dollar relative to other currencies—a favorable development for overseas investors.

- Lack of information. Tracking foreign stocks can be difficult unless you know where to look. But even if you have good sources, the information you receive may still be inadequate. Reporting rules vary from one country to the next. The United States is one of the few countries that require quarterly earnings reports. Some countries ask companies to report earnings only once a year—and those reports often come out many months after the fiscal year-end.

    On the other hand, you may well find that researching foreign stocks is actually easier than you had anticipated. Of the several hundred annual reports I reviewed in researching this book, all but two were in English. All but one of the 100 companies profiled in this book publish English-version reports. (The lone exception is Toyo Seikan Kaisha of Japan, which doesn't even issue a report in Japanese, aside from a few pages of numbers.) Companies around the world have recognized the potential of the global market and the importance of publishing multilingual reports to attract a global following.

- Diversification expense. As every international mutual fund manager I've ever spoken with is quick to point out, if you want a truly diversified global portfolio, you need to begin with a thick cache of investible cash. To be well diversified, you should have investments in several industry groups in several countries around the world. That could mean 20 to 30 stocks (or more). In other words, what you need, say mutual fund managers, is an international mutual fund.

But while diversification is certainly important, let's not get carried away. After all, buying foreign stocks in any quantity is itself a form of diversification. You're not putting your life savings on the line here, just a portion of your investible income. If you can start with a modest investment in two or three stocks—for example, a utility company in Hong Kong, an electronics manufacturer in France, a drug manufacturer in Sweden—then you've already given yourself greater diversity than you would have with a portfolio full of U.S. stocks. In the years ahead, you can buy a few more foreign stocks to further diversify your portfolio.

- Currency exchange. Don't worry, if you buy your stocks through a U.S. broker, your dividend checks will all come in U.S. dollars.
- Global instability. No question about it, most foreign markets are as susceptible to recessions and market downturns as the U.S. market. Many emerging countries are even more volatile, although they also tend to do far better in the good years. A severe national crisis could be a blow to any market—which is another good argument for diversification.

Right now, the global marketplace is as stable as it has ever been. But as Thomas Keyes points out, "War could mess it all up. Right now, though, we're in an economic war, and that's wonderful. It's the ideal environment for a globally oriented investor."

HOW TO INVEST OVERSEAS

The entire world of international stocks is just a phone call away. If you have an account with a major brokerage house (such as Merrill-Lynch, Prudential-Bache, Dean Witter or Shearson-Lehman), there are no limits to the stocks you can buy.

In fact, most full-service brokerage firms of any size can buy stocks for you from just about any country in the world that has an open stock market. The problem with buying foreign stocks through a smaller firm, however, is that unless the brokerage house specializes in foreign stocks, it may have a hard time tracking down research information and even current stock price information for you. A broker at a major firm with international trading operations, on the other hand, will have readily available research information on hundreds—even thousands—of foreign stocks.

And, surprisingly, the commissions you pay for foreign stocks are no higher than the commissions for U.S. stocks—unless you're interested in buying some seldom-traded issue in an exotic foreign market.

American Depository Receipts

Nearly 1,000 foreign stocks are traded in the United States as American Depository Receipts (ADR). Technically speaking, an ADR is a receipt for shares in a foreign corporation issued by a U.S. bank. ADRs entitle the holder to all dividends and stock price appreciation from the stock.

ADRs are traded on U.S. exchanges, which makes them more accessible to the smaller brokerage firms. But only about 200 ADRs are listed on the major exchanges (the New York Stock Exchange, the American Stock Exchange or the NASDAQ over-the-counter exchange). The others trade over the counter in what's known as the "pink sheet" market. Pink sheet stock prices are not published in the newspaper, which tends to make the stocks more difficult to follow.

Even if a stock is not registered as an ADR, you can still buy it through most major full-service brokerage firms. Your broker would be able to buy it either through his or her company's international trading operations or through another brokerage firm that "makes a market" in the stock. A "market-maker" is a brokerage firm that follows a stock and stands ready to buy or sell that stock when orders come in. In the U.S. market, there are market-makers for several thousand foreign stocks.

One problem with buying a less-actively traded foreign stock is that you may have to buy the stock at a slightly higher price and sell at a lower price than what the stock trades for in its own country. The extra cost comes from the higher margins the market-maker builds into the price to cover the extra risk and expense of maintaining an inventory in the stock. But that extra margin is generally minimal, not likely to exceed 1 percent of the total transaction.

Buying Through a Discounter

Buying foreign stocks through a discount broker can range from difficult to impossible unless the stock you're interested in is registered in the United States as an ADR. Some 42 of the 81 non-U.S. stocks profiled in this book trade as ADRs. All ADR stocks are available through discounters.

If the stock does not trade as an ADR, you still may be able to get it through a discounter, but don't count on it. One discounter that does do a lot of trading in foreign stocks is Charles Schwab and Co. But even with Schwab, buying non-ADR stocks can be a hit-or-miss proposition, depending on which broker you happen to get on the phone.

If you go through a Schwab broker to buy a non-ADR stock, you may need to instruct the broker to contact Schwab's trading department in San Francisco to track down the stock, according to Tom Taggart, a Schwab corporate communications spokesman. The trading department will research the stock to try to find a market-maker in that security. "It may take several hours—or even until the next day—to find the market-maker and place the order, but we can usually buy any foreign stocks that the major full-service brokers can buy," says Taggart.

Otherwise, if you've traditionally been a discount brokerage client, you may have to open an account with a full-service broker to trade in the non-ADR stocks you can't get from a discounter.

For smaller volume investors, that can be a problem. While discount brokers welcome trades of $1,000 or less, many full-service brokers consider any orders under $5,000 to be little more than a nuisance. But there are certainly exceptions. You may be able to find a young broker, hungry for clients, who is willing to work with you and accept your smaller orders.

Surprisingly, the full-service firms are nearly as cheap as the discounters on smaller trades. While Schwab (one of the pricier of the discounters) has a minimum commission of $39, Merrill-Lynch's minimum fee is only $35. For trades of $1,000 to $2,000 at the full-commission firms such as Merrill-Lynch, you can expect to pay a commission of $40 to $90, depending on the price of the stock.

Tax Implications

The dividends from most foreign stocks purchased in the United States are subject to income taxes in the countries where the stock is issued (except in Hong Kong, which has no income tax on dividends). Generally speaking, most countries—through reciprocal agreements with the United States—withhold a tax of 15 percent. The money is taken directly out of the dividend, so when the check arrives at your home (after being processed and converted to U.S. currency either by the sponsoring ADR bank, the market-maker or your brokerage firm), the 15 percent has already been withheld.

At tax time, you can claim the 15 percent foreign tax payment as a credit against any other taxes you may owe on your dividend receipts.

Capital gains (profits from the sale of appreciated stocks) are not taxed by the home country. You pay the full tax on your capital gains to the U.S. government.

INVESTING IN INTERNATIONAL MUTUAL FUNDS

The easiest path to a global portfolio is through an international mutual fund. Investors can choose from a growing number of funds—well over 100 are available to American investors, some that invest in stocks from around the world, others that invest strictly in stocks of a single country.

You can buy "closed-end," single-country funds that trade as do stocks on the major stock exchanges, or you can invest in traditional open-end mutual funds, available in both no-load and front-end load varieties.

International mutual funds have some advantages over individual stocks—and some disadvantages. First the benefits:

- Diversification. International mutual funds offer instant diversification. When you buy shares in a mutual fund, you spread your investment to dozens of stocks in perhaps 20 to 25 countries around the world.

  It's impossible to get that type of diversification when you invest in individual stocks. The cost and effort would be too great. With a mutual fund, for as little as $1,000 (or less), you can buy your way into a whole world of stocks.

- Professional management. Investing knowledgeably and trying to stay abreast of the entire world market is no easy task. With a mutual fund, you let the fund manager study the countries, track the companies and make the buying and selling decisions. Mutual funds give you a chance to participate in the global market without devoting your life to it.
- Convenience. You buy in dollars, you sell in dollars, your dividend checks all come in dollars and you pay your taxes in dollars. And, chances are, you can follow your fund in the local newspaper (and certainly in the *Wall Street Journal* or *Investor's Daily*). It's not always that easy to find information on individual foreign stocks.

The Downside

In spite of their many advantages, mutual funds are not for everyone. Among the disadvantages are:

- Annual fees. In addition to the front-end fee that many funds charge (which can total up to $8^1/_2$ percent of your investment), you will also be assessed annual management fees. Annual fees for some no-load international funds can run as high as 2 to 3 percent a year. If a fund is doing well, earning 15 to 30 percent or more, that fee will have little impact. But in a slow year, when the fund goes up only 5 or 6 percent (or less), the annual fee could take a painful bite out of your profit.

   Not all international mutual funds carry high annual fees, but many do. When shopping for funds, find out what annual fee you'll be assessed. All fees are listed in the fund's prospectus, which you can get simply by calling or writing the company. You should also request the annual report; it gives a detailed listing of all of the fund's major stock holdings.
- More taxes. If you invest in an actively traded mutual fund, every time the fund manager sells out a stock at a profit, you, as a shareholder, are subject to income taxes on that gain. On the other hand, if you invest in individual stocks, and take a buy-and-hold approach, your stocks may grow in value for years, but you pay no taxes until you sell.
- Calling the shots. For many investors, part of the thrill of investing is calling their own shots, deciding for themselves in which stocks they want to invest. If you enjoy investing and following the market, you would probably find investing in individual stocks more rewarding.

   While you may not get quite the diversification with individual stocks, the fact is, many investors actually prefer a more focused portfolio. You may be interested in only two or three countries that you feel have the best potential or in a handful of companies you believe will bring you better returns than a wide diversity of stocks from around the world. You might also prefer to switch around from country to country as economic and market conditions change.

If you find that you're caught in the middle—you want diversity, but you also enjoy investing in individual stocks—why not go for a combination. Invest a portion of your money in a broad mutual fund, and put the rest into two or three of your favorite stocks. Then, in the years ahead, beef up your portfolio with new stocks from other countries. Once you've acquired a diverse portfolio of your own, you may decide to sell your mutual fund shares.

Global versus International

Global funds and international funds may sound like the same thing, but there is a difference. While there is no legal distinction, generally speaking *international* funds invest only in stocks outside the United States while *global* funds invest in stocks both in the United States and abroad.

For investors who already have a strong portfolio of U.S. stocks, an international fund would probably be the best choice. But if you are relatively new to the market and want to invest in a single fund that covers the entire world—including the United States—a global fund would be the way to go.

What follows is by no means a complete list of all diversified global and international mutual funds, but it does include many of the better load and no-load funds based on long-term performance records.

NO-LOAD FUNDS

- **Kleinworth Benson International Equity,** 800-233-9164; 200 Park Ave., 24th Floor, New York, NY 10166.
- **Vanguard World International Growth Fund,** 800-662-7447; Vanguard Financial Center, Valley Forge, PA 19482.
- **T. Rowe Price International Stock Fund,** 800-638-5660; 100 East Pratt St., Baltimore, MD 21202.
- **Ivy International Fund,** 800-235-3322; 40 Industrial Park Road, Hingham, MA 02043.
- **Scudder International Fund,** 800-225-2470; 175 Federal St., Boston, MA 02110-2267.
- **Scudder Global Fund** (same phone and address as above).
- **AMA Global Growth Fund,** 800-523-0864; 5 Sentry Parkway West, Suite 120, Blue Bell, PA 19422.
- **Wright International Blue Chip Equities Fund,** 203-330-5000; 1000 Lafayette Blvd., Bridgeport, CT 06604.

LOAD FUNDS

- **Fidelity Overseas Fund,** 800-544-9300.
- **Phoenix International Fund,** 800-243-4361.
- **PaineWebber Classic Atlas** (global fund), 800-544-9300.
- **Oppenheimer Global,** 800-525-7048.
- **Putnam International Equities** (global fund), 800-225-1581.
- **First Investors Global,** 800-423-4026.
- **Templeton World Fund,** 813-823-8712; 700 Central Ave., St. Petersburg, FL 33701. (Templeton also offers a Templeton Global Fund and a Templeton Foreign Fund.)

REGIONAL AND SINGLE-COUNTRY FUNDS

If you want to concentrate on a single country or a region of the world that you believe has superior potential, there is a hybrid type of mutual fund that enables you to do that.

Wright Investors' Service has just introduced (summer of 1990) a series of 14 single-country or regional index funds that enable investors to switch freely from one country to another as economic and market conditions change.

The Wright EquiFunds carry a maximum sales charge of 4 percent if sold through a broker, but they are no-load if purchased by Wright Investors' clients. It has an annual fee of about 1.3 percent.

Investors may choose from any of 14 funds, including Australia (includes some New Zealand stock), Austria, Belgian/Luxembourg, Canada, France, Germany, the Netherlands, Italy, Japan, Pacific Basin (Hong Kong, Singapore and Malaysia), Nordic (Denmark, Finland, Norway and Sweden), Spain, Switzerland and the United Kingdom.

For non-U.S. investors, Wright offers a similar set of funds, with a custodian in Luxembourg, through sponsoring banks in each country or region.

For more information, contact Wright Investors' Service, 203-330-5000, 1000 Lafayette Blvd., Bridgeport, CT 06604.

Other leading single-country funds include:

- **Japan Fund,** 800-53-Japan; 160 Federal St., Boston, MA 02110.
- **Nomura Pacific Basin Fund,** 800-833-0018; 180 Maiden Lane, New York, NY 10038.
- **Financial Strategic Pacific Basin,** 800-525-8085; P.O. Box 2040, Denver, CO 80201.
- **Financial Strategic European** (same phone and address as above).

CLOSED-END FUNDS

About 30 foreign-stock mutual funds are traded like stocks on the New York Stock Exchange or the American Stock Exchange. These *closed-end funds* are managed just like traditional mutual funds—with a portfolio manager handling the buying and selling of a diverse range of stocks—but investing in these funds is exactly the same as buying stock: you order the shares through your broker and pay a commission to your broker for the service.

Most closed-end funds specialize in stocks of a single country such as Brazil, Mexico, Malaysia or Australia, although a few focus on a specific region such as the Pacific Basin or Europe. There is also a Templeton Emerging Markets Fund that invests in stocks of growing Third World countries.

In some cases, the only way to invest in the stocks of certain countries is through a closed-end fund. For instance, you can not buy stocks in Korean or Taiwanese companies, but you can invest in closed-end funds that hold stocks from those countries. The funds are able to invest in those countries through special licensing agreements.

Investing in closed-end funds is a specialty in itself and requires a more studied approach than investing in traditional mutual funds. Closed-end country funds have had a history of outstanding success, but they tend to be very volatile. For example, the Taiwan Fund was up 105 percent in 1989 but down 50 percent through the first six months of 1990.

These funds usually trade at a premium to their net asset value. In other words, the total value of all stocks in a fund's portfolio may equal $10 a share, but the country-fund stock itself may be trading at only $9.50 a share.

Closed-end fund investors must look at potential investments from two angles: is the country that the stock represents due for a period of solid growth, and is the discount to the stock's portfolio value attractive? Shrewd investors will often wait until the discount is particularly steep before jumping into a stock. For instance, if a stock historically has been trading at a discount of about 5 percent and suddenly hits a slow market and drops to a discount of 15 percent, an investor might spot that as an opportunity to scoop up the stock at a bargain price.

Following is a list of most of the leading country funds traded on U.S. exchanges, including ticker symbol and stock exchange:

- Alliance New Europe (ANE), NYSE.
- Asia Pacific (APB), NYSE.
- Austria Fund (OST), NYSE.
- Brazil Fund (BZF), NYSE.
- Central Fund of Canada (CEF), AMEX.
- Chile Fund (CH), NYSE.
- Emerging Germany Fund (FRG), NYSE.
- First Australia (IAF), AMEX.
- First Philippine (FPF), NYSE.

- France Growth Fund (FRF), NYSE.
- Future Germany Fund (FGF), NYSE.
- Germany Fund (GER), NYSE.
- Growth Fund of Spain (GSP), NYSE.
- India Growth (IGF), NYSE.
- Irish Investment Fund (IRL), NYSE.
- Italy Fund (ITA), NYSE.
- Korea Fund (KF), NYSE.
- Malaysia Fund (MF), NYSE.
- Mexico Fund (MXF), NYSE.
- Scudder New Asia Fund (SAF), NYSE.
- Scudder New Europe Fund (NEF), NYSE.
- Spain Fund (SNF), NYSE.
- Taiwan Fund (TWN), NYSE.
- Templeton Emerging Markets Fund (EMF), NYSE.
- Thai Fund (TTF), NYSE.
- Turkish Investment Fund (TKF), NYSE.
- United Kingdom Fund (UKM), NYSE.

TRACKING YOUR GLOBAL INVESTMENTS

Finding timely information on the international stock market is a lot like finding an open table at a good Paris restaurant—if you're willing to look hard and pay dearly, you *might* find what you're looking for.

While Americans interested in U.S. stocks can turn to a wealth of sources—the *Wall Street Journal, Investors' Daily, Barron's, Fortune, Forbes, Value Line* and *Standard & Poor's,* among others—there are no comparable information sources for non-U.S. stocks. You can get stock quotes on several hundred foreign companies in some of the major U.S. newspapers, but more detailed coverage—news reports on the companies, earnings updates and financial histories—simply isn't available from the usual sources.

Using Your Broker

For investors with accounts at major brokerage firms, the best bet in tracking down information on global stocks is to ask your broker. While few stockbrokers have more than a passing knowledge of the international market, they can still serve as a good resource.

For instance, if you're looking for recommendations on non-U.S. stocks, most major brokerage firms keep "recommended" lists of foreign companies, according to Kathy Soule, a financial consultant with Merrill-Lynch. "I've had a lot of investors call me and say, 'I just want something international.' I'll either try to put them in a good international mutual fund or find a good foreign stock from our recommended list," says Soule.

On the other hand, if there's a specific company in which you're interested (perhaps one that you read about in this book), your broker may be able to dig up a research report on the company. "We have research reports on hundreds of foreign companies," says Soule, "and if Merrill-Lynch doesn't have a report out on it, there's a very good chance we can still track down some information on the company through some of our other sources."

But that's not all. Brokerage clients with an interest in global stocks may find their way onto the mailing list of special, internationally oriented brokerage company publications. Merrill-Lynch, for instance, sends its international investors weekly research highlights called "Global Notes" that include articles on international economic and currency developments, investment strategies, technical projections and fixed-income trends.

Going It Alone

For investors who prefer to scout out and track their stocks themselves, the search for information gets a little tougher. Data that are available to individual investors are often very limited—or very expensive—and, often, both.

All is not without hope, however. Following is a list of some of the few global information sources accessible to individual investors:

- Reuters. Although too pricey for all but the most serious investors, this may be the most comprehensive source of international stock market information available. The minimal annual cost for the on-line international information service is about $6,000.

    Your $6,000 gets you about two and a half hours a month of on-line service into the Reuters database of current news reports, press releases and magazine articles on thousands of corporations worldwide. Additional time costs about $175 an hour. If you want stock quotes, however, that's a different service with another additional fee. The service, not surprisingly, is geared more toward the investment professional than the individual investor, but individuals can subscribe. Call: 212-493-7100.
- Dow Jones News Retrieval Service. Dow Jones offers an on-line computer data service similar to Reuters. Its international database is not quite as comprehensive as Reuters, but the service is cheaper. Dow Jones offers news coverage and financial information on several thousand non-U.S. companies. Stock quotes are not included in the basic service. Cost to subscribers of the international service is $2.90 a minute during peak hours ($174 an hour) and $1.80 a minute during off hours ($108 an hour). There is no monthly minimum. The start-up cost is $29.95, and subscribers are billed an annual fee (after the first year) of $18. Call: 800-522-3567.

- *The Financial Times.* A daily newspaper based in London and also sold in the United States, the *Times* is to Great Britain what the *Wall Street Journal* is to the United States. It offers excellent coverage of United Kingdom stocks and daily tables and analyses of world markets. But it does have its limitations. Other than some stock quotes, you won't find much coverage of the Asia-Pacific market. And its coverage of European stocks, while far better than any American paper, still tends to be hit or miss. Cost is $1 an issue. It is available in major news stores in the larger U.S. cities or by subscription. Call: 800-344-1144.

- *Moody's International Stock Market Manual.* You can find this in the form of a thick, two-volume encyclopedia at many major U.S. libraries. Also part of the service is a twice-a-week update newsletter (10 to 15 pages) of articles, earnings and stock information and other data on the roughly 5,000 non-U.S. stocks covered in the Moody's manual. The information, while concise, tends to be fairly dry (most of it comes directly from the financial section of a corporation's annual report) and of limited value to investors who are trying to analyze a given stock. Profiles provide no recommendations, analyses or financial histories (except from the most recent fiscal year). Cost: $1,650 a year. Call: 212-553-0300.

- *International Fund Monitor.* This monthly newsletter tracks international mutual funds—both open- and closed-end funds. Published by John Woronoff, it includes articles on funds, international analyses, currency and economic trends and updated ratings and growth tables of many of the major international mutual funds. It is geared to the individual and professional investor with an interest in investing in international funds. Price: $72 per year. Call: 202-363-3097.

- *Adrian Day's Investment Analyst Monthly.* This publication takes a global approach to a wide range of investments, including U.S. and foreign stocks, mutual funds, gold, currency, etc. Price: $78 per year ($49 for new subscribers). P.O. Box 3217, Silver Spring, MD 20918. Call: 800-673-8485.

- *World Market Perspective.* Focusing on international and U.S. economics and investment, it includes features, editorials, reviews and research on a variety of U.S. and foreign investments. Monthly, 8 pages. Price: $49. (Also available through World Market Perspective is the *Hardaker Forecast Report,* a newsletter covering a range of investments, including international stocks. Price: $95 per year.) For subscription information on both publications: 800-333-5697.

- *The World 100 Report.* This monthly publication is specifically designed for readers of this book (written and published by the author). It tracks financial and corporate developments of the 100 companies profiled here and also reports on dozens of other top international stocks. Although it offers no specific buy and sell recommendations, it does feature practical advice on investing in the world market, global analysis, special company and country focus articles, "Best 100" news, stock price and earnings updates and other features. It well may be the only news publication that concentrates specifically on global stocks. Cost: $79 per year. For sample copy and subscription information, call: 800-927-0964.

- *Value Line Investment Survey. Value Line* provides specific investment information and advice on dozens of foreign stocks and closed-end country funds. 711 Third Ave., New York, NY 10017. Price: $495 a year.

- *Dessauer's Journal of Financial Markets,* a twice-monthly investment advisory letter, is written and published by John P. Dessauer. There are 24 regular issues, 4 special quarterly reports, a twice-weekly telephone hotline and plenty of advice, specific recommendations and readable research reports. Price: $195 per year. P.O. Box 1718, Orleans, MA 02653. Call: 800-272-7550.

- For information on American Depository Receipts for foreign stocks traded in the United States, there are four U.S. money-center banks that act as custodians for ADRs. They are:
  1) The Bank of New York, 90 Washington St., New York, NY 10286;
  2) Citibank, 111 Wall St., 5th Floor, New York, NY 10043;
  3) Morgan Guaranty Trust Company, 23 Wall St., New York, NY 10015;
  4) Chemical Bank, 55 Water St., Room 620, New York, NY 10041.

    Each of the banks publishes a list of ADRs for which it acts as custodian. By writing to the banks, you can obtain copies of their latest listings.

GLOBAL COMPETENCE

What do you need to know to be globally competent, to be able to carry your weight in any water-cooler conversation that suddenly shifts to the world market?

New issues, new forces, new dynamics the past few years have kept the global market hurtling through a blur of change. But a small core of recurring issues has come to dominate current conversation in international investment circles. Getting a grasp of those issues is a big first step toward attaining global competence.

What Are the Investment Prospects for Eastern Europe?   While capitalism is quickly making its way through Eastern Europe, there are no readily available investment opportunities for individual investors. There is only one stock exchange in the Eastern countries, the Budapest Exchange in Hungary, which opened in 1988, and that exchange is not yet prepared to serve the world's investors. It's open only three days a week and has an average daily trading volume of only $16,000.

Throughout most of Eastern Europe, the concept of publicly traded stocks has not yet taken root. When it does, there will be some great opportunities as well as some great disappointments. Unfortunately, telling one from the other will be extremely difficult even for analysts who study the market full time. Most major Eastern manufacturing companies have outdated machinery, poorly trained workers, little or no marketing expertise and no track record in a competitive, capitalistic environment. The long road to capitalism in Eastern Europe is destined to be littered with corporate casualties.

When Eastern companies do begin to trade on public stock exchanges, the best bet for individual investors who want an early jump on the market would be to buy shares in mutual funds that invest in stocks from those countries. To date, there are no such funds. But keep your eyes open. While the Eastern European market is certain to have its ups and downs, it could evolve into one of the most promising ground-floor opportunities of the 20th century.

In the meantime, the best way for individuals to invest in Eastern Europe is to buy stock in Western companies that are likely to do business there. German, Scandinavian and other European companies would seem to have the inside track on business opportunities in the Eastern area. But a number of internationally oriented U.S. and Japanese companies are also vying for position in the Eastern European market.

What types of businesses stand the best chance to cash in on the Eastern market? Banks, construction and building materials businesses, pollution control and waste management operations, machine manufacturers, medical and technology companies and consumer products manufacturers all should find a welcome market in Eastern Europe.

The 1992 Unification of the European Market. At the end of 1992, trade barriers between the 12 European Economic Community (EEC) countries will be removed, creating the world's single largest capitalist market, with 320 million people.

The policy has been enormously difficult to negotiate—the origins of the idea go back as far as 1959—and the benefits are still speculative. But if the unification policy works according to plan, EEC businesses should benefit at the expense of U.S., Japanese and other outside companies that will still face some trade barriers in the European market. Companies from outside the EEC have been scrambling to forge alliances with European companies—or make acquisitions of European companies—to get a foothold in the market before 1993.

The 12 member countries include Great Britain, Ireland, France, Spain, Germany, Italy, Portugal, Belgium, Luxembourg, Denmark, the Netherlands and Greece.

Tariff elimination is just one of the many issues that the European Community has had to wrangle over to forge the barrier-free agreement. Other issues include the standardization of banking policies, food production, electrical appliances, industrial machines, automobile exhausts, television programming, toys, plant and animal health, workers' rights and dozens of other issues. Getting all 12 nations to agree on all 279 separate issues by the deadline of December 31, 1992, will be a miracle in itself.

While the agreement will not prevent outside companies from doing business in Europe, it will put them at a disadvantage to their competitors within the EEC.

For investors, the EEC agreement is one more good reason to invest in European stocks. More importantly, the open border arrangement could add one to two percentage points to the European Market's annual gross product growth.

Is Japan Really Turning the World into Its Own Private Global Colony?   Over the past three decades, Japan has been one of the world's great success stories, pulling itself from the ashes to become a thriving global power. Americans have viewed Japan's rise with a curious paranoia. Awe, amazement, even pride might be more appropriate responses. Japan, after all, is a country that grew up under America's wings, that followed in its footsteps and ultimately proved what Americans have long preached: that an industrious people under a capitalist democracy can grow and prosper.

There is no question of Japan's prosperity. The country is cash rich. Of the world's 10 largest banks, 8 are Japanese. Its biggest brokerage firm, Nomura Securities, earned more in 1989 than America's 10 largest brokerage firms combined. Ten of the world's 15 largest publicly traded companies are Japanese.

How did this island nation of 125 million people suddenly become such a dominant industrial force? Critics point to Japan's protective business environment as a key to its success—and with good reason. Between the Japanese government's stringent regulations and private industry's corporate inbreeding, an impenetrable wall of resistance served for years to seal out all but the most persistent foreign competitors. At the same time, Japanese executives were busy establishing outposts around the globe for their companies' expansion.

But there is more to Japan's success than its protective trade policies. Don't be misled by the country's physical dimensions. Japan has eight times the population of Australia and nearly as many people as Germany and France combined. The Japanese people are well educated, industrious, dedicated and fiercely competitive. They're also big savers, salting away 15 percent of each paycheck into savings and investment accounts (that's four times the savings rate of the average American). The surplus of cash keeps interest rates low, giving Japanese firms an edge on foreign competitors in raising capital.

American consumers also helped fuel Japan's growth, with their appetite for Japan's high-tech gadgetry and well-engineered automobiles. The

American government has been no less gracious with its business. Our country financed its spiraling national debt through the 1980s in large part by selling billions of dollars of T-bills to Japanese investors.

Japan is not the first nation to shake the world with its sudden economic expansion. Americans are quick to forget the dominant role the United States played in the world economy following World War II. Even as late as 1970, U.S. companies accounted for two-thirds of the world's total industrial capitalization.

Now it's Japan's turn in the spotlight. But is it the dominant, infallible empire it seems? It is indeed a powerful industrial and financial force, but Japan claims its dominance and infallibility have been greatly exaggerated.

For instance, many Americans have the impression that Japan is buying up America lock, stock and barrel. Yet, according to a 1989 study by *Forbes* magazine, of the 10 foreign companies with the largest investment stake in the United States, not one was Japanese. The top Japanese company on the list, Honda, ranked only 19th. The top five foreign investors, in order, were Seagram of Canada, Royal Dutch/Shell of the Netherlands, British Petroleum and BAT of the United Kingdom and Tengelmann Group of Germany.

Any envy Americans might have toward their Japanese counterparts might also be misplaced. The standard of living for most Japanese citizens is well below that of the average American. Prices for many consumer goods and foods can run several times higher in Japan than they do in the United States. A meal for a family of four at a good Tokyo restaurant can cost hundreds of dollars. Very few Japanese can afford their own homes. In one posh Tokyo neighborhood, land goes for $245,000 per square meter. It is so difficult for Japanese citizens to finance a new home that one Japanese bank has begun to offer 100-year mortgages, saddling not only the existing family but a couple of generations of descendants with a share of the mortgage.

While the Japanese industrial machine remains strong, the economy has recently shed its image of invulnerability. Since the fall of 1988, the yen has dropped 27 percent relative to the dollar, and through the first half of 1990, the Japanese stock market was down 20 percent. Hit particularly hard was Japan's powerful banking industry. Dai-Ichi Kangyo, the world's largest bank, reported that its net income dropped 35 percent in fiscal 1990; earnings at Mitsubishi Bank were down 26 percent; and Sumitomo Bank was down 20 percent.

The bottom line on Japan: powerful, determined, bent on continued world expansion, yes. An invulnerable, unstoppable force destined to put the world in its pocket: only in its dreams.

Is the United States Washed Up as a World Industrial Power?   There are those who suggest that the emerging strength of Japan, Germany and a unified Europe have helped turn the United States into a second-rate industrial power.

They point out, with great validity, that the United States has let its budget and trade deficits get way out of hand and that other countries around the world have steadily chipped away at America's dominant industrial position. Just 20 years ago, U.S. companies accounted for 70 percent of the world's total industrial capitalization. Now its share has dropped to about 34 percent.

So does that mean America is washed up as a global industrial power?

Three facts:

- Even at 34 percent of the world's total industrial capitalization, the United States still ranks number one in the world. (The Japanese had surpassed the United States but dropped back after severe declines in their currency value and stock market.)
- The United States leads the world in annual gross national product. At $5 trillion, the U.S. GNP exceeds that of Japan and Germany combined.
- Despite its steep trade deficits, the United States ranked as the world's number one exporter in 1989. Germany—not Japan—was number two.

What's Going To Happen to Hong Kong?   Now that Eastern Europe has opened its doors to free enterprise, what will be the next "great wall" to fall?

In Hong Kong, the overriding hope is that the People's Republic of China will soon follow in the footsteps of the world's other Communist regimes. A capitalist China could mean a bonanza of opportunity for Hong Kong, a city/province/country/British Crown Colony of about 6 million people located at the mouth of the Canton River along the southeastern coast of China.

Hong Kong is scheduled to be transferred from British rule to the People's Republic of China July 1, 1997. By all rights, however, 1997 should bring little immediate change. Under the agreement, Hong Kong is to be a special administrative region with its own laws for another 50 years (through 2047).

While the Hong Kong market is expected to remain volatile—tied in part to developments within the People's Republic—it offers extraordinary potential. By itself, Hong Kong is already one of the world's fastest-growing countries, with an annual economic growth rate of about 10 percent. If the People's Republic of China should ultimately join the capitalist revolution, Hong Kong's growth curve could leap off the charts.

Then, of course, there's always the worst-case scenario to consider: that China will renege on its agreement and try to strip Hong Kong of its independence and free enterprise—a scenario those in power seriously doubt but still take very, very seriously. Businesspeople are quietly siphoning cash out of the country. Some of Hong Kong's brightest people have moved elsewhere, and its major multinational corporations, such as Jardine Matheson, have registered their corporations off shore so their operations can continue even if China pulls the plug on Hong Kong.

For investors, Hong Kong is unquestionably a gamble, but lately many investors have been putting their bets on the Crown Colony.

Which National Economies Are Growing the Fastest? Americans don't have to look far to find the world's hottest investment spot. It's in a most unlikely spot—just south of the border. Yes, Mexico. Despite the country's recent bout of instability and hyperinflation, the Mexican stock market has been the world's fastest-growing market the past three years.

Like most emerging markets, however, Mexico offers little in which foreigners can invest their money. The best bet would be the Mexico Fund, a closed-end mutual fund traded on the New York Stock Exchange. It was up 42 percent in 1987, 32 percent in 1988, 112 percent in 1989 and 30 percent through the first six months of 1990.

Other emerging markets include Korea—although the country has been in a slump of late—Taiwan, India, Chile, the Philippines and Thailand. Unfortunately, it ranges from very difficult to impossible for foreign investors to buy individual stocks in any of those countries. But you can buy closed-end funds on the NYSE that invest exclusively in the stocks of each of those countries.

Of all the emerging countries, Hong Kong, Singapore and Malaysia have the best, most accessible stock markets for foreign investors.

With their volatility and uncertainty, the smaller emerging markets are no place for the timid. But aggressive investors in search of vast potential should certainly consider seasoning their portfolio with stocks from some of these rapidly emerging economies.

HOW TO USE THIS BOOK

Consider this book a catalog of world-class stock market prospects. It carries no guarantees, no promises of superior future performance, but each of the 100 stocks profiled here has a history of excellent earnings, revenue and stock price gains.

Most of the 100 stocks will continue to perform well for years to come (barring global disaster). Some, in fact, will provide extraordinary long-term returns. At the same time, a few will flatten out or even lose ground. That's why diversification is so important. Don't put all of your money in one stock, one industry or one country. When you spread your assets around, you also spread your risk and increase your chances of superior long-term performance.

Making Your Selections

When using this book to shop for international stocks, you should consider a three-step approach:

1. Page through the book, read the profiles and try to pick out 5 to 10 stocks you might wish to buy. The profiles cover basic information on each company, including market sector information and financial histories.

Once you've pared your list to the top few prospects, call or write the companies and request their annual reports. Looking through a company's annual report can often give you a better feel for the company. Unfortunately, with foreign stocks, it may take weeks or months to get a report. One company I contacted, BTR of England, never did send me a report even after two letters and seven months of waiting.

If you're in a hurry, and you can't wait several weeks or months for a report, move on to step two.

2. To get further insight into a company, you might want to ask your broker for any research or information he or she has on the firm. If your broker can't help you, or if you use a discounter, you might check for updated news on the company at the library. You may be able to find articles in recent periodicals, or you can check *Moody's International Stock Guide,* which gives periodic updates on about 5,000 companies.

3. After weighing all the available information, you're ready to pare your list down to the final selections. If you plan to buy four or five stocks from the book, it would be advisable to choose stocks from at least two or three countries and industry groups; the more diversified your portfolio, the better your chances of long-term success.

What percentage of your investable assets should be in foreign stocks? One general rule of thumb is that conservative investors should put 5 to 10 percent of their investable assets in foreign stocks while more aggressive investors may prefer keeping 10, 20 or even 30 percent of their assets in international stocks.

MARKET STRATEGIES FOR INVESTORS IN FOREIGN STOCKS

While diversity may be the first rule of international investing, patience is certainly the second. "Investing in international stocks with a time frame of less than two years is ridiculous," says investment author Thomas Keyes. "There are so many variables involved—the currency, the country, the industry and the company—that it could take several years for a stock to reach its potential. I usually look at a four- to five-year time frame although if things change before that—for better or for worse—I may get out of that stock sooner."

Last year, Austria's stock market jumped 150 percent. "If I had had any money in the Austrian market," says Keyes, "by now, I would have taken the money and run. I'd be out of that market."

In evaluating stock opportunities, Keyes suggests that investors look for several fundamental factors: development of a company's products or services, international events and policies that may affect the market, tax changes and political changes within a country. He cites several examples:

- International events. The events in Eastern Europe should have a major impact on many Western European stocks, particularly in Germany. Keyes predicts that by adding East Germany to its economy, Germany's economic growth should nearly double (from just over 2 percent per year to about 4 percent per year). Most of the stocks within Germany should benefit from that growth, adds Keyes.
- New policies. Dismantling the trade barriers within the European Community should add about 1 percent to the annual growth rate of most European countries, boosting the average to about 4 percent per year through the year 2000. "That's a significant increase," says Keyes, "and compounded over 10 years, that's going to make a hell of a difference. The United States is certainly not going to grow at a 4 percent rate. That's why the European market looks so inviting right now."
- Change in tax laws. When the Taiwan government added a capital gains tax on stock profits, its market dropped 40 percent. Keyes suggests that investors be on the lookout for tax changes that will have an effect—pro or con—on a country's market.
- Political and economic changes. A change in immigration policies in Australia, opening up the country to more immigrants, should aid the country's growth. Australia is also pulling out of a recession, which should also bolster its stock market. Now, says Keyes, if the government could tighten securities laws governing publicly traded companies, that could propel the market even further.

Gavin Dobson, president of Murray Johnstone International, says his group takes a similar approach in evaluating investment opportunities for the company's Phoenix International Fund. The group first evaluates the market on a country-by-country basis, deciding how much of the fund's assets should be allocated to each market before making the stock selections. "For instance," says Dobson, "we may decide to put 15 percent of our assets in the Japanese market. Then we give our Japan portfolio manager the money and let him make the individual stock selections."

In evaluating a country's prospects, the group ponders 20 fundamental economic questions on such issues as wages (are wage rates overheating or under control?), money supply (a tight money supply does not bode well for the economy), interest rates (falling rates could spur the stock market), bond returns (high bond rates tend to depress the stock market), stock prices (historically low price-earnings ratios could indicate that stocks are under-priced) and performance of the country's stock market relative to markets elsewhere around the world (a market that is lagging other markets could be poised for a rally).

The system has worked well for the Phoenix Fund, which has provided an average annual return of 29 percent the past five years for its institutional investors. But no system is foolproof, says Dobson. "In 1981 we misjudged the accuracy of the election opinion polls in France that indicated that the conservative candidate would be elected. Instead, François Mitterand (the Socialist candidate who had vowed to nationalize French industry) won in a landslide. The day after the election, the stock market crashed, costing us 25 percent of our investment in the French market."

While international investing can be far more challenging than investing strictly in the domestic market, investors who are able to react to political and economic developments around the world can dramatically increase their chances of reaping exceptional returns.

SELECTING THE "100 BEST"

Paring down the thousands of stocks on the world market to a list of the "100 Best" was a task, predictably, beset by a virtually endless string of problems and complexities. It was like piecing together a puzzle—but with one sadistic twist. There were 20,000 pieces to choose among—scattered around the globe—but only room enough on the board for 100 to fit. Putting the puzzle together and writing the book has taken a full year and a half. If I were a perfectionist, it would probably take another year and a half and end in frustration. The puzzle pieces keep changing, you see, and so does the shape of the board.

I began by trying to track down a good source of research data on international stocks, which in itself was no simple task. I talked to librarians and brokers and analysts who referred me to other librarians and brokers and analysts, who, in turn, referred me to other librarians and brokers and analysts. As I persevered, I got a tip here, a phone number there, until finally I found a source that seemed promising—with limitations. Unfortunately, that company wanted $30,000 for the service, and their research still left much to be desired. I looked harder, made more calls and finally found another source that seemed even more promising. But after weeks of negotiations on the terms and conditions, that one fell through, too.

My trail of calls and tips finally led me to two excellent sources: Wright Investors' Service, a Bridgeport, Connecticut, investment firm that operates the Worldscope Database, with financial data on several thousand non-U.S. companies, and CompuStat, a Colorado-based sister company of Standard & Poor's and a subsidiary of McGraw-Hill. Like Wright, CompuStat has a computer database of several thousand non-U.S. companies.

Henry Herbring of Wright Investors' Service fed me piles of financial information on some of the top companies followed by Wright. Wright's criteria for selecting stocks for its Wright International "True Blue Chip" portfolio were similar to mine. Wright's analysts look for companies with good growth, manageable debt and moderate price-earnings ratios (among other factors).

Bill Griffis at CompuStat took a different tack. I gave him a series of screens to run out on the CompuStat database. The first run-through produced a lengthy list of the fastest-growing companies. Subsequent screens pared that list down to a more manageable group of fast-growing companies that also consistently showed increases in their earnings per share, dividends and stock price.

Next, I collected annual reports of many of the top international mutual funds. I scanned through their lists of stock holdings in search of other good stocks for the book.

The final step in the research process was to request annual reports from all of the finalists on my list—a total of more than 300 companies—and to review both those reports and the financial research data supplied by Wright and CompuStat. The final 100 includes companies from 15 countries. There is also an Honorable Mention list that includes stocks (or single-country mutual funds) from about a dozen other countries.

RATING THE "100 BEST"

Once I had selected the 100 companies, I needed a system to rank the stocks. I used a system similar to the one I set up for *The 100 Best Stocks To Own in America*. Each company is rated for six categories—earnings growth, stock growth, dividend yield, dividend growth, consistency and momentum. There are a maximum of 24 points—4 per category.

Along with the profile for each of the top 100 companies is a rating chart like the one below:

EARNINGS GROWTH	★ ★ ★ ★
STOCK GROWTH	★ ★ ★ ★
DIVIDEND YIELD	★ ★ ★ ★
DIVIDEND GROWTH	★ ★ ★ ★
CONSISTENCY	★ ★ ★ ★
MOMENTUM	★ ★ ★ ★
	24 points

The following guide explains the scoring breakdown for each of the six categories:

KEY
★ = 1 point
Maximum (highest rating) = ★ ★ ★ ★ (4 points)

Earnings Growth/Stock Growth/Dividend Growth

Earnings growth, stock growth and dividend growth are all rated based on growth percentage over the past five years—as follows:

70 to 99% (11–14% per year)	★
100 to 149% (15–19% per year)	★ ★
150 to 199% (20–24% per year)	★ ★ ★
200% and above (25% and up per year)	★ ★ ★ ★

Dividend Yield

This category is based on the dividend yield average over the past two years:

0.5 to 1.4%	★
1.5 to 2.4%	★ ★
2.5 to 3.4%	★ ★ ★
3.5% and above	★ ★ ★ ★

For investors who have no interest in receiving current income from their stock investments, the dividend yield category may be of limited value. Others who look forward to a stream of dividend income from their stocks, however, may find this category particularly useful.

Consistency

Consistency is a fairly subjective category that takes into account a wide range of factors:

- A company that has had a flawless run of increases in earnings per share, revenue, operating income, book value and dividend over the past five years would score four points. The consistency of the stock price growth is not taken into account here because volatility in stock prices can often be dictated by market factors beyond the control of the company. But if the company is strong and growing steadily, the stock price, over time, should reflect that.
- A company that has had a nearly flawless run of increases in the fundamental growth categories would score three points.
- A company that has had a fairly consistent growth record, with occasional lapses in the key categories, would score two points.
- A company that has been somewhat inconsistent, with several ups and downs in the basic growth categories, would score one point in this category.
- Theoretically, a company with a very volatile growth record would score no points here, although the more volatile companies have been weeded out of the top 100 list.

Momentum

Again, momentum is a somewhat subjective category but an important one. This category is intended to indicate whether the company is still growing quickly or may have had a strong growth spurt through the mid-1980s but has slowed down since.

- A company that has increased its growth rate for earnings per share, revenue, operating income and book value over the past couple of years would score four points in this category.
- A company that has maintained strong, sustained growth with no drop-off the past couple of years would score three points.
- A company whose growth has leveled off slightly in the past couple of years would score two points.
- A company whose growth fundamentals have flattened out or declined in recent years would score one point.
- A company that has had earnings or revenue losses in the past year or two would score no points on this one.

Breaking Ties

The 100 companies were ranked in order by points, from the one with the most points, ranked first (Banco Popular Espanol, with a perfect score of 24), through the company with the fewest points. To break a tie, the company with the higher total return (average annual stock price appreciation and reinvested dividends over the past five years) got the higher ranking. If two companies tied on both total points and total return, the company with the higher total revenue got the higher ranking.

Australia

Australia, population 16 million, is a major industrial power in the Southeast Pacific. Its largest stock exchange is in Sydney. It also has exchanges in Melbourne, Adelaide, Brisbane, Hobart and Perth.

Australia's major industries include mining, agriculture, iron, steel, textiles, electrical equipment, chemicals, autos, ships, aircraft, machinery and cattle. Australia is the world's largest wool producer.

The currency is the Australian dollar (AUD 1.28 = US $1, June, 1990). Its GNP was AUD 315 billion (US $270 billion) in 1988. Its inflation rate the past three years has been around 8 percent. Real economic growth the past several years has averaged about 3.5 percent. The market value of stocks traded on the Australian exchanges was AUD 228.9 billion in 1989, up 7 percent from its 1988 total of AUD 213.6 billion.

In 1989 the Australian stock market was up 14 percent in Australian currency (5.6 percent in U.S. currency due to a decline in the value of the Australian dollar). Through the first six months of 1990, the Australian market was in a slump, down 7 percent.

One of the most favorable aspects of the Australian market is that price-earnings ratios are quite low. After a couple of lackluster years, share prices appear to be at bargain levels and could move up quickly when the Australian economy rebounds.

2

MAYNE NICKLESS LIMITED

MAYNE NICKLESS LIMITED

21st Floor
390 St. Kilda Road
Melbourne, Victoria 3004
Australia
Tel: (03) 268-0700
Chairman: Bruce R. Redpath

EARNINGS GROWTH	★ ★ ★ ★
STOCK GROWTH	★ ★ ★ ★
DIVIDEND YIELD	★ ★ ★ ★
DIVIDEND GROWTH	★ ★ ★ ★
CONSISTENCY	★ ★ ★ ★
MOMENTUM	★ ★ ★ ★
MBE	**24 points**

Mayne Nickless operates an array of delivery and security services, including one of the world's largest armored truck businesses. The division has been a cash machine over the years for Mayne Nickless, but it does have its hazards. In the first half of fiscal 1990, the company's England-based Securities Express subsidiary reported a drop in profits "as a result of a significant increase in losses due to armed holdups."

Fortunately, Mayne Nickless has plenty of other profit centers to draw from, most of which deal in some way with the shipping and materials delivery business.

The company was founded in 1886 when John Mayne and Enoch Nickless started a parcel delivery service in Melbourne. Over the years it has expanded into a worldwide transportation business with operations in 13 countries (although its Australian operations still account for about 90 percent of the profit).

The company breaks its operations into three primary segments, including:

- Transport (46 percent of revenues). Mayne Nickless offers freight messenger service, contract distribution, fleet management, container handling and waste management services. Its air delivery division is Australia's leading air express freight carrier. Jetspress Air Couriers and Skyroad Express both operate in Australia, and Express Airborne operates in Canada. Among its leading delivery subsidiaries are Road Express, Mainway Transport, Parceline, Jetsroad, The Overnighters and Ipec Transport.
- Securities services (26 percent of revenues). The company operates several armored car subsidiaries, including Armaguard in Australia and Loomis Armored Car Services in Canada. The company recently sold its U.S. Loomis subsidiary to Brink's after several years of disappointing results. In addition to its armored car services, the firm owns several security guard protection services.
- Computer and health care services (5 percent of revenues). Mayne Nickless operates a payroll service geared to small businesses and has major holdings in 12 Australian hospitals.

EARNINGS GROWTH

The company has had sustained growth the past few years. Its earnings per share increased 216 percent over the past five years, 26 percent per year.

Mayne Nickless reported total revenue of 2.3 billion Australian dollars (1.4 billion in U.S. dollars) in 1989. The company has 40,000 employees.

STOCK GROWTH

The company's stock price has grown quickly over the past five years, increasing 304 percent for the period—32 percent per year.

Including reinvested dividends, a $10,000 investment in Mayne Nickless stock in 1984 would have grown to about $48,000 five years later. Average annual compounded rate of return (including stock growth and reinvested dividends): about 37 percent.

DIVIDEND YIELD

The company generally pays a very good yield, which has averaged about 5 percent over the past five years. During the most recent two-year rating period (1988 and 1989), the stock paid an average annual current return (dividend yield) of 4.8 percent.

DIVIDEND GROWTH

Mayne Nickless raises its dividend most years. The dividend increased 230 percent (27 percent per year) over the five-year period from 1984 to 1989.

CONSISTENCY

The company has had very consistent growth in its earnings per share, revenues and book value per share. Its price-earnings ratio of about 10 is at a very attractive level for a fast-growing company.

MOMENTUM

Mayne Nickless kept up its excellent pace in 1988 and 1989. Its earnings per share rose 26 percent in 1988 and 25 percent in 1989; its operating income rose 88 percent in 1989, and its revenue rose 18 percent. The company anticipated more record returns in fiscal 1990, despite a slow year for the Australian economy.

SUMMARY

Fiscal year ended: July 3
(Australian dollars; revenue and operating income in millions)

	1990*	1989	1988	1987	1986	1985	1984	5-year growth, %† (annual/total)
Revenue	—	2,342	1,994	1,754	1,539	1,167	857	22/173
Operating income	—	163	87	68	64	77	57	23/185
Earnings/share	—	0.57	0.46	0.36	0.28	0.27	0.18	26/216
Dividend/share	0.40	0.33	0.22	0.15	0.13	0.13	0.10	27/230
Dividend yield, %	7.0	5.7	3.9	4.0	5.1	5.2	7.0	—/—
Stock price	5.44	5.74	5.08	3.83	2.57	2.40	1.42	32/304
P/E ratio	9.0	10.0	11.1	10.6	9.3	9.1	7.7	—/—
Book value/share	—	3.00	2.55	2.22	1.89	1.70	1.48	15/102

* 5–1–90
† 1984–89
Source: Company sources and Worldscope.
Note: ADR; stock price quoted in *Barron's,* the *Wall Street Journal, European Wall Street Journal* and the *Financial Times;* 5-year average annual return in U.S. currency: 36%.

4

BRAMBLES INDUSTRIES LIMITED

18th Floor, Gold Fields House
1 Alfred St.
Sydney, NSW 2000
Australia
Tel: (02) 231-8222
Fax: (02) 231-2458
Chairman: Alan W. Coates
Managing Director: Gary M. Pemberton

EARNINGS GROWTH	★ ★ ★ ★
STOCK GROWTH	★ ★ ★ ★
DIVIDEND YIELD	★ ★ ★
DIVIDEND GROWTH	★ ★ ★ ★
CONSISTENCY	★ ★ ★ ★
MOMENTUM	★ ★ ★ ★
MBE, SYD	**23 points**

Whatever the cargo, wherever the port—by truck, by train, by boat or by plane—if it has to be moved, Brambles can do it.

Brambles owns a freight trucking and international transport business based in Sydney, a marine towage and cargo shipping service along the Australian coast and a European railroad transportation group with lines into Eastern Europe. It also has an Australian-based "removalist" division that can pack up your belongings for you and ship them anywhere in the world.

Brambles's leading subsidiaries include:

CHEP, the world leader in "pallet management." In the produce- and goods-hauling industry, cargo is typically stacked on wooden pallets and hauled from shipper to receiver, pallet and all. Brambles claims to have 22 million pallets in use in its transport system worldwide.

Groupe CAIB, European railway rental business. The firm operates about 40,000 railroad cars in Western and Eastern Europe that can be leased to clients who have cargo to move.

Brambles' Marine Group. The company offers a wide range of shipping, towing and shuttle services along the Australian coast. It does a strong business with Australia's off-shore oil industry.

Security Services. Each year, the company transports more than $35 billion in cash, gold and valuables around Australia and overseas for banks, financial institutions, retailers, gold miners and other businesses.

Transport and Freight Forwarding. The company offers a wide range of specialized freight hauling services, including bulk haulage of liquids and gases, foods, computer parts and explosives (for the mining industry).

Grace Removals. The company offers relocation services for individuals and businesses, including packing and storage (if necessary).

Cleanaway. The company offers a variety of waste disposal and waste management services in Australia and Great Britain.

Equipment Services. Brambles leases heavy equipment for the Australian construction and mining industries. It owns more than 300 cranes and 2,000 forklifts.

EARNINGS GROWTH

The company has had excellent growth the past few years. Its earnings per share increased 212 percent over the past five years, 26 percent per year.

Brambles reported total revenue of about AUD 1.6 billion (1.2 billion in U.S. dollars) in 1989.

STOCK GROWTH

The company's stock price has moved up very quickly over the past five years, increasing 444 percent for the period—41 percent per year.

Including reinvested dividends, a $10,000 investment in Brambles stock in 1984 would have grown to about $65,000 five years later. Average annual compounded rate of return (including stock growth and reinvested dividends): about 45 percent.

DIVIDEND YIELD

Brambles generally pays a good yield, which has averaged about 4 percent over the past five years. During the most recent two-year rating period (1988 and 1989), the stock paid an average annual current return (dividend yield) of 3.2 percent.

DIVIDEND GROWTH

Brambles traditionally raises its dividend every year. The dividend increased 213 percent (26 percent per year) over the five-year period from 1984 to 1989.

CONSISTENCY

Over the past five years, the company has had a flawless record of growth in all the key areas—earnings per share, revenues, operating income and book value per share. Its price-earnings ratio of about 13 is a very reasonable level for a company that has been growing as fast as Brambles.

MOMENTUM

Brambles has had excellent growth the past two years. Its earnings per share increased nearly 30 percent in 1988 and 1989.

SUMMARY

Fiscal year ended: June 30
(Australian dollars; revenue and operating income in millions)

	1990*	1989	1988	1987	1986	1985	1984	5-year growth, %† (annual/total)
Revenue	—	1,563	1,426	1,239	1,061	625	539	23/189
Operating income	—	216	193	157	143	81	63	28/242
Earnings/share	—	1.00	0.78	0.61	0.49	0.36	0.32	26/212
Dividend/share	—	0.42	0.32	0.26	0.19	0.16	0.14	25/200
Dividend yield, %	3.0	3.1	3.4	3.0	3.3	4.8	5.7	—/—
Stock price	13.65	13.55	9.40	8.81	5.78	3.33	2.49	41/444
P/E ratio	13.0	13.7	12.0	14.5	11.8	9.4	7.8	—/—
Book value/share	—	4.84	4.28	3.83	3.12	2.36	2.19	17/121

* 6–1–90
† 1984–89
Source: Worldscope.

Note: No ADR; stock price quoted in *Barron's,* the *Wall Street Journal, European Wall Street Journal* and the *Financial Times;* 5-year average annual return in U.S. currency: 44%.

BTR NYLEX Limited

15th Floor
390 St. Kilda Road
Melbourne, Victoria 3004
Australia
Telephone: (03) 823-5700
Chairman: John C. Cahill

EARNINGS GROWTH	★ ★ ★ ★
STOCK GROWTH	★ ★ ★ ★
DIVIDEND YIELD	★ ★ ★
DIVIDEND GROWTH	★ ★ ★ ★
CONSISTENCY	★ ★ ★ ★
MOMENTUM	★ ★ ★
SYD	**22 points**

In terms of sustained, rapid growth, there may be no other company in the world that can compare with the dizzying rise of BTR Nylex. Ten years ago, BTR was a relative unknown among Australian manufacturers. Now it's one of the largest and most dynamic manufacturing concerns in the country.

The company's total sales have grown almost 100-fold over the past decade, increasing from about $37 million (Australian dollars) in 1979 to $3.2 billion in 1988. And operating profit has grown even faster—climbing almost 200-fold during the decade, from about $3 million in 1979 to almost $600 million in 1988. The company had 850 employees in 1979. By 1988, the employee count had jumped to 28,000.

BTR's main corporate division is its polymer group, responsible for producing vinyl products, moldings, textiles and industrial rubber products. Revenues from its polymer groups—based in Australia and Taiwan—account for about 37 percent of the company's $3.2 billion in total revenue. Among the group's key products are synthetic fabrics for furniture, carpets and wall coverings and plastic containers and moldings for automobiles. Its Esky cooler is Australia's top seller, and its Rotomould plastic canoes are becoming popular in waterways throughout the South Pacific region.

BTR's engineering division, which accounts for about 16 percent of revenues, manufactures pumps for power generation, water supply, agriculture and general industrial use. It also makes a variety of automobile components, including axles, transmissions, drive shafts and universal joints.

The company's building products group, which contributes about 18 percent of total sales, specializes in cabinet panels and related products, insulation, tile, laminates and coatings.

BTR also has a packaging division that accounts for about 15 percent of sales and a flatglass group that accounts for about 13 percent of sales.

In all, BTR has about 150 subsidiaries throughout the world. Geographically, its Australian operations account for about 62 percent of annual revenue and Taiwan operations account for about 24 percent. The company also does significant business in the United States (7 percent), Europe (4 percent), Japan (2 percent), Malaysia (2 percent) and elsewhere in Southeast Asia (2 percent).

While BTR has been an aggressive marketer of its existing products—particularly in the Pacific Rim area—its primary growth has been through acquisitions. In 1988 it nearly doubled its size by acquiring ACI International Ltd. for $1.7 billion and Feltrax Ltd. for $750 million.

EARNINGS GROWTH

The company has had phenomenal growth the past few years. Its earnings per share increased 1,900 percent over the past five years, 83 percent per year.

BTR has annual revenue of $3.2 billion (2.7 billion in U.S. dollars).

STOCK GROWTH

The company's stock price has exploded over the past five years, increasing 4,028 percent for the period—110 percent per year.

Including reinvested dividends, a $10,000 investment in BTR Nylex stock in 1984 would have grown to about $440,000 five years later. Average annual compounded rate of return (including stock growth and reinvested dividends): about 113 percent.

DIVIDEND YIELD

The company generally pays a very good yield, which has averaged about 3 percent over the past five years. During the most recent two-year rating period (1987 and 1988), the stock paid an average annual current return (dividend yield) of 3.0 percent.

DIVIDEND GROWTH

BTR Nylex traditionally raises its dividend every year. Like all of the company's other figures, the dividend growth has been phenomenal, climbing 1,900 percent (83 percent per year) over the five-year period from 1983 to 1988.

CONSISTENCY

The company has had very consistent growth in its earnings per share, revenues, operating income and book value per share. Its price-earnings ratio of about 14 is excellent for a company that has been growing as quickly as BTR.

MOMENTUM

While BTR continues to grow, it would be impossible for the company to maintain the kind of spectacular growth it enjoyed through the 1980s.

SUMMARY

Fiscal year ended: Dec. 31
(Australian dollars; revenue and operating income in millions)

	1990*	1989	1988	1987	1986	1985	1984	5-year growth, %† (annual/total)
Revenue	—	—	3,192	1,427	718	371	115	100/3,100
Operating income[1]	—	—	577	235	102	516	16	113/4,338
Earnings/share	—	—	0.18	0.07	0.04	0.02	0.01	83/1,900
Dividend/share	—	—	0.075	0.020	0.010	0.005	0.004	83/1,900
Dividend yield, %	—	—	3.4	2.5	1.7	3.3	6.0	—/—
Stock price	2.95	2.89	2.19	0.87	0.65	0.22	0.07	110/4,028
P/E ratio	—	—	14.6	12.5	16.2	8.6	7.5	—/—
Book value/share	—	—	0.63	0.25	0.17	0.08	0.05	—/—

* 6-1-90
† 1983-88, except stock price (1984-89)
1. Profit before tax
Source: CompuStat, Worldscope and company reports.

Note: No ADR; stock price quoted in *Barron's, European Wall Street Journal* and the *Financial Times;* 5-year average annual return in U.S. currency: 112%.

ROTHMANS HOLDINGS LIMITED

5th Floor
139 Macquarie Street
Sydney, NSW 2000
Australia
Tel: (02) 235-3555
Chairman: J.W. Utz
CEO: W. P. Ryan

EARNINGS GROWTH	★ ★ ★
STOCK GROWTH	★ ★ ★ ★
DIVIDEND YIELD	★ ★ ★ ★
DIVIDEND GROWTH	★ ★ ★ ★
CONSISTENCY	★ ★ ★ ★
MOMENTUM	★ ★ ★
SYD	**22 points**

The increasingly hostile market for tobacco products Down Under has done little to dampen profit growth for Australia's leading cigarette manufacturer.

Rothmans, which produces Winfield cigarettes (Australia's leading brand) and a pack of other Australian favorites, has battled stagnant tobacco consumption, mounting excise taxes and a surge of unfavorable reports on the health effects of tobacco. Yet its earnings, revenues and stock price just keep climbing.

As in the United States, Australian tobacco products face extremely high taxes (nearly 200 percent) and a limited ability to advertise—measures the Australian government has imposed to discourage tobacco consumption. But even with these measures, the Australian tobacco industry—similar to its American counterpart—continues to boost profits through higher per-pack sales margins and increased sales abroad.

But while most U.S. tobacco firms have used the cash flow from their tobacco trade to diversify into other industrial segments, Rothmans still collects 98 percent of its revenue from its tobacco business. The lack of diversity could be cause for concern if tobacco sales continue to slide, as expected. So far, however, Rothmans has enjoyed outstanding sustained success.

The company's leading brands are Winfield, Brandon 40's and Special Mild. The company also does a strong business in cigars, pipe tobaccos and roll-your-own tobaccos.

Along with its strong position in the Australian market, Rothmans is the market leader in New Zealand and has been expanding sales in New Guinea, the Philippines, Fiji and Indonesia.

The company earns 64 percent of its revenue from the sale of its own tobacco products and 34 percent from the distribution of imported tobacco.

EARNINGS GROWTH

Rothmans has had record annual sales and earnings for more than 10 consecutive years. Over the five years, earnings per share have climbed 160 percent—21 percent per year. The company reported annual sales of 1.7 billion Australian dollars ($1.3 billion U.S.) in 1989.

STOCK GROWTH

The company's stock price has increased sharply over the past five years, although like most of the Australian market, its stock price declined in the first half of 1990. Over the past five years, the stock has increased 536 percent (40 percent per year).

Including reinvested dividends, a $10,000 investment in Rothmans stock at its median price in 1985 would have grown to about $64,000 five years later. Average annual compounded rate of return (including stock growth and reinvested dividends): about 45 percent.

DIVIDEND YIELD

The company generally pays an excellent yield, which has averaged about 5 percent the past five years. During the most recent two-year rating period (1988 and 1989), the stock paid an average annual current return (dividend yield) of 4.3 percent.

DIVIDEND GROWTH

The company has traditionally raised its dividend every year. Over the past five years, the dividend climbed 420 percent, an annual increase of 33 percent.

CONSISTENCY

Rothmans's growth in all primary facets has been very consistent for many years, with increases in earnings, revenues, book value and dividend each of the past five years. The company has a very respectable long-term debt-to-capital ratio of 5 percent and a price-earnings ratio of about 8.

MOMENTUM

The company had a 44 percent increase in its earnings per share in 1989 and a 14 percent increase in the first half of fiscal 1990. Its sales revenue has flattened out the past couple of years, but its widening profit margins are keeping earnings on the rise.

SUMMARY

Fiscal year ended: June 30
(Australian dollars; revenue and operating income in millions)

	1990*	1989	1988	1987	1986	1985	1984	5-year growth, %† (annual/total)
Revenue[1]	—	1,731	1,685	1,496	993	758	714	20/142
Operating income	—	164	142	142	103	80	71	18/131
Earnings/share	—	1.04	0.72	0.62	0.55	0.44	0.40	21/160
Dividend/share	—	0.52	0.26	0.20	0.16	0.12	0.10	33/420
Dividend yield, %	6	5.7	2.9	2.9	3.8	5.7	7.0	—/—
Stock price	8.80	9.10	9.00	6.80	4.25	2.05	1.43	40/536
P/E ratio	8.0	8.8	12.5	11.0	7.8	4.7	3.6	—/—
Book value/share	—	3.44	3.05	2.59	2.16	1.77	1.46	6/136

* 5–1–90
† 1984–89
1. Net sales
Source: Worldscope.

Note: No ADR; stock price quoted in the *European Wall Street Journal* and the *Financial Times;* 5-year average annual return in U.S. currency: 44%.

19

EMAIL LIMITED

Joynton Ave.
Waterloo, NSW 2017
Australia
Tel: 690-7333
Chairman: Sir Peter Finley

EARNINGS GROWTH	★ ★ ★ ★
STOCK GROWTH	★ ★ ★ ★
DIVIDEND YIELD	★ ★ ★ ★
DIVIDEND GROWTH	★ ★ ★ ★
CONSISTENCY	★ ★ ★
MOMENTUM	★ ★
SYD, NZL	**21 points**

Wash it, dry it, freeze it or fry it, Email makes it, and Aussies buy it.

Email is one of Australia's leading makers of major home and commercial appliances.

The Waterloo-based manufacturer has had an exceptional run of success the past few years, increasing earnings from about 4 cents a share (split adjusted) in 1983 to 40 cents in 1989.

The company divides its operations into four primary segments:

- Major appliances (50 percent of sales). Email manufactures a wide range of home appliances, including refrigerators, ovens, cooktops, microwaves, washers, dryers, dishwashers and air conditioners. Brand names include Kelvinator, Simpson, Westinghouse (manufactured under agreement with the U.S.-based corporation), Frigidaire, Malleys, Early Kooka and Email. A joint venture in China manufactures washing machines for the Chinese market.
- Industrial products (21 percent of sales). The company makes a variety of industrial and commercial products, including furniture, petro (gasoline) pumps, petroleum meters, large air conditioners, storage systems,

printed circuit boards, communications and control systems and electronic components.

- Building products (27 percent of sales). Email makes bathroom and kitchen products, including sinks, faucets and bathtubs, laundry tubs, spas, aluminum grilles for security doors and windows, plumbing supplies and roofing products. The company's Blunts Homes subsidiary manufactures prefabricated houses.
- Electrical products. Email has a 50–50 joint venture with U.S.-based Westinghouse Electric to manufacture and market electric, gas and water meters, circuit breakers, electric control equipment, ventilation and air filtration products and printed circuit boards.

EARNINGS GROWTH

The company has had excellent growth the past few years. Its earnings per share increased 225 percent over the past five years, 27 percent per year.

Email reported total revenue of $1.4 billion (1.1 billion in U.S. dollars) in 1989.

STOCK GROWTH

The company's stock price has climbed quickly over the past five years, increasing 226 percent for the period—27 percent per year.

Including reinvested dividends, a $10,000 investment in Email stock in 1985 would have grown to about $40,000 five years later. Average annual compounded rate of return (including stock growth and reinvested dividends): about 32 percent.

DIVIDEND YIELD

The company generally pays an excellent yield, which has averaged just over 5 percent over the past five years. During the most recent two-year rating period (1989 and 1990), the stock paid an average annual current return (dividend yield) of 4.7 percent.

DIVIDEND GROWTH

Email traditionally raises its dividend each year. The dividend increased 257 percent (29 percent per year) over the five-year period from 1985 to 1990.

CONSISTENCY

The company has had very consistent growth in all of its key financial categories, with many years of increased earnings through 1989. But in fiscal

1990 the company's fortunes were affected by a sluggish Australian economy, and its earnings per share dipped slightly. The company's price-earnings ratio of 7 is very favorable for a growing company.

MOMENTUM

Despite its slight drop in earnings per share in fiscal 1990, Email still appears to be healthy and growing. Its revenue increased 30 percent in fiscal 1990. When the Australian economy picks up, Email should rebound strongly.

SUMMARY

Fiscal year ended: March 31
(Australian dollars; revenue and operating income in millions)

	1990	1989	1988	1987	1986	1985	1984	5-year growth, %† (annual/total)
Revenue	1,368	1,050	914	794	678	541	391	20/152
Operating income	—	126	102	71	61	38	27	36/367
Earnings/share	0.39	0.40	0.28	0.24	0.18	0.12	0.09	27/225
Dividend/share	0.25	0.23	0.16	0.12	0.09	0.07	0.06	29/257
Dividend yield, %	5.0	4.4	5.2	4.7	6.1	7.2	6.5	—/—
Stock price	3.10	3.52	3.10	2.56	1.41	0.95	0.89	27/226
P/E ratio	7.0	8.2	10.2	10.5	7.6	7.8	10.3	—/—
Book value/share	—	2.00	1.68	1.53	1.32	1.17	1.06	14/89

† 1985–90, except operating income and book value/share, 1984–89
Source: Company sources and Worldscope.

Note: No ADR; stock price quoted in the *Financial Times;* 5-year average annual return in U.S. currency: 31%.

20

THE ADELAIDE STEAMSHIP CO. LTD.

123 Greenhill Road, Unley
South Australia 5061
Australia
Tel: (08) 272-3077
Chairman: K.W. Russell
Managing Director: J.G. Spalvins

EARNINGS GROWTH	★ ★ ★
STOCK GROWTH	★ ★ ★ ★
DIVIDEND YIELD	★ ★ ★ ★
DIVIDEND GROWTH	★ ★ ★ ★
CONSISTENCY	★ ★ ★
MOMENTUM	★ ★ ★
MBE, SYD, NZL	**21 points**

For 100 years, Adelaide Steamship vessels cruised the South Pacific, shuttling cargo and passengers from port to port around the Australian continent. But for Adelaide—which was founded in 1875—the sailing got progressively choppier during the 1960s and 1970s, as the shipping and shipbuilding trade encountered hard times.

To survive the storm, the company did what it had to do: it jumped ship. It bailed out of all of its shipping interests except towage operations and began to diversify into other areas. It's been smooth sailing ever since for Adelaide. The company has increased its operating profit for 13 consecutive years, going from $2.7 million in 1977 to $246 million in 1989—an average annual growth rate of 39 percent.

The Unley-based corporation has a divergent network of wholly and partially owned subsidiaries. Among its principal operations are:

- Food and wine. Among Adelaide's principal subsidiaries and associates are Petersville Sleigh foods (Edgell, Birds Eye, Four'n Twenty, Wedgwood), Penfolds Wines, Allowrie Foods Australia, Australian United Foods and Metro Meat.

- Retailing. The company operates David Jones Ltd. department stores and Clark Rubber Ltd. (sporting goods, furniture and swimming pools).
- Timber, woodchips and building industries (16 percent of revenues). The firm operates several timber operations.
- Towage and port service. The company still operates a towage and shipping service, although it now accounts for only about 3 percent of Adelaide's total annual revenue.
- Real estate. Adelaide has several real estate development subsidiaries involved in the development of housing, commercial properties and hotels.
- Optical goods. Martin Wells optical products, a wholly owned subsidiary of Adelaide, accounts for about 3 percent of the company's annual revenue.

EARNINGS GROWTH

Adelaide has had 13 consecutive years of increased operating profits and six consecutive years of earnings-per-share growth, with a total increase over the past five years of 170 percent (22 percent per year). Most of that growth, however, came in 1986, when the EPS jumped 103 percent.

Adelaide had total annual revenues of $409 million (Australian dollars; $309 million U.S.) in 1989. The company and its associated companies have about 50,000 employees and 16,000 shareholders.

STOCK GROWTH

Adelaide Steamship's shareholders could have gotten a little seasick the past few years just rocking along with the stock. It went from $1.55 in 1984 to almost $6 in 1986, only to drop back under $4 in 1988. Over the past five years, the stock has increased 217 percent (26 percent per year).

Including reinvested dividends, a $10,000 investment in Adelaide stock in 1984 would have grown to about $38,000 five years later. Average annual compounded rate of return (including stock growth and reinvested dividends): about 31 percent.

DIVIDEND YIELD

The company generally pays a very good dividend, which has averaged about 5 percent over the past five years. Because of a special pay-out in 1989, the yield for the year was 14 percent.

DIVIDEND GROWTH

The company traditionally raises its dividend nearly every year. Thanks to the special pay-out in 1989, the dividend increased 678 percent (an average of 56 percent per year) over the five-year period from 1984 to 1989.

CONSISTENCY

The company has increased its earnings per share each of the past six years, but its revenue and operating income have dropped two of the past five years. Its recent price-earnings ratio of about 6 is very attractive.

MOMENTUM

The company's earnings per share have not gone up very quickly since 1986, when it jumped 103 percent, but in 1989 operating income and total assets increased by over 40 percent, and the dividend increased 200 percent.

SUMMARY

Fiscal year ended: June 30
(Australian dollars; revenue and operating income in millions)

	1990*	1989	1988	1987	1986	1985	1984	5-year growth, %† (annual/total)
Revenue	—	409	389	473	366	297	433	–1/–5
Operating income	—	246	173	274	210	103	72	28/241
Earnings/share	—	0.81	0.73	0.71	0.66	0.32	0.30	22/170
Dividend/share	—	0.70	0.23	0.22	0.16	0.11	0.09	56/678
Dividend yield, %	—	14.2	6.0	4.6	2.7	3.7	6.1	—/—
Stock price	4.30	4.91	3.78	4.74	5.93	3.11	1.55	26/217
P/E ratio	5.5	6.1	5.2	6.7	9.0	9.6	5.2	—/—
Book value/share	—	4.59	3.97	3.34	2.71	2.26	1.61	23/185

* 5–1–90
† 1984–89
Source: Worldscope.

Note: No ADR; stock price quoted in *Barron's,* the *European Wall Street Journal* and the *Financial Times;* 5-year average annual return in U.S. currency: 30%.

PACIFIC·DUNLOP

PACIFIC DUNLOP

500 Bourke St.
23rd Floor
Melbourne, Victoria 3000
Australia
Tel: (03) 602-4244
Chairman: Sir Leslie Froggatt

EARNINGS GROWTH	★ ★
STOCK GROWTH	★ ★ ★ ★
DIVIDEND YIELD	★ ★ ★ ★
DIVIDEND GROWTH	★ ★
CONSISTENCY	★ ★ ★ ★
MOMENTUM	★ ★ ★ ★
SYD, TYO, LON, NASDAQ (U.S.)	**20 points**

Pacific Dunlop leads the world in the manufacture of plastic gloves. It also has its fingers in a wide range of other plastic and rubber products, ranking among the world leaders in the production of tires, balloons, condoms, hoses, polystyrene and polyurethane foam products, cables, bedding and car batteries.

The company's operations are located primarily in Australia, the United States and Southeast Asia.

Pacific Dunlop divides its operations into seven business segments:

- Gloves and other latex products (9 percent of sales). Most of its latex products are produced by the company's Ansell subsidiary. It is a world leader in the production of household gloves, industrial gloves, medical, surgical and dental gloves, condoms and balloons.
- Electrical, industrial and automotive parts (21 percent of sales). The company distributes non-technical electrical and industrial parts such as transmission parts, fasteners and engineering and mining supplies through a network of about 50 outlets. It also operates about 230 Repco

Auto Parts stores, 93 Checkpoint brake and clutch outlets and 183 ALH Australia electrical supplies outlets, most of which are located in Australia.

- Batteries (19 percent of sales). Through its GNB group, the company manufactures and markets automotive, traction, stationary and submarine batteries and power packs under the Exide, Chloride, Dunlop, Marshall and Masse brands in Australia and New Zealand, and under the Champion, National, Stowaway and Marshall names in the United States.
- Industrial foam, fiber and cables (15 percent of sales). Pacific Dunlop makes industrial rubber and plastic products, including hoses and fittings, plastic extrusions, adhesives, cables and foam padding for the furniture, bedding, automotive and packaging industries.
- Clothing (21 percent of sales). The firm manufactures popular brands of clothing, shoes and sporting goods, primarily in Australia, with some sales abroad.
- Tires (11 percent of sales). Pacific Dunlop manufactures and markets a large line of tires through its 50 percent ownership of South Pacific Tyres. Brand names include Dunlop, Olympic and Kelly. It also sells Goodyear tires in Australia through special arrangement with the Goodyear company.
- Medical products (5 percent of sales). The company makes heart pacemakers, implantable defibrillators, bionic ear implants, diagnostic ultrasound equipment and blood processing equipment through its recently acquired Nucleus/Telectronics subsidiary.

EARNINGS GROWTH

The company has enjoyed steady growth the past few years. Its earnings per share increased 135 percent over the past five years, 19 percent per year.

Pacific Dunlop reported total revenue of 4.5 billion Australian dollars (3.4 billion in U.S. dollars) in 1989.

STOCK GROWTH

The company's stock price has climbed quickly the past five years, increasing 324 percent for the period—27 percent per year.

Including reinvested dividends, a $10,000 investment in Pacific Dunlop stock in 1984 would have grown to about $40,000 five years later. Average annual compounded rate of return (including stock growth and reinvested dividends): about 32 percent.

DIVIDEND YIELD

The company generally pays a generous yield, which has averaged just under 4 percent over the past five years. During the most recent two-year rating period (1988 and 1989), the stock paid an average annual current return (dividend yield) of 3.6 percent.

DIVIDEND GROWTH

Pacific Dunlop raises its dividend most years. The dividend increased 142 percent (19 percent per year) over the five-year period from 1984 to 1989.

CONSISTENCY

The company has had a flawless record of growth in its earnings per share, revenues, operating income and book value per share the past six years. Its price-earnings ratio of about 10 is a very attractive level for a growing company.

MOMENTUM

The company showed strong growth in just about every key category in fiscal 1989. When the sluggish Australian economy begins to perk again, Pacific Dunlop's stock should be poised for growth.

SUMMARY

Fiscal year ended: June 30
(Australian dollars; revenue and operating income in millions)

	1990*	1989	1988	1987	1986	1985	1984	5-year growth, %† (annual/total)
Revenue	—	4,490	3,579	2,672	2,403	1,851	1,503	24/198
Operating income	—	426	339	263	210	164	128	27/232
Earnings/share	—	0.40	0.32	0.27	0.22	0.21	0.17	19/135
Dividend/share	—	0.17	0.13	0.11	0.09	0.09	0.07	19/142
Dividend yield, %	4.0	3.8	3.4	2.5	3.5	5.5	6.0	—/—
Stock price	4.50	4.50	3.85	4.41	2.55	1.64	1.00	27/324
P/E ratio	10.0	11.2	12.0	16.3	11.6	7.8	5.9	—/—
Book value/share	—	1.56	1.48	1.36	1.22	1.08	0.96	10/62

* 5–1–90
† 1984–89
Source: Company sources and Worldscope.
Note: ADR; stock price quoted in *Barron's,* the *Wall Street Journal,* the *European Wall Street Journal* and the *Financial Times;* 5-year average annual return in U.S. currency: 31%.

45

BORAL LIMITED

10th Floor, Norwich House
6-10 O'Connell Street
Sydney, NSW 2000
Australia
Telephone: (02) 232-8800
Fax: (02) 233-6605
Chairman: Sir Peter Finley
CEO: B.R. Kean

EARNINGS GROWTH	★ ★
STOCK GROWTH	★ ★
DIVIDEND YIELD	★ ★ ★ ★
DIVIDEND GROWTH	★ ★ ★ ★
CONSISTENCY	★ ★ ★
MOMENTUM	★ ★ ★ ★
MBE, SYD, NZL	**19 points**

The construction and building industry, by its very nature, is supposed to be a cyclical business, wed to the ups and downs of the overall economy. But apparently no one ever mentioned that to Boral Ltd. The Sydney-based construction-products manufacturer has posted 17 consecutive years of increased operating profits.

Founded in 1948, Boral has more than 200 subsidiaries and annual sales approaching $4 billion (Australian dollars).

While the company does the major share of its business in Australia (83 percent of sales revenue), it does have operations elsewhere around the world. Its North American operations account for about 11 percent of revenue, and its European operations bring in about 3 percent. Boral breaks its operations into five key segments:

- Construction materials (35 percent of sales revenue). The company operates 90 quarries, sand pits and river gravel sites. One of its subsidiaries, Blue Circle Southern Cement, is Australia's largest cement manufacturer. Boral is also a major player in the asphalt, concrete, limestone and fly ash markets.

- Dwelling products (27 percent of sales revenue). Boral supplies clay bricks, roof tiles, windows, plasterboard, timber and other building materials and supplies for the homebuilding market.
- Building products (17 percent). The company caters to the major aspects of commercial and domestic construction, supplying builders with masonry products, precast concrete, stone, reinforcing steel and scaffolding. Johns Perry Lifts, a Boral subsidiary, is a leading manufacturer of elevators, escalators and moving footways.
- Manufacturing and engineering (16 percent). Through its Johns Perry Engineering subsidiary, the company manufactures heavy mechanical and structural equipment and components. Boral also manufactures prefabricated buildings, hardware (primarily under the Cyclone brand), fencing, packaging, gratings, guard railings, steel castings and other construction-related products.
- Energy (5 percent). The company refines and supplies oil, gas and coal for residential, automotive and industrial uses.

EARNINGS GROWTH

The company has had solid growth the past few years. Its earnings per share rose 121 percent over the past five years, 17 percent per year.

Boral reported total revenue of $3.6 billion (2.7 billion in U.S. dollars).

STOCK GROWTH

The company's stock growth has not measured up to its earnings-per-share growth the past three years. It hit a high of around $4 a share in fiscal 1987 and declined in 1988 and 1989. In 1990, however, it has shown signs of a resurgence. Over the five-year rating period, the stock increased 133 percent, 18 percent per year.

Including reinvested dividends, a $10,000 investment in Boral stock at its median price in 1984 would have grown to about $27,000 five years later. Average annual compounded rate of return (including stock growth and reinvested dividends): about 22 percent.

DIVIDEND YIELD

The company generally pays a good yield, which has averaged about 4.5 percent over the past five years. During the most recent two-year rating period (1988 and 1989), the stock paid an average annual current return (dividend yield) of 6.5 percent.

DIVIDEND GROWTH

Boral traditionally raises its dividend nearly every year. The dividend increased 213 percent (26 percent per year) over the five-year period from 1984 to 1989.

CONSISTENCY

The company has had very consistent growth in its earnings per share, revenues, operating income and book value per share. Its price-earnings ratio of about 8 is a very attractive level for a growing company.

MOMENTUM

Boral has had excellent growth the past year. Its earnings per share increased 31 percent in 1989.

SUMMARY

Fiscal year ended: June 30
(Australian dollars; revenue and operating income in millions)

	1990*	1989	1988	1987	1986	1985	1984	5-year growth, %† (annual/total)
Revenue	—	3,625	2,777	2,372	1,969	1,588	1,364	21/165
Operating income[1]	—	593	455	382	320	239	189	26/214
Earnings/share[2]	—	0.42	0.32	0.30	0.31	0.24	0.19	17/121
Dividend/share[2]	—	0.25	0.18	0.15	0.13	0.09	0.08	26/213
Dividend yield, %	8.0	7.5	3.7	3.6	3.8	4.6	4.5	—/—
Stock price	3.54	3.35	3.72	3.97	2.73	1.69	1.44	18/133
P/E ratio	7.5	8.0	10.5	15.2	12.9	7.6	8.0	—/—
Book value/share[2]	—	1.82	1.71	1.58	1.44	1.27	1.10	11/65

* 6–1–90
† 1984–89
1. Profit before tax and interest expense
2. Adjusted for bonus stock issues
Source: Company sources and Worldscope.

Note: ADR; stock price quoted in *Barron's*, the *Wall Street Journal*, the *European Wall Street Journal* and the *Financial Times*; 5-year average annual return in U.S. currency: 21%.

46 LEND LEASE CORPORATION LIMITED

LEND LEASE CORP. LTD.
Level 46, Australia Square
George St.
Sydney, NSW 2000
Australia
Tel: (02) 236-6111
Chairman: S.G. Hornery, A.O.
Managing Director: J.P. Morschel

EARNINGS GROWTH	★ ★
STOCK GROWTH	★ ★
DIVIDEND YIELD	★ ★ ★ ★
DIVIDEND GROWTH	★ ★ ★ ★
CONSISTENCY	★ ★ ★ ★
MOMENTUM	★ ★ ★
MBE, SYD, NZL	**19 points**

Lend Lease continues to make its mark on the Australian landscape. The 32-year-old operation has become Australia's leading property development and management company.

Based in Sydney, the firm is involved in a wide range of development projects throughout Australia, including construction, refurbishing and management of commercial, industrial, retail and residential properties. Among the company's leading subsidiaries are:

Civil & Civic, Australia's largest construction and reconstruction concern. It reported sales of nearly $1 billion (Australian) in fiscal 1989. The operation is involved in a wide range of activities. Recent projects have included the $120 million Capita Building project in Sydney, the $64 million Charlestown Shopping Square project in Newcastle, and the $32 million Arnott's Biscuits factory/office in Brisbane. It is also involved in construction of a major hospital and of the 720-room, $120 million Corn Exchange Hotel—Australia's biggest.

Lend Lease Interiors.   The division is the Australian market leader in upgrading properties, customizing commercial space and providing business communications systems. Its 1989 revenue was $190 million.

Lend Lease Retail.   It manages 12 shopping centers, four of which are owned by Lend Lease.

Lend Lease Development and Lend Lease Commercial.   Both divisions are involved in the construction and renovation of major retail and commercial properties.

Lend Lease also has divisions in New York, San Francisco, London and Singapore.

In all, Lend Lease's property segment accounts for about 90 percent of the company's revenues and 70 percent of its operating profit. The balance of its profit and revenue comes from the company's financial services division. The company offers a wide range of insurance and financial products and services through its MLC Life subsidiary, which Lend Lease acquired in 1985.

EARNINGS GROWTH

The company has had steady growth the past few years. Its earnings per share increased 139 percent over the past five years, 19 percent per year.

Lend Lease reported total revenue of 1.4 billion Australian dollars (1.05 billion in U.S. dollars) in 1989.

STOCK GROWTH

Although the stock has suffered in the depressed Australian stock market the past couple of years, over the past five years, the stock increased 106 percent, 16 percent per year.

Including reinvested dividends, a $10,000 investment in Lend Lease stock at the end of 1984 would have grown to about $26,000 five years later. Average annual compounded rate of return (including stock growth and reinvested dividends): about 21 percent.

DIVIDEND YIELD

The company generally pays an excellent yield, which has averaged about 5 percent over the past five years. During the most recent two-year rating period (1988 and 1989), the stock paid an average annual current return (dividend yield) of 7.3 percent.

DIVIDEND GROWTH

Lend Lease raises its dividend most years. The dividend increased 283 percent (31 percent per year) over the five-year period from 1984 to 1989.

CONSISTENCY

The company has had very consistent growth in its earnings per share, revenues, operating income and book value per share. Its price-earnings ratio of about 10 to 15 is an attractive level for a growing company.

MOMENTUM

Lend Lease has maintained fairly solid growth the past two years—nearly in line with its five-year growth record.

SUMMARY

Fiscal year ended: June 30
(Australian dollars; revenue and operating income in millions)

	1990*	1989	1988	1987	1986	1985	1984	5-year growth, %† (annual/total)
Revenue	—	1,392	1,255	1,222	816	610	533	21/161
Operating income	—	136	118	98	75	52	41	27/237
Earnings/share	—	0.91	0.80	0.69	0.55	0.46	0.38	19/139
Dividend/share[1]	—	0.69	0.91	0.45	0.36	0.26	0.18	31/283
Dividend yield, %	5.0	7.0	7.6	3.2	4.1	4.4	4.8	—/—
Stock price	12.50	9.80	13.10	14.15	8.70	6.80	4.70	16/108
P/E ratio	12.0	9.8	15.2	22.2	13.5	12.6	11.4	—/—
Book value/share	—	4.59	4.39	3.45	3.33	2.62	2.17	21/156

* 5-1-90
† 1984–89
1. Includes special dividend for 1988 and 1989
Source: Company sources and Worldscope.

Note: No ADR; stock price quoted in *Barron's,* the *European Wall Street Journal* and the *Financial Times;* 5-year average annual return in U.S. currency: 20%.

Coles Myer Ltd.

COLES MYER LTD.

800 Toorak Road
Tooronga, Victoria 3146
Australia
Tel: (03) 829-3687
Chairman and CEO: Brian E. Quinn

EARNINGS GROWTH	★ ★
STOCK GROWTH	★ ★
DIVIDEND YIELD	★ ★ ★ ★
DIVIDEND GROWTH	★ ★
CONSISTENCY	★ ★ ★
MOMENTUM	★ ★ ★
MBE, SYD, NZL, LON, NYSE	**16 points**

Coles Myer opened its first store in 1914. Over the past 75 years, it has grown to more than 1,500 stores—with more than a dozen largely autonomous retail chains—making it Australia's largest retailer and the eleventh largest retailer in the world.

In Australia, it holds the distinction of operating both the K Mart stores and Target stores, which are fierce competitors in the U.S. discount retail market.

Coles Myer owns a variety of different types of stores, including groceries, clothing stores, department stores, discount centers and restaurants.

The company opens nearly 100 new stores per year.

The firm's largest chain is Coles New World supermarkets, with about 350 groceries scattered throughout Australia. Its other major retail chains include:

Bi-Lo. Formerly "Shoeys," Bi-Lo is a discount grocery chain with about 100 outlets.

Liquorland. The liquor store chain has about 150 free-standing outlets and about 120 outlets located inside other stores.

Red Rooster. With 125 outlets, Red Rooster is the largest Australian-owned fast food restaurant chain.

Foodtown. The company operates about 30 Foodtown supermarkets in New Zealand.

3 Guys. Also based in New Zealand, this discount food chain has about 25 stores.

K Mart. Coles Myer operates about 140 K Mart stores throughout Australia and is now expanding into New Zealand.

Katies. The company operates about 170 Katies women's clothing stores. Like K Mart, Katies has been expanding into the New Zealand market.

Coles Fossey. Coles variety stores and the Fossey apparel chain were recently merged to form Coles Fossey—now with about 220 outlets throughout Australia.

Myer Stores. The Myer department store chain has been one of Coles Myer's most profitable divisions. The company operates 40 Myer stores, located throughout Australia.

Grace Bros. Most of the 40 Grace Bros. department stores are located in the New South Wales area.

Target. The company operates about 80 Target discount stores throughout Australia.

Coles Myer also owns seven Georgie Pie restaurants in New Zealand.

EARNINGS GROWTH

The company has had solid growth the past few years. Its earnings per share increased 97 percent over the past five years, 15 percent per year.

Coles Myer reported total revenue of $14 billion (10.6 billion in U.S. dollars) in 1989. The company has 166,000 employees and 53,000 shareholders.

STOCK GROWTH

The company's stock price has moved up well through most of the 1980s, although it has fallen off a bit the past couple of years. Over the past five years, the stock price has increased 122 percent, 17 percent per year.

Including reinvested dividends, a $10,000 investment in Coles Myer stock at the end of 1984 would have grown to about $26,000 five years later. Average annual compounded rate of return (including stock growth and reinvested dividends): about 21 percent.

DIVIDEND YIELD

The company generally pays a good yield, which has averaged about 4 percent over the past five years. During the most recent two-year rating period (1988 and 1989), the stock paid an average annual current return (dividend yield) of 3.7 percent.

DIVIDEND GROWTH

Coles Myer raises its dividend most years. The dividend increased 117 percent (17 percent per year) over the five-year period from 1984 to 1989.

CONSISTENCY

The company has had fairly consistent growth in most of its key financial areas, although its earnings per share declined in 1986. Its price-earnings ratio of about 11 is a very attractive level for a growing company.

MOMENTUM

Coles Myer's growth rate the past couple of years has been about in line with its growth rate over the five-year period. Its stock price, however, has dropped off a bit the past two years, due in large part to a slow Australian stock market.

SUMMARY

Fiscal year ended: July 31
(Australian dollars; revenue and operating income in millions)

	1990*	1989	1988	1987	1986	1985	1984	5-year growth, %† (annual/total)
Revenue	—	14,009	12,774	11,370	10,407	6,132	5,443	22/157
Operating income[1]	—	388	328	218	182	126	106	29/266
Earnings/share	—	0.75	0.64	0.43	0.36	0.42	0.38	15/97
Dividend/share	—	0.37	0.31	0.21	0.19	0.19	0.17	17/117
Dividend yield, %	5.0	4.3	3.1	2.9	4.0	4.7	4.6	—/—
Stock price	7.36	8.45	9.94	7.40	4.70	4.00	3.80	17/122
P/E ratio	10.0	11.3	13.7	15.2	11.6	8.5	8.9	—/—
Book value/share	—	3.82	3.54	3.28	3.01	2.90	2.58	8/48

* 6–1–90
† 1984–89
1. Equity consolidated operating profit (after tax and before extraordinary items)
Source: Company sources and Worldscope.

Note: ADR; stock price quoted in *Barron's,* the *Wall Street Journal,* the *European Wall Street Journal* and the *Financial Times;* 5-year average annual return in U.S. currency: 20%.

Belgium

Located in northwest Europe on the North Sea, Belgium is a country of 10 million people. Its major stock exchange is located in Brussels.

The country's chief industries are steel, glassware, diamond cutting, textiles and chemicals.

The currency is the Belgian franc (BEF 35 = US $1, June, 1990). Belgium's gross domestic product was BEF 5.6 trillion ($150 billion) in 1989. Annual rate of inflation has averaged only about 1.3 percent the past three years. Annual growth rate of industrial production has been about 3 percent.

The market value of equity shares of domestic companies on the Brussels Exchange as of January 1, 1989, was US $59 billion.

The Belgian stock market was up 8.3 percent in Belgian currency in 1989 (13.7 percent in U.S. currency). In the first six months of 1990, the market was up (BEF) 14 percent.

With new markets opening up in nearby Eastern Europe, Belgian companies have the potential to do quite well in the years ahead.

60

DELHAIZE "LE LION" S.A.

Rue Osseghem 53
1080 Brussels
Belgium
Tel: 02 412 2111
Chairman: Henry Stroobant
President and CEO: Guy Beckers

EARNINGS GROWTH	★ ★ ★
STOCK GROWTH	★ ★ ★ ★
DIVIDEND YIELD	★
DIVIDEND GROWTH	★ ★
CONSISTENCY	★ ★ ★
MOMENTUM	★ ★ ★ ★
BRU	**17 points**

There is a statute in Belgium known to the foods industry as the "padlock law." Its intent is to limit the size and number of Belgian groceries. Since the padlock law was enacted in 1975, aggressive growth companies in the Belgian foods industry have had three options: stop growing, change industries or take their business elsewhere.

Delhaize chose option three. It came to America. And in America, it has grown at an astounding pace.

The company owns a 44 percent share of the North Carolina-based supermarket chain Food Lion, which has been America's fastest-growing grocery. The company opens about 100 new stores a year and had 663 stores at the end of 1989. Its stores are located throughout the Southeast—North and South Carolina, Virginia, Georgia, Tennessee, Florida, Maryland and Delaware. Expansion plans called for the company to move into Pennsylvania in 1990.

The key to Food Lion's success has been its low prices and rapid turnover of inventory. This low margins/high volume philosophy is reflected in the company's corporate slogan: "We'd rather make five fast pennies than one slow nickel." To keep costs to a minimum, the company operates its own truck fleet and regional distribution centers.

Elsewhere in the United States, Delhaize also owns a 60 percent share of a group of seven Cub Foods stores in the Atlanta area.

The company has some other holdings outside the United States. In Belgium, Delhaize operates just over 100 Delhaize "Le Lion" supermarkets, 65 AD Delhaize stores, 51 Dial discount food stores and 65 Di drugstores. It also supplies 150 affiliate stores.

In Portugal, Delhaize holds a 38 percent stake in Pingo Doce, a food distribution business with 23 supermarkets and 7 small food stores.

EARNINGS GROWTH

The company has had strong growth the past few years. Its earnings per share increased 187 percent over the past five years, 23 percent per year.

Delhaize reported total revenue of 260 billion Belgian francs (7 billion U.S. dollars) in 1989.

STOCK GROWTH

The company's stock price has moved up very quickly the past five years, increasing 388 percent for the period—37 percent per year.

Including reinvested dividends, a $10,000 investment in Delhaize stock in 1984 would have grown to about $51,000 five years later. Average annual compounded rate of return (including stock growth and reinvested dividends): about 39 percent.

DIVIDEND YIELD

The company generally pays a modest yield, which has averaged just under 2 percent over the past five years. During the most recent two-year rating period (1988 and 1989), the stock paid an average annual current return (dividend yield) of 1.3 percent.

DIVIDEND GROWTH

Delhaize traditionally raises its dividend each year. The dividend increased 140 percent (19 percent per year) over the five-year period from 1984 to 1989.

CONSISTENCY

The company has had steady growth in its earnings per share, revenues, operating income and book value per share, with a couple of exceptions. Revenues declined in 1986 and earnings per share declined in 1985. Its high price-earnings ratio of around 20 is consistent with many other growing companies.

MOMENTUM

Delhaize has had excellent growth the past two years. Its earnings per share increased 57 percent in 1988 and 34 percent in 1989.

SUMMARY

Fiscal year ended: Dec. 31
(Belgian francs; revenue and operating income in billions)

	1990*	1989	1988	1987	1986	1985	1984	5-year growth, %† (annual/total)
Revenue	—	260	211	170	168	187	169	9/52
Operating income	—	—	7.1	5.8	5.4	3.5	3.5	24/197
Earnings/share	—	313.00	234.00	149.00	132.00	83.00	109.00	23/187
Dividend/share	—	60.00	48.00	37.00	30.00	27.00	25.00	19/140
Dividend yield, %	1.5	1.1	1.4	1.6	1.4	1.9	2.7	—/—
Stock price	5,760	5,700	4,790	3,050	2,800	1,718	1,120	37/388
P/E ratio	19	23.0	22.5	20.5	21.2	20.7	10.4	—/—
Book value/share	—	—	966.70	755.00	759.00	773.60	842.60	6/37

* 5–1–90
† 1984–89, except operating income and book value/share, 1983–88
Source: Company sources and Worldscope.

Note: No ADR; stock price quoted in *Barron's,* the *European Wall Street Journal* and the *Financial Times;* 5-year average annual return in U.S. currency: 56%.

Canada

The United States' neighbor to the north, Canada, is the world's second largest country in terms of area (and soon could become the largest if the movement toward the piece-by-piece break-up of the Soviet Union continues). In terms of population, however, Canada is not among the leaders: it has about 25 million people.

Canada's major industries include mining, oil and gas, paper and forest products, consumer products, industrial products, chemicals, real estate, construction, transportation, finance and communications.

The currency is the Canadian dollar (CAD 1.17 = US $1, June, 1990). Its GNP was CAD 599 billion (US $502 billion) in 1988. Canada's inflation rate the past three years has been around 4 percent. Real economic growth the past several years has also averaged about 4 percent per year. The market value of all domestic stocks traded on the Toronto Exchange, the major exchange in Canada, was US $241.5 billion as of January 1, 1989. The country also has exchanges in Montreal, Calgary, Winnipeg and Vancouver.

In 1989 the Canadian stock market was up 17.8 percent in Canadian currency (21.4 percent in U.S. currency). Through the first six months of 1990, the Canadian market was in a slump, down (CAD) 8.7 percent.

27

LAIDLAW

LAIDLAW, INC.

3221 North Service Road
P.O. Box 5028
Burlington, Ontario L7R 3Y8
Canada
Tel: (416) 336-1800
Chairman and CEO: Michael G. DeGroote
President and COO: Douglas R. Gowland

EARNINGS GROWTH	★ ★ ★ ★
STOCK GROWTH	★ ★ ★ ★
DIVIDEND YIELD	★
DIVIDEND GROWTH	★ ★ ★ ★
CONSISTENCY	★ ★ ★ ★
MOMENTUM	★ ★ ★
TOR, NASDAQ (U.S.)	**20 points**

Laidlaw hauls solid waste and school children. The Burlington, Ontario, company operates North America's largest school bus service and third largest solid waste disposal service.

One of the most profitable companies in North America, Laidlaw has experienced outstanding growth the past few years in both of its primary segments. Its net income grew 25-fold during the 1980s, and its earnings per share rose 12-fold.

Laidlaw's largest segment is waste services, which accounts for about 55 percent of the company's revenues. Its hottest growth area is chemical waste services. Through its GSX Chemical Services subsidiary, the company collects, treats and reclaims or disposes of a variety of chemical wastes. The firm has established a national network of treatment facilities throughout the United States, along with seven regional service centers.

In all, Laidlaw provides disposal services for more than 155,000 commercial and industrial customers and 1.7 million residential customers in 20 states and 6 Canadian provinces. It operates about 40 landfills.

69

The company claims to have initiated North America's first residential recycling program in Kitchener, Ontario. Today, Laidlaw collects recyclables from half a million homes in the United States and Canada. It also recently completed a gas recovery plant in California that burns the methane created from decaying landfill refuse to generate electricity for the Coyote Canyon area.

Laidlaw Transit, the company's school bus operation, accounts for about 43 percent of the firm's total revenues. Its 22,000 buses and vans transport more than a million children to school each day.

EARNINGS GROWTH

The company has had outstanding growth the past few years. Its earnings per share increased 422 percent over the past five years, 39 percent per year.

Laidlaw reported total revenue of $1.4 billion (Canadian dollars) in 1989.

STOCK GROWTH

The company's stock price has moved up very quickly the past five years, increasing 510 percent for the period—42 percent per year.

Including reinvested dividends, a $10,000 investment in Laidlaw stock at the end of 1984 would have grown to about $59,000 five years later. Average annual compounded rate of return (including stock growth and reinvested dividends): about 43 percent.

DIVIDEND YIELD

The company generally pays a modest yield, which has averaged about 1 percent over the past five years. During the most recent two-year rating period (1988 and 1989), the stock paid an average annual current return (dividend yield) of 1.4 percent.

DIVIDEND GROWTH

Laidlaw traditionally raises its dividend every year. The dividend jumped 666 percent (51 percent per year) over the five-year period from 1984 to 1989.

CONSISTENCY

The company has had very consistent growth in its earnings per share, revenues, operating income and book value per share. Its price-earnings ratio of about 18 to 20 is consistent with other fast-growing North American companies.

MOMENTUM

Laidlaw has maintained strong growth the past two years, with a gain in earnings per share of 31 percent in 1988 and 24 percent in 1989.

SUMMARY

Fiscal year ended: Aug. 31
(Canadian dollars; revenue and operating income in millions)

	1990*	1989	1988	1987	1986	1985	1984	5-year growth, %† (annual/total)
Revenue	—	1,413	1,183	964	517	400	320	35/341
Operating income	—	258	198	135	81	65	—	41/296
Earnings/share	—	0.94	0.76	0.58	0.30	0.23	0.18	39/422
Dividend/share	—	0.23	0.15	0.10	0.05	0.05	0.03	51/666
Dividend yield, %	1.1	1.6	1.1	0.8	0.9	1.3	1.5	—/—
Stock price	22.60	18.30	13.40	13.00	7.00	4.00	3.00	42/510
P/E ratio	20.0	15.6	18.1	20.2	18.5	16.3	11.2	—/—
Book value/share	—	6.09	3.98	3.73	1.94	1.19	0.98	43/521

* 5–1–90
† 1984–89, except operating income, 1985–89 (4 yrs.)
Source: Company sources.

Note: No ADR; stock price quoted in *Barron's,* the *Wall Street Journal,* the *European Wall Street Journal* and the *Financial Times;* 5-year average annual return in U.S. currency: 47%.

89

THE OSHAWA GROUP LTD.

302 The East Mall
Etobicoke, Ontario M9B 6B8
Canada
Tel: (416) 236-1971
Fax: (416) 236-2071
Chairman and CEO: Allister P. Graham
President and COO: Jonathan A. Wolfe

EARNINGS GROWTH	★
STOCK GROWTH	★ ★
DIVIDEND YIELD	★ ★
DIVIDEND GROWTH	★
CONSISTENCY	★ ★ ★ ★
MOMENTUM	★ ★ ★
MON, TOR	**13 points**

Oshawa helps keep Canada's pantries stocked and its prescriptions filled. With annual revenue of about $5 billion (Canadian dollars), Oshawa is one of Canada's leading food suppliers.

The company's main line of business is as a food wholesaler for IGA supermarkets and independent grocers and convenience stores throughout Canada. It also owns several of its own grocery stores as well as two drug store chains and a major Canadian department store operation.

Oshawa breaks its operations into three primary divisions including:

- Wholesale and retail food (79 percent of sales). The company serves as a wholesale food supplier for about 500 franchised IGA stores and 40 company-owned IGAs, 1,400 convenience stores and 800 other groceries. The company has operations in four geographic regions: in Ontario as Oshawa Foods (Toronto), Dutch Boy (Kitchener) and Elliott Marr (London); in Quebec as Hudon et Deaudelin ltee; in Atlantic Canada as Bolands; and in Western Canada as Codville Distributors.

- Food service and produce (5 percent of sales). Through several subsidiaries, Oshawa distributes groceries, frozen foods and meats to the food service industry and juice and coffee to the dispenser services.
- General merchandise (16 percent of sales). The company owns 51 Towers Department stores in locations throughout Canada. It also owns Kent Drugs Limited, which operates 45 stores in Ontario, Manitoba, New Brunswick and Nova Scotia under the names Drug City and Metro Drugs. Oshawa recently purchased 107 Pharma Plus Drugmarts. It also operates 25 pharmacies within other, larger stores.

EARNINGS GROWTH

The company has enjoyed steady growth the past few years. Its earnings per share increased 85 percent over the past five years, 13 percent per year.

Oshawa reported total revenue of 4.9 billion Canadian dollars (4 billion U.S. dollars) in fiscal 1990.

STOCK GROWTH

The company's stock price has moved up consistently the past five years, increasing 126 percent for the period—18 percent per year.

Including reinvested dividends, a $10,000 investment in Oshawa stock in 1984 would have grown to about $25,000 five years later. Average annual compounded rate of return (including stock growth and reinvested dividends): about 20 percent.

DIVIDEND YIELD

The company generally pays a modest yield, which has averaged about 1.5 percent over the past five years. During the most recent two-year rating period (1988 and 1989), the stock paid an average annual current return (dividend yield) of 1.5 percent.

DIVIDEND GROWTH

Oshawa traditionally raises its dividend each year. The dividend increased 95 percent (14 percent per year) over the five-year period from 1984 to 1989.

CONSISTENCY

The company has had very consistent growth in all of the key categories— earnings per share, revenues, operating income and book value per share. Its price-earnings ratio of about 13 is consistent with other growing Canadian companies.

MOMENTUM

Oshawa is continuing its steady growth with earnings-per-share and revenue gains the past couple of years that exceed slightly its five-year average.

SUMMARY

Fiscal year ended: Jan. 28
(Canadian dollars; revenue and operating income in millions)

	1990	1989	1988	1987	1986	1985	1984	5-year growth, %† (annual/total)
Revenue	4,948	4,274	3,804	3,526	3,102	2,665	2,434	13/85
Operating income	107	95	89	79	67	58	43	13/84
Earnings/share	2.11	1.78	1.56	1.48	1.29	1.14	0.92	13/85
Dividend/share	0.39	0.35	0.31	0.27	0.24	0.20	0.16	14/95
Dividend yield, %	1.4	1.5	1.5	1.5	1.5	1.2	1.8	—/—
Stock price	28.25	24.25	20.38	18.75	16.63	12.50	8.38	18/126
P/E ratio	13.5	13.6	13.1	12.1	11.2	8.7	7.0	—/—
Book value/share	15.42	12.13	10.67	9.39	8.17	7.11	6.16	17/116

† 1985–90
Source: Company sources and Worldscope.

Note: No ADR; stock price quoted in *Barron's,* the *Wall Street Journal,* the *European Wall Street Journal* and the *Financial Times;* 5-year average annual return in U.S. currency: 24%.

France

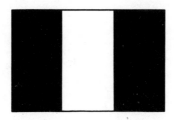

A Western European nation of 56 million people, France's major industries include steel, chemicals, autos, textiles, wine, perfume, aircraft and electronic equipment.

The currency is the French franc (FRF 5.64 = US $1, June, 1990). Its gross domestic product was FRF 5.7 trillion (US $933 billion) in 1988. France's inflation rate the past three years has been around 2.7 percent. Real economic growth the past several years has also averaged about 3 percent per year. The market value of all domestic stocks traded on the Paris Exchange, the major exchange in France, was US $223 billion as of January 1, 1989. The country also has smaller exchanges in Bordeaux, Lyon, Nancy, Lille, Marseille and Nantes.

In 1989 the French stock market was up 28.1 percent in French currency (34.2 percent in U.S. currency). Through the first six months of 1990, the French market was in a mild slump, down (FRF) 1.5 percent.

The country stands to benefit in the future from both the opening of Eastern Europe and the organization of the European Economic Community.

17

CMB PACKAGING

88 rue du Dôme
BP 7
92101 Boulogne-sur-Seine
France
Tel: (1) 47 61 25 25
President: Jean-Marie Descarpentries

EARNINGS GROWTH	★ ★ ★ ★
STOCK GROWTH	★ ★ ★ ★
DIVIDEND YIELD	★ ★ ★
DIVIDEND GROWTH	★ ★ ★ ★
CONSISTENCY	★ ★ ★ ★
MOMENTUM	★ ★
PAR, LON	**21 points**

After a remarkable decade of growth—capped by its 1989 merger with British-based Metalbox Packaging—CMB has wrapped up the dominant position in the European packaging industry.

With its enormous volume of bottles and boxes, cartons and cans, CMB (formerly Carnaud) is now Europe's largest packaging company and the third largest in the world.

CMB stock is traded on both the Paris stock exchange (in francs) and the London exchange (in pounds) as a result of the merger that brought Metalbox and Carnaud together.

While the greatest share of its business is still based in France (37 percent of revenue) and Britain (21 percent of revenue), CMB has a number of subsidiaries elsewhere in Europe, Africa and the Far East. It also owns U.S.-based Risdon Corp. and holds a 50 percent share of Genesis Packaging Systems (also based in the United States). In all, the company operates 145 factories in 29 countries.

CMB is involved in the manufacture of a wide range of packaging products. It controls a 35 percent share of the European food packaging industry, a 22 percent share of the beverage cans market, a 10 percent share of the health and beauty products market and a 19 percent share of the European industrial packaging market.

Based on materials used, the company breaks its operations into three segments:

- Metal packaging (72 percent of revenue). The company produces food and beverage cans and a variety of industrial packaging.
- Plastic packaging (21 percent of revenue). CMB produces plastic wrappers, bottles, tubes and other types of containers for foods, cosmetics and other consumer goods and industrial products.
- Others (7 percent of revenue). The company handles a variety of packaging needs for glass bottles, cardboard boxes and other materials.

EARNINGS GROWTH

The company has had tremendous growth the past few years. Its earnings per share increased 216 percent over the past five years, 26 percent per year.

CMB reported total revenue of 21 billion francs (3.7 billion in U.S. dollars) in 1989. The company has 37,000 employees.

STOCK GROWTH

The company's stock price has exploded over the past five years, increasing 909 percent for the period—60 percent per year.

Including reinvested dividends, a $10,000 investment in CMB stock in 1984 would have grown to about $275,000 five years later. Average annual compounded rate of return (including stock growth and reinvested dividends): about 63 percent.

DIVIDEND YIELD

The company generally pays a fairly good yield, which has averaged about 3 percent over the past five years. During the most recent two-year rating period (1988 and 1989), the stock paid an average annual current return (dividend yield) of 2.2 percent.

DIVIDEND GROWTH

CMB traditionally raises its dividend every year. The dividend jumped 237 percent (27 percent per year) over the five-year period from 1984 to 1989.

CONSISTENCY

The company has had very consistent growth in its earnings per share, revenues, operating income and book value per share. Its price-earnings ratio of about 10 to 14 is very attractive for a rapidly growing company.

MOMENTUM

CMB's growth has begun to flatten out somewhat over the past couple of years. Its earnings per share were up 13 percent in 1989—far short of the 26 percent average annual growth rate the company had posted over the five-year period.

SUMMARY

Fiscal year ended: Dec. 31
(French francs; revenue and operating income in millions)

	1990*	1989	1988	1987	1986	1985	1984	5-year growth, %† (annual/total)
Revenue	—	21,316	9,456	7,231	6,585	6,572	6,265	28/240
Operating income	—	2,084	1,042	749	605	652	600	28/247
Earnings/share	—	17.10	15.07	10.80	7.14	5.61	5.40	26/216
Dividend/share	—	5.40	4.50	3.20	2.50	1.70	1.60	27/237
Dividend yield, %	3	2.2	2.2	3.7	2.5	2.6	6.7	—/—
Stock price	211.00	240.00	197.43	85.42	97.33	63.97	23.78	60/909
P/E ratio	10.0	14.0	13.1	7.9	13.6	11.4	4.4	—/—
Book value/share	—	—	72.60	49.84	43.79	37.55	35.77	15/102

* 6–1–90
† 1984–89, except book value/share, 1983–88
Source: Company sources and CompuStat.

Note: No ADR; stock price quoted in the *Financial Times;* 5-year average annual return in U.S. currency: 82%.

37

LVMH

MOËT HENNESSY . LOUIS VUITTON

LVMH MOËT HENNESSY LOUIS VUITTON
30 Avenue Hoche
75008 Paris
France
Tel: (1) 45 63 01 01
Chairman: Frédéric Chandon de Briailles
President: Bernard Arnault

EARNINGS GROWTH	★ ★ ★
STOCK GROWTH	★ ★ ★
DIVIDEND YIELD	★ ★
DIVIDEND GROWTH	★ ★ ★ ★
CONSISTENCY	★ ★ ★ ★
MOMENTUM	★ ★ ★ ★
PAR	**20 points**

With its champagnes and vintage wines, its custom leather goods and fine perfumes, LVMH lays claim to the title of the corporate world's "luxury leader."

Born of the 1987 merger between wines-and-spirits giant Moët-Hennessy and leather-goods leader Louis Vuitton, LVMH has combined forces to market its growing list of fine French frills from one corner of the globe to the other.

The Paris-based manufacturer, which also owns Christian Dior and Givenchy perfumes and Roc beauty products, has well over 100 subsidiaries in more than 30 countries.

The company breaks its operations into four primary segments:

- Champagne and wines (30 percent of sales). The company produces Dom Perignon, Moët & Chandon, Mercier and Ruinart champagnes. Moet & Chandon, the leading champagne exporter, sells nearly 30 million bottles of the bubbly a year, about 80 percent of which is sold outside of France. The United States is the division's largest export market.

- Cognac and spirits (25 percent of sales). LVMH sells about 35 million bottles of cognac a year. Its sales come primarily from Hennessy and Hine cognac. The company's Pellisson division sells about 8 million bottles of brandy a year.
- Luggage, leather goods and accessories (21 percent of sales). Founded in 1854, Louis Vuitton (Malletier) is one of the leading producers of luggage and leather goods. The division has experienced exceptional growth recently, as the popularity of leather has soared worldwide. In addition to its manufacturing operations, the company operates about 130 stores, primarily in Europe and the United States.
- Perfumes and beauty products (23 percent of sales). Parfums Christian Dior produces six fragrance lines for women and three for men. Parfums Givenchy produces four fragrance lines for women and three for men. Roc specializes in pharmaceutical skin-care products, including a wide range of hypoallergenic treatments.

EARNINGS GROWTH

The company has had outstanding growth the past few years. Its earnings per share increased 191 percent over the past five years, 24 percent per year.

LVMH has total revenue of 16 billion francs (2.7 billion in U.S. dollars).

STOCK GROWTH

The company's stock price has also been exceptional, increasing 190 percent the past five years—24 percent per year.

Including reinvested dividends, a $10,000 investment in LVMH stock in 1984 would have grown to about $31,000 five years later. Average annual compounded rate of return (including stock growth and reinvested dividends): about 25 percent.

DIVIDEND YIELD

The company generally pays a modest yield, which has averaged just over 1 percent over the past five years. During the most recent two-year rating period, the stock paid an average current return (dividend yield) of 1.7 percent.

DIVIDEND GROWTH

LVMH traditionally raises its dividend every year. The dividend increased 216 percent (26 percent per year) over the recent five-year period.

CONSISTENCY

The company has had a flawless record of growth in its earnings per share, revenues, operating income and book value per share for many years. Its price-earnings ratio of about 20 is a bit high but should not be a problem if the firm continues its strong growth.

MOMENTUM

LVMH has continued to grow quickly the past two years. Its earnings per share increased 48 percent in 1988, and its stock price climbed 110 percent in 1988 and 15 percent in 1989.

SUMMARY

Fiscal year ended: Dec. 31
(French francs; revenue and operating income in millions)

	1990*	1989	1988	1987	1986	1985	1984	5-year growth, %† (annual/total)
Revenue	—	—	16,442	13,247	8,051	7,689	6,841	25/208
Operating income	—	—	4,240	3,166	1,715	1,762	1,493	31/284
Earnings/share	—	—	173.15	117.16	111.22	78.83	76.65	24/191
Dividend/share	—	—	44.00	32.00	25.00	15.97	15.97	26/216
Dividend yield, %	—	1.5	1.3	2.0	1.3	1.0	1.2	—/—
Stock price	4,685	3,798	3,302	1,570	1,983	1,635	1,301	24/190
P/E ratio	—	20.0	19.1	13.4	17.8	20.7	17.0	—/—
Book value/share	—	—	825.52	673.02	580.58	506.52	458.14	17/117

* 5-1-90
† 1983–88, except stock growth, 1984–89
Source: Worldscope.

Note: ADR; stock price quoted in the *Wall Street Journal* and the *Financial Times;* 5-year average annual return in U.S. currency: 38%.

41

ACCOR

33 avenue du Maine
Tour Maine-Montparnasse
75755 Paris Cedex 15
France
Tel: (1) 43 20 13 26
Fax: (1) 45 38 71 34
Co-chairman: Gérard Pélisson
Co-chairman: Paul Dubrule

EARNINGS GROWTH	★ ★
STOCK GROWTH	★ ★ ★ ★
DIVIDEND YIELD	★ ★
DIVIDEND GROWTH	★ ★ ★
CONSISTENCY	★ ★ ★ ★
MOMENTUM	★ ★ ★ ★
PAR	**19 points**

Accor has been spreading French hospitality around the world. The Paris-based company operates more than 800 hotels in 53 countries; it owns one of the world's largest catering services, an international network of restaurants and the world's largest voucher service.

Among Accor's more prominent hotel chains are the Hotel Sofitel, Novotel, Hotel Mercure, Hotel Ibis economy hotels, Hotel Urbis, Hotel Formule 1, Hotelia (geared to seniors), PanSea resort hotels and Parthenon serviced apartment hotels. It recently purchased the large U.S. motel chain, Motel 6.

Accor has even made in-roads into the Chinese hotel market. Through a joint venture with a Chinese construction firm, Accor operates six Travel Inns and a Novotel Hotel in the Peoples Republic of China and is completing plans to open more hotels there.

The company opens about 100 new hotels a year around the world. Its hotel business accounts for 50 percent of total revenues.

Its other business segments include:

- Restaurants (15 percent of revenues). The company operates about 400 restaurants, about 70 of which are located outside France. Primary chains include Pizza Del Arte (23 restaurants), Courte-Paille (100 units), Churrasco (30 restaurants in Germany), Le Boeuf Jardinier (11 units in France), B & Burger and Lenotre.
- Institutional catering (24 percent of revenues). Accor's institutional catering business serves 200 million meals a year in more than 2,000 institutional cafeterias and restaurants. Its strongest markets outside of France are Brazil, Italy, Spain and Germany.
- Service vouchers (26 percent of operating profit). The company's Ticket Restaurant division is the world's leading issuer of service vouchers. It issues about 700 million vouchers worldwide. The vouchers are typically used for corporate incentive and perks programs. The company's client base includes 75,000 businesses and 250,000 participating restaurants and supermarkets.

EARNINGS GROWTH

The company has had solid growth the past few years. Its earnings per share increased 120 percent over the past five years, 17 percent per year.

Accor has annual revenue of 12 billion francs (2 billion in U.S. dollars).

STOCK GROWTH

The company's stock price has moved up very quickly the past five years, increasing 279 percent for the period—30 percent per year.

Including reinvested dividends, a $10,000 investment in Accor stock in 1984 would have grown to about $40,000 five years later. Average annual compounded rate of return (including stock growth and reinvested dividends): about 32 percent.

DIVIDEND YIELD

The company generally pays a moderate yield, which has averaged about 2 percent over the past five years. During the most recent two-year rating period, the stock paid an average annual current return (dividend yield) of 2.3 percent.

DIVIDEND GROWTH

Accor traditionally raises its dividend every year. The dividend increased 150 percent (20 percent per year) over the recent five-year period.

CONSISTENCY

The company has had a very consistent record of growth in its earnings per share, revenues, operating income and book value per share for the past five years. Its price-earnings ratio of about 20 is high for a French company but should not be a problem if the company continues its strong growth.

MOMENTUM

Accor has had excellent growth the past two years. Its earnings per share increased 21 percent in 1988, and its stock price jumped 88 percent in 1988 and 52 percent in 1989.

SUMMARY

Fiscal year ended: Dec. 31
(French francs; revenue and operating income in millions)

	1990*	1989	1988	1987	1986	1985	1984	5-year growth, %† (annual/total)
Revenue	—	—	12,337	11,120	9,558	8,053	6,755	16/109
Operating income	—	—	828	719	642	322	200	32/305
Earnings/share	—	—	29.22	24.32	21.35	19.04	15.95	17/120
Dividend/share	—	—	10.50	8.50	6.50	5.80	4.90	20/150
Dividend yield, %	—	—	1.8	2.7	1.4	2.0	2.1	—/—
Stock price	935.00	904.00	594.00	316.00	478.00	295.00	238.00	30/279
P/E ratio	—	—	20.3	13.0	22.4	15.5	14.9	—/—
Book value/share	—	—	252.26	229.31	144.38	115.32	89.58	27/236

* 5–1–90
† 1983–88, except stock price, 1984–89
Source: Company sources and Worldscope.
Note: No ADR; stock price quoted in *Barron's,* the *Wall Street Journal,* the *European Wall Street Journal* and the *Financial Times;* 5-year average annual return in U.S. currency: 46%.

LAFARGE COPPÉE

28 rue Émile Ménier
75116 Paris
France
Tel: (1) 47 04 11 11
Chairman and CEO: Bertrand Collomb

EARNINGS GROWTH	★ ★ ★ ★
STOCK GROWTH	★ ★ ★ ★
DIVIDEND YIELD	★ ★
DIVIDEND GROWTH	★ ★
CONSISTENCY	★ ★ ★
MOMENTUM	★ ★ ★
PAR, CON, DUS, FRA	**18 points**

Lafarge Coppee has paved itself a prominent place in the world cement market. The Paris-based conglomerate pours about 30 million metric tons of cement per year—making it the third largest producer in the world.

Originally established in 1833, Lafarge Coppee hit its stride over the past decade. It has grown both through aggressive internal expansion and through a rapid-fire series of acquisitions. Lafarge now comprises about 400 companies in 20 countries.

Lafarge generates more than half its revenues from operations outside of France. About 47 percent of revenues come from its French divisions, 38 percent from North America, 10 percent from other European countries and 5 percent from scattered locations around the world.

While Lafarge has been moving toward greater diversification, the company still draws the major share of its income from the cement, concrete and aggregates trade. Cement accounts for about 39 percent of the company's revenues, and concrete and aggregates (sand, gravel and crushed stone used to mix with cement) account for about 30 percent.

Lafarge Coppee has two other divisions:

- Building materials (22 percent of sales revenue). The company produces gypsum wall board, plastic blocks, exterior wall finishes, sealants, calcium aluminate cements, bathroom furnishings, paints and a variety of other building materials.
- Biotechnology (9 percent of sales). The company's Orsan subsidiary concentrates on the agricultural biogenetics market. It is one of the world's top producers of amino acids (including monsodium glutamate, which is used as a food flavor enhancer) and lysine, an animal feed supplement. Orsan is also a leading European seed producer and is active in developing improved hybrids of wheat and other plants.

EARNINGS GROWTH

The company has had exceptional growth the past few years. Its earnings per share jumped 414 percent over the past five years, 39 percent per year.

Lafarge has annual revenue of 23 billion francs (3.7 billion in U.S. dollars).

STOCK GROWTH

The company's stock price has climbed quickly the past five years, increasing 385 percent for the period—37 percent per year.

Including reinvested dividends, a $10,000 investment in Lafarge stock in 1984 would have grown to about $51,000 five years later. Average annual compounded rate of return (including stock growth and reinvested dividends): about 39 percent.

DIVIDEND YIELD

The company generally pays a moderate yield, which has averaged about 2 percent over the past five years. During the most recent two-year rating period, the stock paid an average annual current return (dividend yield) of 2.1 percent.

DIVIDEND GROWTH

Lafarge traditionally raises its dividend each year. The dividend increased 144 percent (19 percent per year) over the recent five-year period.

CONSISTENCY

The company has had very consistent growth in its earnings per share and book value per share. Its revenue, however, declined two of the past five years.

MOMENTUM

Lafarge has continued to enjoy solid growth the past couple of years. Its price-earnings ratio of about 10 is very favorable for a growing French company.

SUMMARY

Fiscal year ended: Dec. 31
(French francs; revenue and operating income in millions)

	1990*	1989	1988	1987	1986	1985	1984	5-year growth, %† (annual/total)
Revenue	—	—	22,684	19,080	16,897	17,443	18,883	5/25
Operating income	—	—	3,576	2,688	2,067	1,551	1,369	18/130
Earnings/share	—	—	37.85	31.00	27.62	19.78	13.66	39/414
Dividend/share	—	—	7.50	6.25	5.25	4.31	3.52	19/144
Dividend yield, %	—	2.0	2.1	2.1	1.5	2.4	4.3	—/—
Stock price	415.00	397.75	354.25	291.25	342.50	181.81	82.04	37/385
P/E ratio	—	10.0	9.4	9.4	12.4	9.2	6.0	—/—
Book value/share	—	—	168.24	147.73	131.27	98.78	83.84	17/124

* 5–1–90
† 1983–88, except stock price, 1984–89
Source: Worldscope.

Note: No ADR; stock price quoted in *Barron's,* the *Wall Street Journal,* the *European Wall Street Journal* and the *Financial Times;* 5-year average annual return in U.S. currency: 54%.

 MERLIN GERIN

MERLIN GERIN

2 chemin des Sources
38240 Meylan
France
Tel: (1) 76 57 60 60
Chairman: Jean Vaujany

EARNINGS GROWTH	★ ★
STOCK GROWTH	★ ★ ★ ★
DIVIDEND YIELD	★ ★
DIVIDEND GROWTH	★ ★
CONSISTENCY	★ ★ ★ ★
MOMENTUM	★ ★ ★ ★
PAR	**18 points**

Merlin Gerin has found hundreds of ways to tap into the electrical equipment market—and the steady current of profits that comes with it.

The company manufactures everything from fuses and switches to electrical substation equipment and nuclear power plant reactor controls.

It has operations throughout Europe (61 percent of revenue), Asia (18 percent), North and South America (10 percent), Africa (8 percent) and Australia (3 percent).

While the company offers no break-down in revenues from its various market segments, it has operations in about a dozen different electrical products sectors, including:

- Extra-high-voltage transmission and distribution. The company builds circuit breakers, isolaters, metal-clad substations and compartmentalized substations.
- Medium-voltage distribution. Merlin Gerin manufactures capacitors, transformers and a line of circuit breakers for the medium-voltage market.

89

- Transformer stations. The company manufactures factory-built substations and on-pole substations for the transformer market, as well as medium-voltage cubicles, switches, fuses, transformers and other components.
- Low-voltage distribution. The company offers circuit breakers and other equipment for this segment.
- Electrical automation systems. The company builds programmable controls for electrical distribution systems and industrial processes.
- Electronic safety systems and radiation protection. Merlin Gerin builds components to enhance safety in nuclear power plants and other industrial applications.

The company also manufactures low-voltage capacitors, power supply interfaces, insulation monitors, remote control devices and a wide range of other electrical systems and equipment.

EARNINGS GROWTH

The company has had steady growth the past five years, with an earnings-per-share increase of 132 percent, 18 percent per year.

Merlin Gerin has annual revenue of 11 billion francs (1.9 billion in U.S. dollars).

STOCK GROWTH

The company's stock price has climbed very quickly the past five years, rising 295 percent for the period—32 percent per year.

Including reinvested dividends, a $10,000 investment in Merlin Gerin stock in 1984 would have grown to about $43,000 five years later. Average annual compounded rate of return (including stock growth and reinvested dividends): about 34 percent.

DIVIDEND YIELD

The company generally pays a moderate yield, which has averaged about 2 percent over the past five years. During the most recent two-year rating period, the stock has paid an average annual current return (dividend yield) of 1.2 percent.

DIVIDEND GROWTH

Merlin Gerin traditionally raises its dividend every year. The dividend increased 117 percent (17 percent per year) over the recent five-year period.

CONSISTENCY

The company has had very consistent growth in its earnings per share, revenues and book value per share for several years.

MOMENTUM

Merlin Gerin has had excellent earnings gains and stock price appreciation the past two years.

SUMMARY

Fiscal year ended: Dec. 31
(French francs; revenue and operating income in millions)

	1990*	1989	1988	1987	1986	1985	1984	5-year growth, %† (annual/total)
Revenue	—	—	11,368	9,770	8,725	7,468	6,246	13/86
Operating income	—	—	450	505	308	265	181	5/30
Earnings/share	—	—	251.28	180.37	169.47	146.94	119.76	18/132
Dividend/share	—	—	48.00	40.00	36.00	32.00	25.73	17/117
Dividend yield, %	—	1.1	1.3	3.2	1.3	1.1	2.0	—/—
Stock price	5,790	4,999	3,640	1,240	2,685	2,840	1,263	32/295
P/E ratio	—	18.0	14.5	6.9	15.8	19.3	10.5	—/—
Book value/share	—	—	1,427	1,318	1,133	959	671	21/156

* 5-1-90
† 1983–88, except stock price, 1984–89
Source: Worldscope.

Note: No ADR; stock price quoted in the *Financial Times;* 5-year average annual return in U.S. currency: 48%.

BSN GROUPE

7 rue de Téhéran
75381 Paris Cedex 08
France
Tel: (1) 42 99 10 10
Fax: (1) 42 25 67 16
Chairman: Antoine Riboud
Vice-Chairman and President: Georges Lecallier

EARNINGS GROWTH	★ ★ ★
STOCK GROWTH	★ ★ ★ ★
DIVIDEND YIELD	★ ★
DIVIDEND GROWTH	★ ★
CONSISTENCY	★ ★ ★ ★
MOMENTUM	★ ★ ★
PAR, BRU, LON, ZUR, BAS, GEN	**18 points**

BSN is not your typical milk and biscuits food company—although it does do a huge business in both. It also sells beer and ale (Kronenbourg is its leading brand), champagne, mineral water, sauces, seasonings, pastas and desserts.

The Paris-based company is one of the world's largest food processors—with total sales of $8 billion (48.7 billion francs)—and one of the fastest growing. Its assets have doubled over the past five years, and its operating earnings have tripled.

BSN has achieved its outstanding growth primarily through acquisitions of other food and beverage companies throughout Europe. It also owns several U.S. food companies, including Dannon (dairy foods), General Bisquits of America and Lea & Perrins.

The company divides its operations into six segments:

- Dairy products (26 percent of revenues). The company makes a variety of cheeses, desserts, yogurts and other milk-based products. Its main product line is Gervais Danone France.
- Grocery products (24 percent of revenues). The company makes a variety of pasta products (including Panzani noodles), jams, baby foods, mustards (Amora), vinegars, sauces, soups and prepared dishes.
- Biscuits (17 percent of revenues). BSN sells over $1 billion a year in crackers and biscuits, primarily under its LU and L'Alsacienne brands.
- Beer (14.5 percent of revenues). The company is the brewer of several brands of beer, including Kronenbourg, Kanterbräu and Obernai.
- Champagne and mineral water (8 percent of revenues). BSN sells about 13 million bottles of champagne a year under the Pommery and Lanson labels. It also does a strong business in bottled water; its leading brand is Evian.
- Containers (11.5 percent of revenues). The company is a leading manufacturer of glass containers for foods and beverages.

EARNINGS GROWTH

The company has had strong growth the past few years. Its earnings per share increased 144 percent over the past five years, 20 percent per year.

BSN reported total revenue of 49 billion francs (8 billion in U.S. dollars) in 1989.

STOCK GROWTH

The company's stock price has grown quickly the past five years, increasing 222 percent for the period—27 percent per year.

Including reinvested dividends, a $10,000 investment in BSN stock in 1984 would have grown to about $37,000 five years later. Average annual compounded rate of return (including stock growth and reinvested dividends): about 30 percent.

DIVIDEND YIELD

The company generally pays a moderate yield, which has averaged about 2.5 percent over the past five years. During the most recent two-year rating period (1988 and 1989), the stock paid an average annual current return (dividend yield) of 2.3 percent.

DIVIDEND GROWTH

BSN traditionally raises its dividend each year. The dividend increased 109 percent (16 percent per year) over the five-year period from 1984 to 1989.

CONSISTENCY

The company has had a flawless five years of growth in all of the key areas—earnings per share, revenues, operating income and book value. Its price-earnings ratio of about 15 is near average for a growing company.

MOMENTUM

BSN enjoyed sustained growth throughout the past five years, including the two most recent years. Earnings per share increased 23 percent in 1988 and 19 percent in 1989—about in line with its five-year growth rate.

SUMMARY

Fiscal year ended: Dec. 31
(French francs; revenue and operating income in millions)

	1990*	1989	1988	1987	1986	1985	1984	5-year growth, %† (annual/total)
Revenue	—	48,669	42,177	37,156	33,623	28,475	27,293	12/78
Operating income	—	5,022	4,527	3,296	2,724	1,863	1,660	25/202
Earnings/share	—	49.70	41.70	34.00	27.00	21.00	20.30	20/144
Dividend/share	—	11.50	10.00	8.50	7.00	6.00	5.50	16/109
Dividend yield, %	2.0	2.2	2.3	2.9	2.4	3.3	3.4	—/—
Stock price	798.00	774.00	648.00	434.00	435.00	275.00	240.00	27/222
P/E ratio	14.0	15.6	15.5	12.7	16.0	13.1	11.8	—/—
Book value/share	—	348.00	302.60	266.16	219.80	198.60	186.70	13/87

* 5–1–90
† 1984–89
Source: Company sources and Worldscope.

Note: ADR; stock price quoted in *Barron's,* the *Wall Street Journal,* the *European Wall Street Journal* and the *Financial Times;* 5-year average annual return in U.S. currency: 44%.

59

ARJOMARI

GROUPE ARJOMARI

3 rue du Pont de Lodi
75006 Paris
France
Tel: (1) 43 29 21 84
Fax: (1) 43 29 11 91
Chairman, CEO and President: Yves de Courlon

EARNINGS GROWTH	★ ★ ★
STOCK GROWTH	★ ★ ★ ★
DIVIDEND YIELD	★ ★
DIVIDEND GROWTH	★ ★ ★
CONSISTENCY	★ ★ ★
MOMENTUM	★ ★
PAR	**17 points**

Even the most pessimistic Arjomari shareholders can take heart in knowing that if business at the Paris paper producer should ever take a sudden turn for the worse, to make ends meet, the firm could simply print up its own money.

One of Arjomari's specialties is fiduciary and security papers used for bank notes, currency, stock certificates, traveler's checks, lottery tickets and savings documents. Arjomari is the second largest exporter of bank-note papers in the world.

There's little chance, however, that Arjomari will ever have to resort to printing francs to stay afloat. The company has a long history of exceptional earnings, stock price and dividend gains.

Arjomari has patented several anti-counterfeit features for its specialty papers—watermarks and security threads that can be detected either by close inspection or through special detection equipment. The company sells its papers to banks and government printing offices in dozens of countries.

In fact, that crumpled dollar bill in your pocket may well have come from Arjomari.

The company's line of fiduciary and security papers is just one of several lines of paper products Arjomari markets. (Fiduciary papers account for only about 5 percent of the company's total revenue.) The company's other four primary product groups include:

Products for the printing industry and deluxe publications (49 percent of total sales). Arjomari claims to be Europe's largest producer of "premium quality papers." The company produces coated and uncoated papers for use in books, magazines, brochures, playing cards, stationery and packaging.

Office papers (13 percent of sales). The firm produces carbonless chemical papers, photocopier and blueprint papers, fax papers, laser and ink jet papers and optical reader papers.

Technical and industrial papers (24 percent of sales). Arjomari produces decorative papers with printed patterns and designs such as woodgrain and stone, flexible papers for grinding and sanding, mineral base papers for wall and floor coverings, artificial leather, special papers for architectural drawings and other products for household and hygienic applications.

Fine art and technical drawing papers (9 percent). Through its Canson subsidiary, the company produces a wide range of papers for technical drawing and commercial art. It also produces colored sheets and drawing pads.

EARNINGS GROWTH

The company has had excellent growth the past five years, with earnings per share rising 157 percent for the period, 21 percent per year.

Arjomari reported total annual revenue of 10 billion francs (1.7 billion in U.S. dollars) in 1989.

STOCK GROWTH

The company's stock price has moved up very quickly the past five years, increasing 420 percent for the period—40 percent per year.

Including reinvested dividends, a $10,000 investment in Arjomari stock in 1984 would have grown to about $58,000 five years later. Average annual compounded rate of return (including stock growth and reinvested dividends): about 42 percent.

DIVIDEND YIELD

The company generally pays a moderate yield, which has averaged about 2 percent over the past five years. During the most recent two-year rating period, the stock paid an average annual current return (dividend yield) of 1.4 percent.

DIVIDEND GROWTH

Arjomari traditionally raises its dividend each year. The dividend rose 159 percent (21 percent per year) over the recent five-year period.

CONSISTENCY

The company has had consistent growth in its earnings per share, revenues and book value per share, although its earnings did decline in 1989. Its price-earnings ratio of about 13 is consistent with other growing French companies.

MOMENTUM

After a strong 1988, when earnings per share were up 34 percent, the company's earnings dropped about 10 percent in 1989. But revenue and book value per share continued to rise in 1989, as did the shareholder dividend.

SUMMARY

Fiscal year ended: Dec. 31
(French francs; revenue and operating income in millions)

	1990*	1989	1988	1987	1986	1985	1984	5-year growth, %† (annual/total)
Revenue	—	10,056	8,258	6,101	5,232	4,885	4,309	18/133
Operating income	—	840	857	539	604	408	358	18/134
Earnings/share	—	215.80	233.08	174.23	177.72	99.10	83.87	21/157
Dividend/share	—	40.00	35.00	30.00	22.73	20.00	15.45	21/159
Dividend yield, %	1.5	1.3	1.6	2.0	1.2	2.0	2.6	—/—
Stock price	2,560	3,090	2,231	1,530	1,855	986	590	40/423
P/E ratio	13.0	14.3	9.6	8.8	10.4	10.0	7.0	—/—
Book value/share	—	1,232	1,004	787	660	499	401	25/207

* 6–1–90
† 1983–88, except stock price, 1984–89
Source: Company sources and Worldscope.

Note: No ADR; stock price quoted in the *Financial Times;* 5-year average annual return in U.S. currency: 57%.

71 L'ORÉAL

L'ORÉAL

41 rue Martre
92117 Clichy
France
Tel: (1) 47 56 70 00
Chairman and CEO: Lindsay Owen-Jones

EARNINGS GROWTH	★ ★
STOCK GROWTH	★ ★ ★
DIVIDEND YIELD	★
DIVIDEND GROWTH	★ ★
CONSISTENCY	★ ★ ★ ★
MOMENTUM	★ ★ ★ ★
PAR	**16 points**

L'Oreal is an international merchant of glamour. Its 250 consolidated companies spread mascara, blush, gel, mousse, perfume and other beauty aids throughout Europe, North America and the Pacific Rim.

The French beauty concern divides its business into two primary divisions, consumer and salon (48 percent of sales) and perfumes and beauty (34 percent of sales). The company also operates some pharmaceutical research and development businesses that have generated about 15 percent of its revenue.

- Consumer and salon division. The company produces a variety of haircare products that are sold through beauty hair styling salons such as Kerastase, Dulcia Vital and Majirel. It also offers a line of hair products available through normal retail outlets—primarily in Europe. Popular brands include Studio Line, Elseve and Jojoba shampoos and conditioners.

  The division also markets deodorant, shaving products, men's perfumes, setting gels, hair coloring dyes, nail varnish, blushes and other beauty products.

- Perfumes and beauty division. L'Oreal markets a wide range of perfumes for both men and women. Leading lines include Ralph Lauren, Armani, Paloma Picasso and Drakkar Noir.

  The firm also produces a variety of skin-care products, including Biotherm, Vichy, Phas and Helena Rubinstein. In the United States, L'Oreal's Armani, Chaps and Vanderbilt lines have also been popular.

EARNINGS GROWTH

The company has had solid growth the past few years. Its earnings per share increased 97 percent over the past five years, 15 percent per year.

L'Oreal reported total revenue of 27 billion francs (4.5 billion in U.S. dollars) in 1989.

STOCK GROWTH

The company's stock price has moved up steadily the past five years, increasing 160 percent for the period—21 percent per year.

Including reinvested dividends, a $10,000 investment in L'Oreal stock in 1984 would have grown to about $27,000 five years later. Average annual compounded rate of return (including stock growth and reinvested dividends): about 22 percent.

DIVIDEND YIELD

The company generally pays a modest yield, which has averaged just over 1 percent over the past five years. During the most recent two-year rating period (1988 and 1989), the stock paid an average annual current return (dividend yield) of 1.2 percent.

DIVIDEND GROWTH

L'Oreal traditionally raises its dividend each year. The dividend increased 113 percent (16 percent per year) over the five-year period from 1984 to 1989.

CONSISTENCY

The company has had very consistent growth in its earnings per share, revenues, operating income and book value per share. Its price-earnings ratio of about 20 is relatively high but not out of line for a fast-growing company.

MOMENTUM

L'Oreal has picked up its pace of growth the past two years. Its earnings per share increased 16 percent in 1988 and 19 percent in 1989.

SUMMARY

Fiscal year ended: Dec. 31
(French francs; revenue and operating income in millions)

	1990*	1989	1988	1987	1986	1985	1984	5-year growth, %† (annual/total)
Revenue	—	27,170	24,445	20.095	18,130	16,430	15,804	11/71
Operating income[1]	—	2,929	2,499	2,029	1,727	1,721	1,657	12/76
Earnings/share	—	252.00	212.40	182.60	144.00	139.00	128.00	15/97
Dividend/share	—	60.00	50.00	37.00	33.00	30.00	28.15	16/113
Dividend yield, %	1.3	1.2	1.1	1.5	1.0	1.2	1.5	—/—
Stock price	5,240	4,869	4,400	2,545	3,208	2,383	1,867	21/160
P/E ratio	19.0	19.3	20.7	13.9	22.2	14.3	14.5	—/—
Book value/share	—	1,464	1,234	1,061	865	775	660	17/121

* 5–1–90
† 1984–89
1. Operating profit is given here.
Source: Company sources and Worldscope.

Note: ADR; stock price quoted in *Barron's,* the *Wall Street Journal,* the *European Wall Street Journal* and the *Financial Times;* 5-year average annual return in U.S. currency: 35%.

⁷⁸ L˥ legrand

LEGRAND

128 avenue de Lattre de Tassigny
B.P. 523
87045 Limoges Cedex
France
Tel: (1) 55 33 71 33
Chairman: François Grappotte

EARNINGS GROWTH	★ ★ ★ ★
STOCK GROWTH	★ ★ ★ ★
DIVIDEND YIELD	★ ★
DIVIDEND GROWTH	★
CONSISTENCY	★ ★ ★ ★
MOMENTUM	★ ★
PAR	**16 points**

Legrand operates in a single market segment—electrical fittings and accessories—but within that segment, its offerings are vast and varied.

The French manufacturer produces everything from simple switches, power sockets and connectors to circuit breakers, alarm monitoring systems and sophisticated electronic control centers.

Legrand has operations in 23 countries. About a third of its 13,000 employees work in operations outside of France. The company's U.S. subsidiaries (Pass & Seymour and Slater—now merged—and Power Controls) generate about 12 percent of Legrand's total revenue.

Among Legrand's leading subsidiaries are:

Legrand Limoges. The division makes a variety of products, ranging from simple switches, power sockets and fuses to sophisticated high-tech devices such as remote control systems and cordless switches.

101

Legrand Normandy. This manufacturing plant produces industrial products such as metal cabinets, wiring and connection devices, transformers and uninterruptible power units.

Arnould-Fae and Sute.   The division makes electric and telephone fittings, under-floor distribution systems, cable ducts and trunkings.

Other key subsidiaries include Inovac (manufactures plugs, cord set switches and adapters), Martin & Lunel (a major manufacturer of antiexplosive devices and similar products), Planet-Wattohm (makes baseboards, cable ducts and trunking systems) and Legrand Antibes (specializes in magneto-thermic and earth-leakage circuit breakers).

EARNINGS GROWTH

The company has had excellent growth the past few years. Its earnings per share increased 275 percent over the past five years, 30 percent per year.

Legrand reported total revenue of 8.7 billion francs (1.4 billion in U.S. dollars) in 1989.

STOCK GROWTH

The company's stock price has moved up quickly the past five years, increasing 308 percent for the period—32 percent per year.

Including reinvested dividends, a $10,000 investment in Legrand stock in 1984 would have grown to about $45,000 five years later. Average annual compounded rate of return (including stock growth and reinvested dividends): about 35 percent.

DIVIDEND YIELD

The company has paid a good yield in the past—an average of about 3 percent over the past five years—but the yield has dropped in recent years. During the most recent two-year rating period (1988 and 1989), the stock paid an average annual current return (dividend yield) of 1.6 percent.

DIVIDEND GROWTH

Legrand traditionally raises its dividend each year, but not by much. The dividend increased 67 percent (11 percent per year) over the five-year period from 1984 to 1989.

CONSISTENCY

The company has had very consistent growth in the past five years, but it did have declines in earnings per share in 1983 and 1984. Its price-earnings ratio of about 17 is consistent with other growing companies.

MOMENTUM

Legrand had exceptional revenue growth in 1989—a 55 percent increase—but its earnings per share rose only 4 percent.

SUMMARY

Fiscal year ended: Dec. 31
(French francs; revenue and operating income in millions)

	1990*	1989	1988	1987	1986	1985	1984	5-year growth, %† (annual/total)
Revenue	—	8,715	5,616	4,936	4,557	4,470	3,407	21/155
Operating income	—	1,613	1,114	1,002	679	562	334	37/382
Earnings/share	—	225.00	216.00	170.00	135.00	82.13	60.00	30/275
Dividend/share	—	47.50	42.50	38.00	34.00	30.74	28.28	11/67
Dividend yield, %	1.2	1.3	1.8	2.7	2.0	3.5	4.6	—/—
Stock price	4,270	3,735	3,551	2,150	2,630	1,303	915	32/308
P/E ratio	17.0	16.6	16.4	12.6	19.5	15.9	15.2	—/—
Book value/share	—	1,231	1,103	916	797	695	651	13/89

* 5–1–90
† 1984–89
Source: Company sources and Worldscope.
Note: No ADR; stock price quoted in *Barron's,* the *European Wall Street Journal* and the *Financial Times;* 5-year average annual return in U.S. currency: 49%.

L'AIR LIQUIDE

75 quai d'Orsay
75321 Paris Cedex 07
France
Tel (1) 40 62 55 55
Chairman and CEO: Edouard de Royere

EARNINGS GROWTH	★
STOCK GROWTH	★
DIVIDEND YIELD	★ ★ ★
DIVIDEND GROWTH	★
CONSISTENCY	★ ★ ★
MOMENTUM	★ ★ ★
FRA, PAR, OTH	**12 points**

You could call it the invisible empire.

L'Air Liquide has built an international corporate conglomerate with products that are virtually weightless and entirely invisible. But the company's rising profits have kept its shareholders floating on air for many years. The Paris-based company is one of the leading gas-producing companies in the world.

L'Air Liquide produces and distributes a wide variety of gases—combustive gases, fuel gases, pure gases, safety gases, tool gases, life-supporting gases and industrial gases, to name a few. Its biggest sellers include oxygen, nitrogen, argon, helium, hydrogen, acetylene and carbon dioxide.

Founded in 1902, L'Air Liquide now has subsidiaries throughout Europe (55 percent of sales), North and South America (30 percent), Australia, New Zealand and Southeast Asia (13 percent) and Africa (2.5 percent). In all, it has 120 subsidiaries in more than 50 countries on 5 continents. The company employs 27,000 people—11,000 in France and 16,000 elsewhere around the world.

While gas sales constitute the majority of its income (69 percent of sales), L'Air Liquide also does a strong international business in several related areas. Chemicals and pharmaceuticals account for 15 percent of its sales. Most of its pharmaceutical business is generated by its subsidiary, the LIPHA company (Lyonnaise Industrielle Pharmaceutique).

L'Air Liquide also has an equipment operation that specializes in metal welding equipment, surgical equipment and deep-sea diving equipment. That division accounts for about 12 percent of sales. An engineering and construction division, which specializes in the construction of gas-production facilities, accounts for about 5 percent of the company's sales.

In the United States, its main subsidiaries are Liquid Air Corp. and Big Three.

EARNINGS GROWTH

The company has had solid growth the past few years. Its earnings per share increased 77 percent over the past five years, 12 percent per year.

L'Air Liquide has annual revenue of 26 billion francs (4.2 billion in U.S. dollars).

STOCK GROWTH

The company's stock price has increased 90 percent over the past five years, 14 percent per year.

Including reinvested dividends, a $10,000 investment in L'Air Liquide in 1984 would have grown to about $21,000 five years later. Average annual compounded rate of return (including stock growth and reinvested dividends): about 16 percent.

DIVIDEND YIELD

The company generally pays a moderate yield, which has averaged about 2 percent over the past five years. During the most recent two-year rating period (1988 and 1989), the stock paid an average annual current return (dividend yield) of 2.1 percent.

DIVIDEND GROWTH

L'Air Liquide raises its dividend most years. The dividend increased 77 percent (12 percent per year) over the recent five-year period.

CONSISTENCY

The company has had fairly consistent growth in most of its key areas, with a couple of exceptions; earnings per share stayed even in 1987 and operating income declined twice in the past six years. Its price-earnings ratio of about 18 is consistent with other growing French companies.

MOMENTUM

L'Air Liquide has maintained solid growth over the last couple of years—well in line with its level of growth during the past six years.

SUMMARY

Fiscal year ended: Dec. 31
(French francs; revenue and operating income in millions)

	1990*	1989	1988	1987	1986	1985	1984	5-year growth, %† (annual/total)
Revenue	—	—	25,828	23,460	20,639	19,904	19,829	9/51
Operating income	—	—	3,775	4,799	2,859	2,639	2,578	7/38
Earnings/share	—	—	35.73	31.36	30.93	28.00	20.74	12/77
Dividend/share	—	—	13.00	11.82	11.82	9.91	8.26	12/77
Dividend yield, %	—	2.0	2.2	2.7	1.9	2.0	2.3	—/—
Stock price	712.00	688.00	599.00	435.45	637.27	495.41	362.03	14/90
P/E ratio	—	18.0	16.8	13.9	20.6	17.7	17.5	—/—
Book value/share	—	—	237.85	197.85	244.21	182.02	162.52	8/46

* 5–1–90
† 1983–88, except stock price, 1984–89
Source: Worldscope.

Note: ADR; stock price quoted in *Barron's,* the *Wall Street Journal,* the *European Wall Street Journal* and the *Financial Times;* 5-year average annual return in U.S. currency: 28%.

Germany

(Federal Republic of Germany)

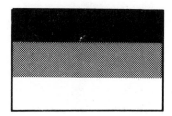

The German machine is purring at high speed. No country stands in a better position to gain from Eastern Europe's capitalist transformation than Germany—where East, literally, meets West. As it assimilates into West Germany, the East German economy is expected to grow at a rate of 8 to 10 percent a year—two to three times higher than the rate of growth of most other industrialized countries.

Economists predict that as East Germany grows, West German corporations should reap a bonanza in sales and earnings. In all, the rebuilding of East Germany's infrastructure is expected to cost about $500 billion.

Located in central Europe, Germany has about 78 million people—62 million in the West and 16 million in the East. Its major industries include steel, ships, autos, machinery, coal and chemicals.

The currency is the German deutsche mark (DEM 1.68 = US $1, June, 1990). Germany's GNP was DEM 2,121 billion (US $1,192 billion) in 1988. Its inflation rate the past three years has been just under 1 percent (although the currency exchange with East Germany was expected to boost inflation; on the other hand, cheap labor in East Germany could keep inflation down for some years to come).

Real economic growth the past several years has also averaged about 3.5 percent per year—which should rise by at least a percentage point as a result of the merger between East and West. The market value of all domestic stocks traded on the German stock exchanges was $251 billion as of January 1, 1989. Germany's largest exchange is Frankfurt, but it also has exchanges in Hamburg and Munich, plus regional exchanges in Berlin, Dusseldorf, Hanover, Bremen and Stuttgart.

In 1989 the German stock market was up 37 percent in German currency (44 percent in U.S. currency). Through the first six months of 1990, the German market was up 4 percent.

Suitable stock investments are fairly rare in Germany. The shares of most companies' stocks are not freely traded on the exchanges but are held by tightly controlled private groups or banks. Of the 600 companies listed on the stock exchanges, only about 100 issues are suitable for investor trading. (By comparison, in the United States there are more than 5,000 publicly traded stocks.)

34

CONTINENTAL AG
Königsworther Platz 1
Postfach 169
3000 Hanover 1
Germany
Tel: (511) 765-1
Chairman: Horst W. Urban

EARNINGS GROWTH	★ ★ ★ ★
STOCK GROWTH	★ ★ ★ ★
DIVIDEND YIELD	★ ★ ★
DIVIDEND GROWTH	★ ★ ★ ★
CONSISTENCY	★ ★ ★
MOMENTUM	★ ★
FRA, DUS, GVA, VIE	**20 points**

While most American tire makers have been spinning their wheels the past few years, as competition in the industry heated up, German tire giant Continental has been burning rubber, making up ground between itself and the industry frontrunners.

Through acquisitions and internal expansion, the company has doubled its revenues and tripled its earnings over the past five years. Continental is now the fourth largest tire maker in the world, behind Goodyear, Michelin and Bridgestone. It controls about 8 percent of the world tire market.

In addition to its flagship Continental line of tires, the company also owns General Tire, which it acquired in 1987, Semperit, which it bought in 1985, and the Uniroyal Englebert division, which it acquired in 1979.

The bulk of the company's business comes from Germany, the rest of Europe and North America, where General Tire generates about a third of Continental's total revenue.

General Tire is the largest of Continental's subsidiaries, with plants and sales offices throughout the United States (including about 90 dealer outlets), plus Mexico, Canada, Ecuador, Pakistan, Mozambique, Portugal, Morocco and Angola.

The Continental line of tires is the company's second largest money-maker, accounting for about 20 percent of sales. The company has plants and sales offices in Germany, France and Spain.

Uniroyal Englebert (12 percent of sales) and Semperit (11 percent) are also considered part of the Continental group. Uniroyal has plants and sales centers in Germany, Belgium, France and England, and Semperit has operations in Austria, Ireland and Yugoslavia.

The company's other division, ContiTech Group, accounts for about 19 percent of sales. ContiTech manufactures rubber and plastic products for a wide variety of applications, including hoses, sound-proofing foam and foam for furniture and auto interiors.

EARNINGS GROWTH

The company has had excellent growth the past few years. Its earnings per share increased 261 percent over the past five years, 29 percent per year.

Continental reported total revenue of 8.4 billion marks (4.7 billion in U.S. dollars) in 1989.

STOCK GROWTH

The company's stock price has moved up quickly the past five years, increasing 213 percent for the period—26 percent per year.

Including reinvested dividends, a $10,000 investment in Continental stock in 1984 would have grown to about $36,000 five years later. Average annual compounded rate of return (including stock growth and reinvested dividends): about 29 percent.

DIVIDEND YIELD

The company generally pays a good yield, which has averaged about 3 percent over the past five years. During the most recent two-year rating period (1988 and 1989), the stock paid an average annual current return (dividend yield) of 2.7 percent.

DIVIDEND GROWTH

Continental raises its dividend most years, and recently the increases have been substantial. The dividend increased 203 percent (25 percent per year) over the five-year period from 1984 to 1989.

CONSISTENCY

The company has been fairly consistent in the key financial categories, although it did have a bad year in 1987, when earnings dropped 36 percent and operating income dropped 55 percent. Its price-earnings ratio of about 10 to 12 is good for a growing company.

MOMENTUM

Continental had a big year in 1988 (earnings per share rose 43 percent) and a fair year in 1989, when the EPS rose 15 percent. But revenues rose only 6 percent in 1989, and operating income dropped 32 percent.

SUMMARY

Fiscal year ended: Dec. 31
(deutsche mark; revenue and operating income in millions)

	1990*	1989	1988	1987	1986	1985	1984	5-year growth, %†(annual/total)
Revenue	—	8,382	7,906	5,098	4,969	5,003	3,534	119/137
Operating income	—	323	474	160	359	262	172	14/87
Earnings/share	—	26.18	22.93	16.00	25.08	14.96	7.25	29/261
Dividend/share	—	8.00	8.00	7.00	5.29	4.41	2.64	25/203
Dividend yield, %	3.2	2.5	2.9	3.4	1.8	3.0	2.6	—/—
Stock price	287.00	322.00	272.00	205.00	302.00	146.00	103.00	26/213
P/E ratio	10.0	12.2	11.8	12.8	12.0	9.7	14.2	—/—
Book value/share	—	184.00	177.00	163.00	108.00	87.00	78.00	19/135

* 5–1–90
† 1984–89
Source: Worldscope.

Note: ADR; stock price quoted in *Barron's,* the *Wall Street Journal,* the *European Wall Street Journal* and the *Financial Times;* 5-year average annual return in U.S. currency: 46%.

67

METALLGESELLSCHAFT AG

Reuterweg 14
Postfach 101501
D-6000 Frankfurt 1
Germany
Tel: (069) 159-0
Chairman, Supervisory Board: Dr. Wolfgang Röller
Chairman, Executive Board: Dr. Heinz Schimmelbusch

EARNINGS GROWTH	★ ★ ★ ★
STOCK GROWTH	★ ★
DIVIDEND YIELD	★ ★
DIVIDEND GROWTH	★ ★
CONSISTENCY	★ ★ ★
MOMENTUM	★ ★ ★ ★
FRA, DUS, OTH	**17 points**

Metallgesellschaft has been a leading player in the world metals market for over 100 years. Since it was established in 1881, the Frankfurt-based operation has been involved in the mining, processing and trading of a wide range of metals.

The company has operations worldwide, with 125 subsidiaries and nearly $11 billion a year in total revenue. About 38 percent of its revenue comes from its German operations, 31 percent comes from elsewhere in Europe, 20 percent comes from North America and the remaining 10 percent comes from operations in Africa, Asia, Australia and the Middle East.

Nearly 70 percent of Metallgesellschaft's revenue is generated by its trade and financial services sector. The company is active in the worldwide metal commodities trading market and is involved in the mining, processing and shipping of metals. Among its major metal groups are zinc, iron and copper.

The firm's financial services group is involved in banking services, commodities trading, futures, insurance and real estate.

Engineering services account for about 8 percent of the company's revenues. Metallgesellschaft is heavily involved in the waste treatment industry, providing services in sewage treatment, air pollution control and landfill management.

Metallgesellschaft also builds electrical power-generating plants, engineers the construction of chemical processing plants and has developed new processes to treat and refine a variety of metals.

The company's other operations, which account for about 18 percent of its revenues, include mining operations, construction of metals processing plants and metals recovery plants, scrap metal recycling operations and chemical production operations.

EARNINGS GROWTH

The company has had tremendous growth the past few years, with an increase in earnings per share of 530 percent over the past five years, 45 percent per year.

Metallgesellschaft reported total revenue of 20.1 billion marks (11 billion in U.S. dollars) in 1989. The firm has 25,000 employees worldwide.

STOCK GROWTH

The company's stock price has enjoyed steady growth, moving up 105 percent over the past five years—15 percent per year.

Including reinvested dividends, a $10,000 investment in Metallgesellschaft stock in 1984 would have grown to about $22,000 five years later. Average annual compounded rate of return (including stock growth and reinvested dividends): about 17 percent.

DIVIDEND YIELD

The company generally pays a moderate yield, which has averaged about 2.2 percent over the past five years. During the most recent two-year rating period (1988 and 1989), the stock paid an average annual current return (dividend yield) of 2.2 percent.

DIVIDEND GROWTH

Metallgesellschaft paid no dividend until 1985. It only increased its dividend twice since then, but the increases were sizable. In all, the dividend went up 74 percent over the four-year period from 1985 to 1989, an average of 15 percent per year.

CONSISTENCY

Because of its heavy reliance on the metals commodities market, Metallgesellschaft can sometimes be volatile. Its growth in most key categories the past few years, however, has been pretty steady, including five consecutive years of increased earnings per share. But the company has had drops in revenues, book value per share and operating income one time each during the past five years.

MOMENTUM

Metallgesellschaft has been on a roll lately. Its earnings per share increased 42 percent in 1988 and 33 percent in 1989.

SUMMARY

Fiscal year ended: Sept. 30
(deutsche mark; revenue and operating income in millions)

	1990*	1989	1988	1987	1986	1985	1984	5-year growth, %† (annual/total)
Revenue	—	20,126	15,235	13,329	14,901	11,207	10,491	14/92
Operating income	—	235	133	1,334	994	166	114	15/106
Earnings/share	—	23.65	17.74	12.51	12.18	8.80	3.75	45/530
Dividend/share	—	9.33	7.13	5.35	5.35	5.35	0.00	15/74[1]
Dividend yield, %	2.0	2.1	2.3	2.5	1.8	2.1	0.0	—/—
Stock price	610.00	472.00	338.00	235.00	325.00	273.00	230.00	15/105
P/E ratio	20.0	19.2	15.7	16.7	23.8	27.7	51.2	—/—
Book value/share	—	216.86	168.29	138.65	135.47	136.09	118.11	13/83

* 5–1–90
† 1984–89
1. Dividend growth percentages are calculated based on four years' growth, 1985–89.
Source: Worldscope.

Note: No ADR; stock price quoted in *Barron's,* the *Wall Street Journal,* the *European Wall Street Journal* and the *Financial Times;* 5-year average annual return in U.S. currency: 32%.

LINDE AG

Abraham-Lincoln-Strasse 21
6200 Wiesbaden 1
Germany
Tel: (0 61 21) 770-0
Chairman, Supervisory Board: Dr. Wolfgang Schieren
Chairman, Executive Board: Dr. Hans Meinhardt

EARNINGS GROWTH	★ ★
STOCK GROWTH	★ ★ ★
DIVIDEND YIELD	★ ★
DIVIDEND GROWTH	**(no points)**
CONSISTENCY	★ ★ ★ ★
MOMENTUM	★ ★ ★ ★
FRA, DUS, GVA, OTH	**15 points**

Linde has established its own small niche in the transportation industry, but you won't see its vehicles cruising the *autobahn*. Linde's track is the factory floor, the stockyard and the warehouse aisleway.

The company is a major manufacturer of fork lifts, side loaders, tractors and platform trucks, horizontal and vertical pickers, reach trucks, pedestrian stackers, high-rise stackers and automated guided vehicles. It also builds hydraulics systems, transmissions and piston pumps and motors for farm and construction equipment.

Forklifts and related material handling equipment account for 52 percent of Linde's total revenue. The company does the bulk of its business in Europe—including 42 percent of revenues from Germany and 47 percent from elsewhere in Europe. The balance of its sales come from North America (6 percent), Asia and Australia (4 percent) and Africa (1 percent).

In addition to its forklift and hydraulics operations, the company does business in three other primary market sectors, including:

• Process plant engineering and construction (16 percent of revenue). The company is involved in the engineering and construction of chemical and petrochemical plants, synthesis gas plants, gas treatment plants, natural gas plants, air separation plants, environmental engineering plants, catalytic process plants and petrochemical process and refinery furnaces.

The company also manufactures liquid gas tanks, heat exchangers, catalytic converters and a wide range of equipment for the gas-processing industry.

- Industrial gases (20 percent of revenue). Linde produces gases for a variety of industries, including welding and cutting—which accounts for 40 percent of its industrial gas business—refrigeration, medical applications and other industrial uses.
- Refrigeration (12 percent). The company builds refrigerated and freezer display cases for grocery stores, cold rooms, non-refrigerated shop equipment, space and process cooling systems, heat recovery systems and air conditioning and ventilation systems.

EARNINGS GROWTH

The company has had steady growth the past few years. Its earnings per share increased 123 percent over the past five years, 18 percent per year.

Linde reported total revenue of 5.5 billion marks (3.2 billion in U.S. dollars) in 1989.

STOCK GROWTH

The company's stock price climbed 159 percent over the past five years—21 percent per year.

Including reinvested dividends, a $10,000 investment in Linde stock in 1984 would have grown to about $28,000 five years later. Average annual compounded rate of return (including stock growth and reinvested dividends): about 23 percent.

DIVIDEND YIELD

The company generally pays a good yield, which has averaged about 2 percent over the past five years. During the most recent two-year rating period (1989 and 1990), the stock paid an average annual current return (dividend yield) of 1.5 percent.

DIVIDEND GROWTH   (no points)

Linde traditionally raises its dividend each year, but not by much. The dividend increased 60 percent (10 percent per year) over the five-year period from 1984 to 1989.

CONSISTENCY

The company has had very consistent growth in its earnings per share, revenues and book value per share. Its price-earnings ratio of about 30 is a bit on the high side, creating more downside risk for the stock. But if the company continues its strong growth, the high P/E should not be a factor.

MOMENTUM

Linde had exceptional growth in 1989. Its earnings per share increased 26 percent, its revenues 53 percent, operating income 64 percent and book value per share 36 percent.

SUMMARY

Fiscal year ended: Dec. 31
(deutsche mark; revenue and operating income in millions)

	1990*	1989	1988	1987	1986	1985	1984	5-year growth, %† (annual/total)
Revenue	—	5,453	3,564	3,131	2,930	2,708	2,602	16/109
Operating income	—	260	159	142	237	194	178	8/46
Earnings/share	—	30.84	24.50	23.57	21.19	15.83	13.79	18/123
Dividend/share	—	14.00	12.38	11.90	11.43	10.48	8.70	10/60
Dividend yield, %	1.3	1.6	1.7	2.4	1.7	1.8	2.5	—/—
Stock price	950	888.00	733.33	497.14	680.95	571.43	341.72	21/159
P/E ratio	30.0	28.5	29.9	21.1	32.1	36.1	24.8	—/—
Book value/share	—	301.99	222.15	209.16	196.73	179.21	147.45	15/104

* 5–1–90
† 1984–89
Source: Worldscope.

Note: ADR; stock price quoted in *Barron's,* the *Wall Street Journal,* the *European Wall Street Journal* and the *Financial Times;* 5-year average annual return in U.S. currency: 33%.

93 BASF

BASF AG

6700 Ludwigshafen-Rhein
Germany
Tel: (49) 621-601
Chairman Supervisory Board: Dr. Matthias Seefelder
Chairman, Executive Board: Dr. Hans Albers

EARNINGS GROWTH	★
STOCK GROWTH	(no points)
DIVIDEND YIELD	★ ★ ★ ★
DIVIDEND GROWTH	(no points)
CONSISTENCY	★ ★
MOMENTUM	★ ★ ★ ★
FRA, ZRH, OTH	**11 points**

Soon after it was established in 1865, BASF quickly emerged as a major player in the colors and chemicals markets. Today, the company continues to be a world leader in the production of dyes, pigments and a wide variety of other chemical products for the industrial, agricultural, plastics and consumer markets.

With $28 billion (47 billion marks) a year in total revenues, BASF is one of Germany's largest companies. It operates production sites in 35 countries and conducts business in more than 160 countries. It has well over 100 wholly or partially owned subsidiaries, with 340 separate companies.

The firm operates in six primary market segments, including:

- Consumer products (20 percent of sales). BASF is probably best known to most consumers through its audio and video tape cassettes, which sell worldwide. The company's consumer division also produces paints, coatings, printing systems, electronic data processing equipment and pharmaceuticals. Its pharmaceuticals include a line of medications for the treatment of cardiovascular ailments, hypertension and neurological problems.

- Chemicals (21 percent of sales). The company manufactures a broad range of industrial chemicals, such as plasticizers, solvents and laminating resins.
- Plastics (18 percent of sales). BASF makes a wide range of plastics, vinyls and foam products, including nylons, polystyrene, polyurethane and polyvinyl chloride.
- Dyes and finishing products (17.5 percent of sales). The company makes dyes and finishing products for the coatings market as well as for office supplies, printing inks, electroplating, adhesives, plastics processing, finishes, leather, paper, polishes, detergents and the textile industry (clothing, linens, etc.).
- Raw materials and energy (13 percent of sales). Production of oil, natural gas and bituminous coal and petroleum refining are conducted by the company's Wintershall AG and Gewerkschaft Auguste Victoria affiliates.
- Agricultural chemicals (11 percent of sales). BASF makes a line of fertilizers, pesticides and fungicides.

EARNINGS GROWTH

The company has had up and down growth the past few years. Its earnings per share increased 79 percent over the past five years, 12 percent per year.

BASF reported total revenue of 48 billion marks (28 billion in U.S. dollars) in 1989.

STOCK GROWTH   (no points)

The company's stock price has moved up in fits and starts the past five years, increasing 62 percent for the period—10 percent per year.

Including reinvested dividends, a $10,000 investment in BASF stock in 1984 would have grown to about $19,000 five years later. Average annual compounded rate of return (including stock growth and reinvested dividends): about 14 percent.

DIVIDEND YIELD

The company generally pays an excellent yield, which has averaged about 4 percent over the past five years. During the most recent two-year rating period (1989 and 1990), the stock paid an average annual current return (dividend yield) of 4.2 percent.

DIVIDEND GROWTH   (no points)

BASF rarely raises its dividend. The dividend increased 45 percent (8 percent per year) over the five-year period from 1984 to 1989.

CONSISTENCY

The company has been one of the more erratic companies among the top 100. It had drops in earnings per share in 1985 and 1986, drops in operating income in 1986, 1988 and 1989 and a drop in revenue in 1986.

MOMENTUM

And now for the good news: BASF is on a roll. Despite drops in operating income, the company's earnings per share increased 31 percent in 1988 and 43 percent in 1989.

SUMMARY

Fiscal year ended: Dec. 31
(deutsche mark; revenue and operating income in millions)

	1990*	1989	1988	1987	1986	1985	1984	5-year growth, %† (annual/total)
Revenue	—	47,617	43,868	40,238	40,471	44,377	40,400	4/17
Operating income	—	2,351	2,840	3,751	2,517	3,072	2,994	–5/–27
Earnings/share	—	35.35	24.74	18.94	17.00	19.35	19.70	12/79
Dividend/share	—	13.00	12.00	10.00	10.00	10.00	8.91	8/45
Dividend yield, %	4.0	4.3	4.3	3.9	3.6	3.7	4.8	—/—
Stock price	299.50	300.00	279.60	255.50	274.70	270.50	184.30	10/62
P/E ratio	—	8.5	11.3	13.5	16.2	14.0	9.4	—/—
Book value/share	—	242.78	219.43	213.51	218.74	207.03	191.64	5/26

* 5–1–90
† 1984–89
Source: Worldscope.

Note: ADR; stock price quoted in *Barron's,* the *Wall Street Journal,* the *European Wall Street Journal* and the *Financial Times;* 5-year average annual return in U.S. currency: 29%.

Hoechst

HOECHST AG

Box 80 03 20
D-6230 Frankfurt AM Main 80
West Germany
Tel: (49) 69 3050
Chairman: Dr. Rolf Sammet

EARNINGS GROWTH	★ ★
STOCK GROWTH	**(no points)**
DIVIDEND YIELD	★ ★ ★ ★
DIVIDEND GROWTH	★
CONSISTENCY	★ ★
MOMENTUM	★ ★
FRA, DUS, AMS, BRU	**11 points**

Hoechst has long been recognized as a world leader in the development of breakthrough medications. It has treatments for cancer, heart disease, diabetes and bacterial infections.

But no formula it has ever concocted compares to its latest and unquestionably most controversial "breakthrough" drug. Mifepristone, as the drug is officially labeled, is medical science's first commercially available abortion pill.

The drug, produced by Hoechst's French subsidiary, Roussel-Uclaf, terminates a pregnancy in 80 to 90 percent of the cases, when used according to directions. Administered along with an injection of a second drug, Mifepristone becomes 96 percent effective. (When it doesn't work, the abortions are completed surgically.)

Mifepristone is available now only in France and only under strict supervision of a physician. The drug may soon be sold elsewhere in Europe but is not expected to be available in the United States any time soon—primarily because of the powerful anti-abortion faction in the U.S.

Hoescht is one of the world's largest medical products companies. It has a medical research staff of 5,000 scientists and technicians. About $5 billion of the Frankfurt conglomerate's $25 billion a year in annual revenue comes from its health products division.

The company is involved in a number of other industrial segments, including chemicals, fibers, polymers, agricultural products and engineering projects. The company's activities include:

- Chemicals and color (26 percent of revenues). The company produces a wide range of organic chemicals, including methanol, formaldehyde, acetic acid, vinyl acetate, ethylene glycol and acrylates. It is also a major producer of dyes and pigments for clothing, inks, paints and plastics.
- Fabrics and plastic film (20 percent of sales). Hoechst produces various fibers for clothing and other textile products. It controls about 10 percent of the worldwide polyester market. It also produces plastic products for audio and video tapes, food packaging and a variety of industrial applications.
- Polymers (18 percent of revenues). The company produces plastics and waxes for the production of automotive, electrical and electronic parts. It also produces paints and resins for the industrial and automotive market. Its polymer emulsions and vinyls are used for construction products, adhesives, special paper and printing ink.
- Engineering and technology (12 percent of revenues). The company manufactures products for the printing business (such as printing plates) as well as for photocopiers and fax machines. Hoechst also manufactures optical storage disks and circuit-board film.
- Agriculture (6 percent of revenues). Hoechst produces herbicides (Arelon, Illoxan, Derosal, Excel and Puma), insecticides (Thiodan and Hostathion) and fertilizers.

EARNINGS GROWTH

The company has had solid growth the past few years. Its earnings per share increased 117 percent over the past five years, 18 percent per year.

Hoechst has total annual revenue of 41 billion marks (23 billion in U.S. dollars).

STOCK GROWTH   (no points)

The company's stock price has increased 60 percent over the past five years, 10 percent per year.

Including reinvested dividends, a $10,000 investment in Hoechst stock in 1984 would have grown to about $19,000 five years later. Average annual compounded rate of return (including stock growth and reinvested dividends): about 14 percent.

DIVIDEND YIELD

The company generally pays a good yield, which has averaged about 4 percent over the past five years. During the most recent two-year rating period (1988 and 1989), the stock paid an average annual current return (dividend yield) of 4.0 percent.

DIVIDEND GROWTH

Hoechst traditionally raises its dividend nearly every year. The dividend increased 81 percent (13 percent per year) over the recent five-year rating period.

CONSISTENCY

The company has had earnings per share increases four of the past five years, but it has also had declines in revenue and operating income two of the past four years. Its price-earnings ratio of about 9 is consistent with other major German manufacturers.

MOMENTUM

Hoechst's revenue and operating income growth has been very flat the past few years, but its earnings per share jumped 31 percent in 1988, and its book value rose 15 percent.

SUMMARY

Fiscal year ended: Dec. 31
(deutsche mark; revenue and operating income in millions)

	1990*	1989	1988	1987	1986	1985	1984	5-year growth, %† (annual/total)
Revenue	—	—	40,964	36,956	38,014	42,722	41,457	2/10
Operating income	—	—	4,000	3,258	3,803	4,006	3,976	5/22
Earnings/share	—	—	32.21	24.63	22.47	23.14	21.10	18/117
Dividend/share	—	—	12.00	11.00	10.00	9.94	8.95	13/81
Dividend yield, %	—	4.0	3.9	4.4	3.7	3.4	4.7	—/—
Stock price	*289.00	306.00	305.50	250.00	269.40	292.80	190.10	10/60
P/E ratio	—	9.0	9.5	10.0	12.0	12.7	9.0	—/—
Book value/share	—	—	178.90	155.40	169.90	157.50	156.60	6/36

* 5-1-90
† 1983–88, except stock price, 1984–89
Source: Worldscope.

Note: ADR; stock price quoted in *Barron's,* the *Wall Street Journal,* the *European Wall Street Journal* and the *Financial Times;* 5-year average annual return in U.S. currency: 29%.

97 Bayer

BAYER AG

5090 Leverkusen-Bayerwerk
Germany
Tel: (49) 214 301
Chairman, Supervisory Board: Dr. Herbert Grünewald
Chairman, Board of Management: Herman J. Strenger

EARNINGS GROWTH	★ ★
STOCK GROWTH	(no points)
DIVIDEND YIELD	★ ★ ★ ★
DIVIDEND GROWTH	(no points)
CONSISTENCY	★ ★
MOMENTUM	★ ★
FRA, DUS, NYSE, LON	**10 points**

In the United States—and throughout much of the world—Bayer has long been synonymous with aspirin. In fact, "Aspirin" is a registered trade name of the Bayer company. The German manufacturer is also the maker of another traditional American remedy—Alka-Seltzer.

But over-the-counter medications account for just a fraction of Bayer's total revenue. The company is a huge ($25 billion a year in sales) and highly diversified conglomerate, with prominent positions in seven industrial segments.

Bayer's health-care segment accounts for about 16 percent of the company's total revenue. In addition to its over-the-counter medications, the company produces a wide range of prescription drugs, particularly for the treatment of cardiovascular ailments, infections and diabetes. Bayer's diagnostics division (headquartered in the United States at Miles, Inc., formerly Miles Laboratory, which was recently acquired by Bayer) is among the world leaders in the development of diagnostic systems for diabetes management and urinalysis.

The company is also a major producer of citric acid, industrial enzymes and dairy additives.

Bayer's other business sectors include:

- Polymers (18 percent of revenue). The company is a leading producer of plastic and rubber products and synthetic fibers primarily for the automotive, electrical engineering, electronics, construction, information technology and textile industries.
- Industrial products (22 percent of revenue). Bayer produces inorganic chemicals, pigments, ceramics, polyurethanes and coating raw materials for a wide range of industrial uses.
- Organic products (14 percent of revenue). The company produces organic chemicals, dyes and pigments and a variety of specialty chemicals.
- Agrochemicals (13 percent of revenue). Bayer produces fertilizers, insecticides and fungicides for the agricultural industry. It also produces a line of consumer products, including household insecticides, scouring creams, disinfectants, air freshners and cosmetics. Bayer also produces health and nutritional products for farm animals and pets.
- Imaging technologies (17 percent of revenue). Bayer manufactures film, photofinishing products, magnetic tapes, graphic information systems and a line of other graphics-related products.

EARNINGS GROWTH

The company's earnings per share increased 50 percent over the past three years, 15 percent per year.

Bayer has total revenue of 43 billion marks (25 billion in U.S. dollars).

STOCK GROWTH   (no points)

The company's stock price has increased 62 percent over the past five years, 10 percent per year.

Including reinvested dividends, a $10,000 investment in Bayer stock in 1984 would have grown to about $19,000 five years later. Average annual compounded rate of return (including stock growth and reinvested dividends): about 14 percent.

DIVIDEND YIELD

The company generally pays a good yield, which has averaged about 4 percent over the past five years. During the most recent two-year rating period (1988 and 1989), the stock paid an average annual current return (dividend yield) of 4 percent.

DIVIDEND GROWTH   (no points)

Bayer raises its dividend most years. The dividend increased 30 percent (9 percent per year) over the recent five-year period.

CONSISTENCY

The company has not been particularly consistent the last few years. Its growth in most key financial areas has been flat. But book value per share has gone up for at least six consecutive years. Its price-earnings ratio of about 10 is about average for a German company.

MOMENTUM

Bayer's stock price and revenues have not moved substantially in several years, but its earnings per share increased 35 percent over the past two years (1988 and 1989). And with new markets opening up next door in Eastern Europe, Bayer could enjoy greater success in the future.

SUMMARY

Fiscal year ended: Dec. 31
(deutsche mark; revenue and operating income in millions)

	1990*	1989	1988	1987	1986	1985	1984	3-year growth, %† (annual/total)
Revenue	—	43,299	40,468	37,143	38,284	45,926	43,032	5/13
Operating income	—	4,290	4,002	3,276	3,286	3,957	4,898	9/30
Earnings/share	—	32.60	29.25	24.24	22.44	24.09	26.20	15/50
Dividend/share	—	13.00	12.00	11.00	10.00	10.00	9.00	9/30
Dividend yield, %	—	4.19	3.91	4.14	3.15	3.71	4.68	—/—
Stock price	301	310	307	265.50	317.50	269.50	192.50	10/61
P/E ratio	—	9.51	10.50	10.95	14.15	11.19	7.35	—/—
Book value/share	—	249.38	240.27	227.05	207.31	209.75	172.88	7/20

* 5–1–90
† 1986–89 Except stock price, 1984–89. Amounts for 1986 through 1989 are stated in accordance with the new German Commercial Code; amounts for years prior to 1986 are not comparable.
Source: Company sources.

Note: ADR; stock price quoted in *Barron's,* the *Wall Street Journal,* the *European Wall Street Journal* and the *Financial Times;* 5-year average annual return in U.S. currency: 29%.

Hong Kong

Located at the mouth of the Canton River along the southeastern coast of China, Hong Kong is a British Crown Colony with a population of about 6 million. Its major industries include textiles, apparel, tourism, shipbuilding, iron and steel, fishing, cement and small manufacturing.

The languages of trade are English and Cantonese. Its currency is the Hong Kong dollar (HKD 7.80 = US $1, June, 1990). Its gross domestic product was HKD 426 billion (US $55 billion) in 1988. Hong Kong's inflation rate the past three years has been around 4 percent. Real economic growth the past several years has averaged about 10 percent per year (a very high rate by world standards). The market value of all domestic stocks traded on the Hong Kong Stock Exchange was US $74 billion as of January 1, 1989.

In 1989 the Hong Kong stock market was up 3.3 percent in Hong Kong currency (3.4 percent in U.S. currency). Through the first six months of 1990, the Hong Kong market was the world's best performing major market, up HKD 15 percent.

Hong Kong's capitalist sector faces the future with some uncertainty. The province is scheduled to be transferred from British rule to the People's Republic of China on July 1, 1997. By all rights, however, 1997 should bring little immediate change. Under the agreement, Hong Kong is to be a special administrative region with its own laws for another 50 years (through 2047).

While the Hong Kong market is expected to remain volatile—tied in part to developments within the People's Republic—it offers extraordinary potential. If China should eventually follow the lead of its fellow-communist regimes and turn to an open capitalist structure, Hong Kong would be in a perfect position to profit from the change.

6

HONG KONG & CHINA GAS COMPANY LTD.

24th Floor Leighton Centre
77 Leighton Road
Causeway Bay
Hong Kong
Tel: 890 1433
Chairman: Shau Kee Lee

EARNINGS GROWTH	★ ★ ★ ★
STOCK GROWTH	★ ★ ★ ★
DIVIDEND YIELD	★ ★ ★
DIVIDEND GROWTH	★ ★ ★ ★
CONSISTENCY	★ ★ ★ ★
MOMENTUM	★ ★ ★ ★
HKG	**23 points**

In Hong Kong, the Hong Kong & China Gas Company is referred to simply as "Towngas." For many years, Towngas has provided a steadily increasing flow of natural gas for its customers and a steadily increasing flow of profits for its stockholders.

Over the past 10 years, the company's customer base has grown dramatically, from 130,000 customers in 1979 to over 600,000 customers in 1988. Its gas sales have quadrupled during that period, from 3 million megajoules to 12 million megajoules.

The company's profitability has grown at an even faster clip, with earnings per share rising nearly 10-fold over the past 10 years.

That growth is expected to continue well into the future, as Hong Kong's population and industrial segment grow and develop. The company projects an increase of about 70,000 new customers a year and an increase in gas sales of about 14 percent.

Towngas supplies natural gas for most of Hong Kong island, Kowloon and several communities on the edge of the New Territories area.

EARNINGS GROWTH

The company has had excellent growth the past few years. Its earnings per share increased 218 percent over the past five years, 26 percent per year.

Towngas reported total revenue of 1.8 billion in Hong Kong dollars (233 million in U.S. dollars) in 1989.

STOCK GROWTH

The company's stock price has climbed very quickly the past five years, increasing 341 percent for the period—35 percent per year.

Including reinvested dividends, a $10,000 investment in Towngas stock at the end of 1984 would have grown to about $48,000 five years later. Average annual compounded rate of return (including stock growth and reinvested dividends): about 37 percent.

DIVIDEND YIELD

The company generally pays a fairly good yield, which has averaged about 2.5 percent over the past five years. During the most recent two-year rating period (1988 and 1989), the stock paid an average annual current return (dividend yield) of 2.5 percent.

DIVIDEND GROWTH

Towngas raises its dividend each year. The dividend jumped 500 percent (43 percent per year) over the five-year period from 1984 to 1989.

CONSISTENCY

The company has had very consistent growth in its earnings per share, revenues, operating income and book value per share. Its price-earnings ratio of about 18 to 20, although a little on the high side, is still a very comfortable level for a quickly growing company.

MOMENTUM

The company has continued to grow at a robust pace the past two years, with earnings-per-share increases of 32 percent in 1988 and 27 percent in 1989.

SUMMARY

Fiscal year ended: Dec. 31
(Hong Kong dollars; revenue and operating income in millions)

	1990*	1989	1988	1987	1986	1985	1984	5-year growth, %† (annual/total)
Revenue	—	1,816	1,526	1,309	989	994	874	15/107
Operating income[1]	—	593	478	359	270	216	159	30/272
Earnings/share	—	1.18	0.93	0.71	0.52	0.42	0.37	26/218
Dividend/share	—	0.84	0.45	0.37	0.26	0.18	0.14	43/500
Dividend yield, %	2.7	2.3	2.7	2.5	1.8	1.8	3.0	—/—
Stock price	20.10	20.50	16.90	14.80	14.64	10.00	4.65	35/341
P/E ratio	18.0	19.0	18.2	20.8	28.1	23.8	12.6	—/—
Book value/share	—	4.27	3.63	3.15	2.81	2.48	1.70	20/151

* 5–1–90
† 1984–89
1. Pre-tax income is used here.
Source: Company sources and Worldscope.

Note: ADR; stock price quoted in *Barron's,* the *European Wall Street Journal* and the *Financial Times;* 5-year average annual return in U.S. currency: 37%.

11

Hang Lung Development Company Limited

恒隆有限公司

HANG LUNG DEVELOPMENT CO. LTD.

25th Floor, Hanglung Centre
2-20 Paterson Street
Causeway Bay
Hong Kong
Tel: (5) 579 4111
Chairman: Tseng Tao Thomas Chen

EARNINGS GROWTH	★ ★ ★ ★
STOCK GROWTH	★ ★ ★ ★
DIVIDEND YIELD	★ ★ ★ ★
DIVIDEND GROWTH	★ ★ ★ ★
CONSISTENCY	★ ★ ★
MOMENTUM	★ ★ ★
HKG	**22 points**

Whether it was sound corporate planning or merely a matter of being in the right place at the right time, Hang Lung Development has taken advantage of Hong Kong's booming expansion the past five years to bolster its own stellar record of sales and earnings growth.

Founded in 1960, Hang Lung is one of Hong Kong's leading property developers. It builds residential high-rise apartment buildings and commercial and industrial complexes, primarily in the Hong Kong area.

With the demand for housing, office and industrial space still outpacing development of new properties, Hang Lung's potential for sustained growth seems promising.

The company divides its operations into four segments:

- Property development (46 percent of revenues). Residential development accounts for about 75 percent of the company's property development segment. Among its leading recent projects is the Tai Hing Gardens apartments, a 960-unit high-rise complex, Handsome Court, a 900-unit residential high rise, and Tuen Mun industrial building, a 77,000-square-meter industrial complex.

- Property investment (37 percent of revenues). The company buys existing buildings—primarily in the office and commercial segment—and refurbishes them for lease or resale. The business has been growing rapidly.
- Hotels (10 percent of revenues). Hang Lung owns a group of three Grand Hotels in the Hong Kong area, with a total of 1,241 rooms. A fourth Grand Hotel is expected to open in 1991.
- Other operations (7 percent of revenues). The company has a number of joint ventures in the foods and retail trade, including ventures with Matsuzakaya Department Store in Japan and Denny's American Cafe in the U.S. Hang Lung is also active in food processing under the Amoy brand through a joint venture with Pillsbury (now a subsidiary of Grand Metropolitan).

EARNINGS GROWTH

The company has enjoyed tremendous growth the past few years. Its earnings per share increased 583 percent over the past five years, 48 percent per year.

Hang Lung reported total revenue of 2.8 billion Hong Kong dollars (363 million in U.S. dollars) in 1989.

STOCK GROWTH

The company's stock price climbed rapidly the past five years, increasing 270 percent for the period—30 percent per year.

Including reinvested dividends, a $10,000 investment in Hang Lung stock at the end of 1984 would have grown to about $45,000 five years later. Average annual compounded rate of return (including stock growth and reinvested dividends): about 35 percent.

DIVIDEND YIELD

The company generally pays a very good yield, which has averaged about 5 percent over the past five years. During the most recent two-year rating period (1988 and 1989), the stock paid an average annual current return (dividend yield) of 8 percent.

DIVIDEND GROWTH

Hang Lung traditionally raises its dividend each year. The dividend increased 516 percent (43 percent per year) over the five-year period from 1984 to 1989.

CONSISTENCY

The company has had steady growth in its key financial areas over the past few years, with a few exceptions—a drop in earnings per share in 1984, a drop in revenue and a big drop in operating earnings in 1989.

MOMENTUM

Hang Lung's growth in earnings per share continues to be impressive—it increased 32 percent in 1989—but both revenues and operating income decreased in 1989. The stock price, after falling by more than 50 percent from 1987 to 1989, has begun to rebound. And with a price-earnings ratio of about 6, the stock would seem to be an excellent value.

SUMMARY

Fiscal year ended: June 30
(Hong Kong dollars; revenue and operating income in millions)

	1990*	1989	1988	1987	1986	1985	1984	5-year growth, %† (annual/total)
Revenue	—	2,828	3,430	2,921	1,612	747	619	35/356
Operating income	—	323	1,167	1,086	669	447	369	−7/−14
Earnings/share	—	0.82	0.66	0.58	0.30	0.17	0.12	48/583
Dividend/share	—	0.37	0.30	0.25	0.15	0.10	0.06	43/516
Dividend yield, %	—	10.6	5.5	3.4	4.5	3.8	6.0	—/—
Stock price	4.95	3.48	5.45	7.35	3.35	2.72	0.94	30/270
P/E ratio	6.0	4.2	8.3	12.7	11.2	15.8	7.9	—/—
Book value/share	—	6.02	5.33	3.97	2.61	2.45	0.75	52/702

* 5-1-90
† 1984-89
Source: Worldscope.

Note: ADR; stock price quoted in *Barron's,* the *European Wall Street Journal* and the *Financial Times;* 5-year average annual return in U.S. currency: 35%.

23

JARDINE MATHESON HOLDINGS LIMITED

Jardine House
48th Floor, Connaught Center
Connaught Road Central
Hong Kong
Tel: (5) 843 8388
Chairman: Henry Keswick

EARNINGS GROWTH	★ ★ ★ ★
STOCK GROWTH	★ ★ ★
DIVIDEND YIELD	★ ★ ★ ★
DIVIDEND GROWTH	★ ★ ★ ★
CONSISTENCY	★ ★
MOMENTUM	★ ★ ★ ★
HKG	**21 points**

You name it, Jardine Matheson can probably get it for you.

Established in 1832, the Hong Kong trading company sells sugar, furniture, medical supplies, Mercedes Benz automobiles, wines and liquor, optical products, food, clothing, leather and luggage. It owns insurance, financial services and brokerage divisions, operates 180 Pizza Hut restaurants throughout the Pacific area, a chain of Taco Bells in Hawaii and some Sizzler Steak Houses in Canada and Australia.

Through its subsidiaries and affiliated companies, it manages seven grand luxury hotels in the Hong Kong area, operates an aviation and shipping service, has a land development firm, owns Hong Kong's largest supermarket chain, runs a network of Seven-Eleven stores in Singapore, Hong Kong and Malaysia and is involved in engineering and construction projects throughout the Asia-Pacific region.

Jardine generates about half of its revenue from its operations in Hong Kong, China and Asia. The other half comes from Europe (23 percent of revenues), North America (14 percent) and Australia (8 percent).

The company breaks its operations into four primary segments, dominated by its marketing and distribution segment, which accounts for nearly

135

70 percent of its revenues. The marketing and distribution segment, under the name Jardine Pacific, handles the marketing of most of the company's wide range of products. Other segments include:

- Financial services (16 percent of revenue). The company offers a wide range of financial advisory and brokerage services through various subsidiaries.
- Engineering and construction (10 percent of revenue). Jardine is involved in a variety of construction projects throughout the Asia-Pacific region.
- Aviation and shipping services (4 percent). The company has several freight shipping and air transportation subsidiaries in Europe and the Far East.

EARNINGS GROWTH

The company has had tremendous growth the past few years. Its earnings per share increased 2,007 percent over the past five years, 86 percent per year.

Jardine reported total revenue of 15 billion Hong Kong dollars (2 billion in U.S. dollars) in 1989.

STOCK GROWTH

The company's stock price has climbed 197 percent for the period—24 percent per year.

Including reinvested dividends, a $10,000 investment in Jardine stock in 1984 would have grown to about $33,000 five years later. Average annual compounded rate of return (including stock growth and reinvested dividends): about 27 percent.

DIVIDEND YIELD

The company has been paying an excellent dividend the past few years. During the most recent two-year rating period (1989 and 1990), the stock paid an average annual current return (dividend yield) of 4.5 percent.

DIVIDEND GROWTH

Jardine has raised its dividend dramatically the past few years. The dividend increased 1,257 percent (68 percent per year) over the five-year period from 1984 to 1989.

CONSISTENCY

The company has been somewhat inconsistent over the past few years, with declines in every key financial category in 1983 and 1984, plus declines in revenue in 1986 and operating income in 1987. However, it has had five consecutive years of increased earnings through 1989. Its price-earnings ratio of about 8 is excellent for a fast-growing company.

MOMENTUM

Jardine has had excellent growth the past two years. Its earnings per share increased 39 percent in 1988 and 44 percent in 1989.

SUMMARY

Fiscal year ended: Dec. 31
(Hong Kong dollars; revenue and operating income in millions)

	1990*	1989	1988	1987	1986	1985	1984	5-year growth, %† (annual/total)
Revenue	—	15,058	14,817	12,720	10,416	10,497	8,881	11/69
Operating income	—	—	877	543	1,325	1,053	1,026	−5/30
Earnings/share	—	2.95	2.04	1.47	0.90	0.27	0.14	86/2,007
Dividend/share	—	0.95	0.65	0.48	0.29	0.07	0.07	68/1,257
Dividend yield, %	4.0	5.1	4.5	4.6	1.8	0.7	1.2	—/—
Stock price	28.20	18.40	14.60	10.30	16.07	9.79	6.18	24/197
P/E ratio	8.0	6.2	7.2	7.0	17.9	36.1	45.5	—/—
Book value/share	—	—	15.83	10.12	8.67	8.27	7.32	12/78

* 5-1-90
† 1984–89, except operating income and book value/share 1983–88
Source: Company sources and Worldscope.
Note: ADR; stock price quoted in *Barron's,* the *Wall Street Journal,* the *European Wall Street Journal* and the *Financial Times;* 5-year average annual return in U.S. currency: 27%.

Swire Pacific Limited
The Swire Group

SWIRE PACIFIC LIMITED

Swire House, 4th Floor
9 Connaught Road, Central
Hong Kong
Tel: (5) 840 8888
Chairman: David A. Gledhill

EARNINGS GROWTH	★ ★ ★
STOCK GROWTH	★ ★ ★ ★
DIVIDEND YIELD	★ ★ ★ ★
DIVIDEND GROWTH	★ ★
CONSISTENCY	★ ★ ★ ★
MOMENTUM	★ ★
HKG	**19 points**

It was in 1816 that British cloth merchant John Swire opened his textile business near the docks in Liverpool. As the company developed, its reach extended around the globe. It imported goods from Australia, cotton from America and in 1867 the company opened a trading shop in China.

Today, the London-based Swire Group is a vast and diversified manufacturing and merchandising empire. It has offices or subsidiaries throughout the United States and Australia, as well as in Europe, Japan and Taiwan. But nowhere is its influence greater than in Hong Kong, where its spin-off corporation, Swire Pacific, has blossomed into a multinational conglomerate in its own right.

Swire Pacific (which is publicly traded, independently of Swire Group) is one of Hong Kong's largest concerns. It has more than 40 subsidiaries and operates offices in the United States, Australia, Denmark, Panama, Singapore, Taiwan, China and Japan.

Aviation is Swire Pacific's primary profit area. It operates Swire Air Caterers, which prepares about 30,000 meals a day for airline passengers, Hong Kong Air Cargo Terminals Ltd., Hongkong Air Terminal Services and Securair, an airport security service.

The company also has substantial interests in Cathay Pacific Airways, a separate publicly traded company that offers cargo and passenger flights from Hong Kong to Europe, Australia, Asia and the United States.

Revenues from its aviation division account for about 60 percent of the company's total revenue.

Swire Pacific also operates several other divisions:

- Properties (12 percent of revenues). The company builds and operates office towers and residential high rises in the Hong Kong area and owns majority interest in the new Hong Kong Marriott Hotel. The company also owns a handful of properties in the United States.
- Industries (15 percent of revenues). Swire Pacific operates two large Coca-Cola bottling plants in the Hong Kong area. It also has a video and audio cassette manufacturing operation, a canning plant, a semiconductor assembly plant, a sugar packaging operation and several other businesses.
- Trading (11 percent of revenues). The firm has several subsidiaries involved in the import-export business. It exports clothing and home furnishings and imports a wide variety of commodities for the Hong Kong market, including Chrysler cars, trucks and jeeps and Reebok shoes, as well as a variety of pharmaceuticals, foods and household products. It also sells Volvos in Taiwan and operates several Kentucky Fried Chicken franchises in Hong Kong.

Swire owns several insurance subsidiaries and operates a shipping division with about 50 ships.

EARNINGS GROWTH

The company has had excellent sustained growth the past few years. Its earnings per share increased 178 percent over the past five years, 23 percent per year.

Swire reported total revenue of nearly 28 billion Hong Kong dollars (3.5 billion in U.S. dollars) in 1989.

STOCK GROWTH

The company's stock price has grown rapidly the past five years, increasing 205 percent for the period—25 percent per year.

Including reinvested dividends, a $10,000 investment in Swire Pacific stock in 1984 would have grown to about $37,000 five years later. Average annual compounded rate of return (including stock growth and reinvested dividends): about 30 percent.

DIVIDEND YIELD

The company generally pays a very good yield, which has averaged about 5 percent over the past five years. During the most recent two-year rating period (1988 and 1989), the stock paid an average annual current return (dividend yield) of 5.0 percent.

DIVIDEND GROWTH

Swire traditionally raises its dividend each year. The dividend increased 128 percent (18 percent per year) over the five-year period from 1984 to 1989.

CONSISTENCY

The company has had very consistent growth in its earnings per share, revenues, operating income and book value per share for the past several years. Its price-earnings ratio of about 8 is very favorable for a fast-growing company.

MOMENTUM

Swire's earnings per share increased less than 3 percent in 1989, but its book value rose 18 percent. Its stock price was up 30 percent the first half of 1990.

SUMMARY

This information refers to Class B shares; Class A shares, which are also actively traded and are followed in the stock tables of the *Wall Street Journal* and the *Financial Times,* are valued at (and typically trade at) approximately five times the price of Class B shares.

Fiscal year ended: Dec. 31
(Hong Kong dollars; revenue and operating income in millions)

	1990*	1989	1988	1987	1986	1985	1984	5-year growth, %† (annual/total)
Revenue	—	27,676	25,108	20,166	16,604	13,692	11,997	18/130
Operating income	—	5,350	5,651	4,565	2,929	1,852	1,919	23/178
Earnings/share	—	0.39	0.38	0.31	0.23	0.16	0.14	23/178
Dividend/share	—	0.16	0.15	0.12	0.10	0.08	0.07	18/128
Dividend yield, %	4.0	5.3	4.7	4.6	3.2	7.3	9.5	—/—
Stock price	3.88	2.75	3.23	2.73	3.00	1.42	0.90	25/205
P/E ratio	9.0	7.7	8.5	8.9	7.9	6.4	5.7	—/—
Book value/share	—	3.41	2.89	1.90	1.16	0.80	0.60	41/468

* 6–1–90
† 1984–89
Source: Company sources and Worldscope.
Note: ADR; stock price (Class A shares) quoted in *Barron's*, the *Wall Street Journal*, the *European Wall Street Journal* and the *Financial Times;* 5-year average annual return in U.S. currency: 30%.

65

中華電力有限公司

CHINA LIGHT & POWER CO., LTD.

147 Argyle St.
Kowloon
Hong Kong
Tel: (3) 760 6111
Fax: 852 760 4448
Chairman: The Lord Kadoorie

EARNINGS GROWTH	★ ★	
STOCK GROWTH	★ ★	
DIVIDEND YIELD	★ ★ ★ ★	
DIVIDEND GROWTH	★ ★ ★	
CONSISTENCY	★ ★ ★ ★	
MOMENTUM	★ ★	
HKG	**17 points**	

As the Hong Kong area expands and develops, its appetite for electricity continues to grow. China Light & Power's steady, persistent record of earnings gains reflects that growth.

Over the past 10 years, electricity sales by the Hong Kong utility have more than doubled, and the demand continues to grow at about 8 percent per year. The firm generated about 18 million kilowatts of electricity in 1989.

Founded in 1901, China Light supplies electricity to about 1.4 million customers in Kowloon and the New Territories. It also exports power to the Guangdong Province of the People's Republic of China.

The company uses both the traditional coal-burning plants and nuclear plants to generate electricity.

As Hong Kong's 1997 reunification with China nears, the company—like Hong Kong itself—faces an uncertain future. The reunification could bring new opportunities for China Light to expand its operations, or it could bring tighter restrictions under the Chinese regime.

China Light's chairman, Lord Kadoorie, puts it this way: "As to the future, two broad generalizations can be made. The first is that the current political instability could endure for some time. The second is that the economic austerity measures now taking place in China will continue to be enforced. While this may cause the present uncertainty to continue in the near term, taking the longer view, mutual interest and the fact that Hong Kong meets the need for a neutral point of contact between East and West strengthens my belief that we can look forward to the future with optimism."

EARNINGS GROWTH

The company has had steady growth the past few years. Its earnings per share increased 103 percent over the past five years, 15 percent per year.

China Light reported total revenue of $9.8 billion (1.3 billion in U.S. dollars) in 1989.

STOCK GROWTH

The company's stock price has had strong growth the past five years, increasing 123 percent for the period—17 percent per year.

Including reinvested dividends, a $10,000 investment in China Light stock at the end of 1984 would have grown to about $26,000 five years later. Average annual compounded rate of return (including stock growth and reinvested dividends): about 21 percent.

DIVIDEND YIELD

The company generally pays a good yield, which has averaged about 4 percent over the past five years. During the most recent two-year rating period (1989 and 1990), the stock paid an average annual current return (dividend yield) of 5.3 percent.

DIVIDEND GROWTH

China Light raises its dividend about 20 percent every year. The dividend increased 150 percent (20 percent per year) over the five-year period from 1984 to 1989.

CONSISTENCY

The company has had very consistent growth in its earnings per share, revenues, operating income and book value per share. Its price-earnings ratio of about 10 is an attractive level for a growing company.

MOMENTUM

While the company is still growing, its growth has tapered off somewhat during the past couple of years.

SUMMARY

Fiscal year ended: Sept. 30
(Hong Kong dollars; revenue and operating income in millions)

	1990*	1989	1988	1987	1986	1985	1984	5-year growth, %† (annual/total)
Revenue	—	9,755	8,873	8,331	7,538	6,859	6,405	9/52
Operating income	—	2,310	2,019	2,116	1,866	1,381	1,126	15/105
Earnings/share	—	1.22	1.10	1.01	0.89	0.77	0.60	15/103
Dividend/share	—	0.60	0.50	0.42	0.35	0.29	0.24	20/150
Dividend yield, %	5.0	5.5	4.6	2.4	3.3	4.0	4.8	—/—
Stock price	13.00	10.92	10.76	17.51	10.59	7.28	4.88	17/123
P/E ratio	10.0	9.0	9.7	17.4	11.9	9.5	8.1	—/—
Book value/share	—	5.35	4.74	4.14	3.55	3.00	2.51	16/113

* 5–1–90
† 1984–89
Source: Worldscope.

Note: ADR; stock price quoted in *Barron's,* the *Wall Street Journal,* the *European Wall Street Journal* and the *Financial Times;* 5-year average annual return in U.S. currency: 21%.

Japan

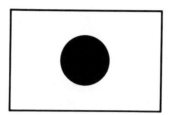

A cluster of islands off the east coast of Asia, Japan is small in terms of square miles but large in terms of population, which is estimated at about 125 million (nearly the size of France and all of Germany combined).

Japan's major industries include banking and financial services, autos, electrical and electronic equipment, machinery and chemicals. In 1989 the world's 10 largest banks were all Japanese.

The currency is the Japanese yen (JPY 155 = US $1, June, 1990). Its GNP was JPY 366 trillion (US $2.9 trillion) in 1988. Japan's inflation rate the past three years has been under 1 percent—a misleading figure because prices of goods in Japan are enormously inflated. A motel room can cost hundreds of dollars, dinner at a good restaurant for a Japanese family can cost hundreds of dollars and land and housing prices are astronomical. While the country is cash rich, the standard of living for most Japanese is substantially below that of the average American.

Real economic growth the past several years has averaged about 5 percent per year. The market value of all domestic stocks traded on the Tokyo Stock Exchange was US $3.8 trillion as of January 1, 1989. The Tokyo exchange is the largest of eight Japanese exchanges.

Price-earnings ratios of Japanese stocks have been enormously inflated compared with stocks of other countries around the world. While a P/E of 20 is considered fairly high by U.S. or European standards, Japanese stocks have carried P/Es of 50 to 150. In other words, the stock of a company that earned a mere $1 per share could sell for as much as $100 to $150, while in the United States the stock of a company that earned $1 a share is likely to sell for only about $10 to $20 a share.

But Japanese investors—avid savers who could earn an interest rate of only about 2 to 3 percent in Japanese banks—continued to plow their money into stocks as the market climbed at a breathtaking pace. The rationale for their continuing investment was the same as that of all markets that eventually crash: this market is different; the basic fundamentals of the past no longer matter; this market can sustain these high prices because the economy is growing at such a fast pace.

Ultimately, however, what goes up must come down, and the Japanese market proved to be no exception. The yen began its descent in 1989, and the stock market soon followed. In 1989 the Japanese yen dropped 17 percent relative to the U.S. dollar. And in the first nine months of 1990, the Japanese stock market was down 37 percent, and the yen was down another 7 percent.

For many Japanese investors, this cut substantially into the big gains they had made over the past few years. For example, investors in Mitsubishi Bank paid more for the stock in 1987 than it was selling for three years later in 1990. Yamanouchi Pharmaceutical—one of the top stocks listed in this book—was selling for about the same price in 1985 as it was in 1990. On the other hand, a few stocks (such as Nintendo) continued to grow even through the crash.

One more misconception outsiders have about corporate Japan is that all Japanese auto makers are thriving at the expense of sagging American and European car makers. The fact is, despite their growing market share, the stock of Japanese car companies has not fared all that well. Honda Motors stock, for instance, was selling only 22 percent higher in 1990 than it was in 1985 (that's an average annual increase of only 4 percent in Japanese currency; in U.S. currency, factoring in currency changes, the growth rate would be several percentage points higher).

In reviewing the Japanese stocks listed on the following pages, you'll notice that most score very low on the rating system. The low scores are due partly to the crash and partly to the fact that Japanese stocks pay very low dividends.

For prospective investors, the Japanese crash could be considered an opportunity to buy stocks at a substantial discount to previous prices. Just be aware that price-earnings ratios in Japan continue to be much higher than they are elsewhere and that compared to its rising interest rates (now approaching 5 percent), the average stock dividend yields in Japan (under 1 percent) are extremely low.

54

Nintendo Co., Ltd.

NINTENDO CO., LTD.

60 Fukuine Kamitakamatsu-cho
Higashiyama-ku
Kyoto 605
Japan
Tel: 075 541 6112
Fax: 075 541 6127
President: Hiroshi Yamauchi

EARNINGS GROWTH	★ ★ ★ ★
STOCK GROWTH	★ ★ ★ ★
DIVIDEND YIELD	**(no points)**
DIVIDEND GROWTH	★ ★
CONSISTENCY	★ ★ ★ ★
MOMENTUM	★ ★ ★ ★
TYO	**18 points**

Green monsters stand behind every corner; mazes, trap doors and land mines lay in wait for the unsuspecting. Young eyes, nimble fingers weave the trails, shoot the targets, forge the traps, catch the prizes—and then come back for more. All of which helps explain Nintendo's amazing success.

Nintendo has run roughshod over the home entertainment industry, capturing an 80 percent share of the burgeoning U.S. and Japanese home video game market. One in every four American homes now owns a Nintendo Entertainment System, according to the company. For the past three Christmases, Nintendo has been America's best-selling toy.

Rarely in the toy industry has any game so dominated the market—which leads analysts to wonder how long Nintendo can continue to weave its magic. Is there a trap door in Nintendo's future—a burnout point for video-game consumers? It happened in 1985, when video game sales dropped to almost nothing after cresting a couple of years earlier at the $3 billion mark.

It could happen again. Sales of Nintendo's game cartridge player were expected to fall this year for the first time ever. Mounting industry competition—from upstart systems by NEC and Sega—could also make things tougher on Nintendo.

Just the same, the Kyoto-based game maker is hardly ready to flash the "game over" sign. This is no overnight operation. Few investors realize it, but the Nintendo Company was founded more than a century ago, in 1889, as a manufacturer of Japanese playing cards known as *Hanafuda*.

In 1970 it introduced Japan's first hand-held video game, featuring a liquid-crystal screen. It first brought its current model home video system to America in 1985—just as Atari was crashing.

Nintendo sells both hardware and software for its games and holds licensing rights over other software makers that design and market games for the Nintendo system. There are now well over 300 different Nintendo games available in the United States. Its Super Mario Brothers game is the all-time favorite.

In recent years, the company has brought some new electronic toy products to market, including a hot-selling portable Nintendo Game Boy that can be played by one individual or hooked up with other games for group competition.

Where to next? More games and more markets. Having taken Japan and the United States by storm, Nintendo has been aggressively spreading its brand of fun to the European market. Nintendo can hardly take credit for knocking down the Berlin Wall, but it well may have a video game on the drawing boards that does just that.

EARNINGS GROWTH

The company has had excellent growth the past few years. Its earnings per share increased 201 percent over the past five years, 25 percent per year.

Nintendo reported total revenue of 250 billion yen (2 billion in U.S. dollars) in 1989.

STOCK GROWTH

The company's stock price has continued to climb—even through the recent Japanese market crash. Over the past five years, the stock price has climbed 259 percent—29 percent per year.

Including reinvested dividends, a $10,000 investment in Nintendo stock at its median price in 1984 would have grown to about $37,000 five years later. Average annual compounded rate of return (including stock growth and reinvested dividends): about 30 percent.

DIVIDEND YIELD   (no points)

The company generally pays a very modest yield, which has averaged about 0.5 percent over the past five years. During the most recent two-year rating

period (1988 and 1989), the stock paid an average annual current return (dividend yield) of 0.4 percent.

DIVIDEND GROWTH

Nintendo raises its dividend most years. The dividend increased 119 percent (17 percent per year) over the five-year period from 1984 to 1989.

CONSISTENCY

The company has had very consistent growth in its earnings per share, revenues, operating income and book value per share. Its price-earnings ratio of about 50 is not especially high by Japanese standards, but it is substantially higher than its average over the past few years. That should not be a problem if the company continues its strong growth.

MOMENTUM

Nintendo has continued to grow quickly the past two years and had particularly strong growth in earnings and revenue through the latter part of 1989 and into 1990.

SUMMARY

Fiscal year ended: Aug. 31
(Japanese yen; revenue and net income in billions)

	1990*	1989	1988	1987	1986	1985	1984	5-year growth, %† (annual/total)
Revenue	—	250	178	140	117	77	65	31/284
Operating income[1]	—	30	27	25	16	10	9	27/233
Earnings/share	—	282	254	234	153	97	93	25/201
Dividend/share	—	33	27	24	20	15	15	17/119
Dividend yield, %	—	0.3	0.5	0.6	0.4	0.7	0.6	—/—
Stock price	20,900	8,913	5,379	5,510	4,710	2,337	2,478	29/259
P/E ratio	56.0	43.5	21.1	16.6	30.7	24.0	26.5	—/—
Book value/share	—	—	—	—	—	—	—	—/—

* 3–31–90
† 1984–89
1. Net income is given here.
Source: Nikko Securities, Inc.

Note: ADR; stock prices quoted in *Barron's,* the *Wall Street Journal* and the *European Wall Street Journal;* 5-year average annual return in U.S. currency: 46%.

61

⊛ 大和ハウス工業株式会社

DAIWA HOUSE INDUSTRY CO., LTD.

5-16, 1-chome, Awaza
Nishi-ku
Osaka 550
Japan
Tel: (06) 532-5111
Fax: (06) 532-5806
Chairman: Nobuo Ishibashi
President: Shunichi Ishibashi

EARNINGS GROWTH	★ ★ ★
STOCK GROWTH	★ ★ ★ ★
DIVIDEND YIELD	★
DIVIDEND GROWTH	★
CONSISTENCY	★ ★ ★ ★
MOMENTUM	★ ★ ★ ★
TYO, OSA, CIN, OTH	**17 points**

When Daiwa House Industry first started turning out its line of factory-built, prefabricated homes back in the 1950s, the houses were very cheap and *very basic*. But the prefab housing market has come a long way over the past 35 years—and so has Daiwa House.

The company is now Japan's second leading home builder, and, while it still offers the basic one-story starter home, many of its houses are elaborate two- and three-story models, with bay windows, spacious decks and posh interiors.

Daiwa House has also become a leading resort and hotel developer, with luxury properties throughout Japan.

The company produces thousands of prefabricated, single-family homes each year as well as a wide range of multi-family homes and large urban housing complexes, such as the 8,500-unit Okayama Neopolis in western Japan.

Daiwa has also adapted its prefabricated construction techniques to the commercial and industrial market. The company builds shopping centers, warehouses, factories, office buildings and educational and recreational centers.

The company's other key profit center is the resort business. Since 1972, Daiwa has built 3 golf courses and 15 resort hotels. Its chain of Daiwa Royal Hotels is located in scenic areas throughout Japan and often include tennis courts, swimming pools, conference centers, vacation villas and, in some cases, beach access.

In addition to its Japanese operations, the company has begun to expand to other countries. It is currently at work on major projects in China and Australia.

EARNINGS GROWTH

The company has had excellent growth the past few years. Its earnings per share increased 181 percent over the past five years, 23 percent per year.

Daiwa reported total revenue of 562 billion yen (4.2 billion in U.S. dollars) in 1989.

STOCK GROWTH

The company's stock price has moved up very quickly the past five years, increasing 254 percent for the period—29 percent per year.

Including reinvested dividends, a $10,000 investment in Daiwa House stock in 1985 would have grown to about $37,000 five years later. Average annual compounded rate of return (including stock growth and reinvested dividends): about 30 percent.

DIVIDEND YIELD

The company generally pays a modest yield—typical of Japanese stocks—which has averaged under 1 percent over the past five years. During the most recent two-year rating period (1988 and 1989), the stock paid an average annual current return (dividend yield) of 0.7 percent.

DIVIDEND GROWTH

Daiwa is not in the habit of raising its dividend each year. The dividend increased 88 percent (13 percent per year) over the five-year period from 1984 to 1989.

CONSISTENCY

The company has had very consistent growth in its earnings per share, revenues and book value per share. Its price-earnings ratio of about 40 is consistent with most growing Japanese stocks.

MOMENTUM

Daiwa has had excellent growth the past two years. Its earnings per share increased 59 percent in 1988 and 38 percent in 1989.

SUMMARY

Fiscal year ended: Mar. 31
(Japanese yen; revenue and operating income in billions)

	1990	1989	1988	1987	1986	1985	1984	5-year growth, %† (annual/total)
Revenue	—	562	465	386	355	318	285	15/97
Operating income	—	47	30	20	23	23	19	20/147
Earnings/share	—	51	37	24	21	19	18	23/181
Dividend/share	—	14	12	11	9	9	8	13/88
Dividend yield, %	0.9	0.7	0.7	0.5	0.7	1.6	1.6	—/—
Stock price	1,980	2,000	1,740	2,100	1,250	560	475	29/254
P/E ratio	40.0	39.3	46.6	89.3	59.6	30.1	26.0	—/—
Book value/share	—	466	412	368	330	305	281	11/65

† 1984–89, except stock price, 1985–90
Source: Worldscope.

Note: ADR; stock price quoted in *Barron's,* the *Wall Street Journal,* the *European Wall Street Journal* and the *Financial Times;* 5-year average annual return in U.S. currency: 46%.

NATIONAL HOUSE INDUSTRIAL CO., LTD.

1-12, 1 Chome, Shinsenri Nishimachi
Toyonaka City, Osaka 565
Japan
Tel: 06 834 5111
President: Minoru Nishio

EARNINGS GROWTH	★ ★ ★ ★
STOCK GROWTH	★ ★ ★ ★
DIVIDEND YIELD	★
DIVIDEND GROWTH	(no points)
CONSISTENCY	★ ★ ★
MOMENTUM	★ ★ ★ ★
TYO, OSA	**16 points**

National House Industrial began as a home builder but has evolved to a higher plane, claims company president Minoru Nishio. Now, he says, the company is a builder of life cultures.

"We firmly believe that a home should not only be a safe, convenient life tool," says Nishio, "it should also be a place where the dreams of a rich life are fulfilled, a place full of health and human relationship."

The company's philosophy is a response to what Nishio calls the "age of sensitivity, the age of feeling." It's also—for National House—the age of quickly rising profits. The company's emphasis on the human element in home building is apparently working well with consumers. National has reported 12 consecutive years of increased sales and earnings.

The company builds upscale homes and apartments under the Pana-Home trademark. The typical PanaHome house features an airy, open room-to-room environment, hardwood floors and an emphasis on storage-space efficiency.

In addition to its on-site construction of homes and apartments, National House operates factories that turn out building materials and furniture for use in the construction and furnishing of its homes.

With each new home, the company tries to put into practice its philosophy of "creating life cultures." Before the contract is signed, the company investigates the plot and the neighborhood, assesses the client's needs and draws a "life culture sketch" of the proposed home. Then the construction manager visits each of the surrounding homes to inform the neighbors that construction is soon to begin.

Before work starts, the parties meet at the site for a traditional Japanese blessing of the site and putting of the ridgepole. Once construction is finished, again the parties gather at the home for a "completion ceremony" to "give thanks for the safe completion of the construction work and to pray for many long years of happiness in the new home."

EARNINGS GROWTH

National House has enjoyed strong earnings growth the past five years, with an excellent earnings-per-share gain of 316 percent for the period—32 percent per year. The company in 1989 had total annual sales of 176 billion yen, about 1.34 billion in U.S. dollars. National is a spin-off of the Matsushita Group.

STOCK GROWTH

The company's stock price has increased four of the past five years. During the recent Japanese market crash, National House stock held firm. Over the past five years, the stock has jumped 420 percent (39 percent per year).

Including reinvested dividends, a $10,000 investment in National House stock at its median price in 1985 would have grown to about $55,000 five years later. Average annual compounded rate of return (including stock growth and reinvested dividends): about 40 percent.

DIVIDEND YIELD

Like most Japanese companies, National pays a low yield, which has averaged about 1.5 percent over the past five years. During the most recent two-year rating period (1989 and 1990), the stock paid an average annual current return (dividend yield) of 0.8 percent.

DIVIDEND GROWTH   (no points)

The company has raised its dividend only 25 percent over the past five years, an annual increase of only 5 percent.

CONSISTENCY

National has had 12 consecutive years of increased revenues and earnings, although its earnings per share and book value have each had modest declines in the past five years. All in all, however, the company has been a very consistent performer. Its price-earnings ratio of about 28 is very favorable for the Japanese market.

MOMENTUM

The company has maintained strong increases in revenues and operating earnings the past two years. Its earnings per share has more than doubled in the past two years.

SUMMARY

Fiscal year ended: Mar. 31
(Japanese yen; revenue and operating income in billions)

	1990	1989	1988	1987	1986	1985	1984	5-year growth, %† (annual/total)
Revenue	—	176	156	129	114	105	97	13/81
Operating income	—	16	13	10	7	6	5	26/220
Earnings/share	—	57	42	26	21	17.5	18	32/316
Dividend/share	—	13	13	10	10	10	10	5/25
Dividend yield, %	0.8	0.8	0.7	0.7	1.1	2.3	2.0	—/—
Stock price	1,600	1,524	1,558	1,102	657	308	343	39/420
P/E ratio	28.0	28.6	44.9	55.7	45.3	24.9	26.11	—/—
Book value/share	—	322	269	213	184	175	187	12/72

† 1984–89, except stock price, 1985–90
Source: Company sources and Worldscope.
Note: No ADR; stock price quoted in the *Financial Times;* 5-year average annual return in U.S. currency: 57%.

81

SEVEN-ELEVEN JAPAN CO., LTD.

1-4 Shibakoen 4-chome
Minato-ku
Tokyo 105
Japan
Tel: 03 459-3711
Chairman and CEO: Masatoshi Ito
President: Toshifumi Suzuki

EARNINGS GROWTH	★ ★ ★
STOCK GROWTH	★ ★
DIVIDEND YIELD	**(no points)**
DIVIDEND GROWTH	★ ★ ★
CONSISTENCY	★ ★ ★ ★
MOMENTUM	★ ★ ★
TYO, OTC	**15 points**

It's little wonder that when U.S.-based Southland Corporation, which operates America's chain of Seven-Eleven stores, found itself on the verge of bankruptcy in March, 1990, it turned to its friends from Japan for a bailout.

U.S. Seven-Eleven stores, which constitute the nation's largest convenience store chain, could take a few lessons from their Japanese counterparts. Seven-Eleven Japan has set new income records every year since 1974, when the company was established (under the wings of Southland), and new Seven-Eleven outlets continue to spread like locusts across Japan.

There are already about 4,000 Seven-Eleven stores in Japan, with another 350 or so being added each year. It is the largest convenience store chain in Japan.

Under an agreement with Southland Corporation, Seven-Eleven Japan and its parent company, Ito-Yokado, agreed to purchase a 75 percent stake in Southland for $400 million. Southland had been struggling under heavy debt.

Seven-Eleven Japan has fared significantly better than its U.S. counterpart. The chain sells more pastries, more boxed lunches and more magazines than any other retailer in Japan. In fact, in 1989 it became Japan's leading retailer of food products.

In addition to its pastries and boxed lunches, Seven-Elevens do a strong business in a wide range of packaged foods, canned coffee (a favorite in Japan), sundries, drugs and cosmetics, cards, school supplies and a variety of other goods. Food items account for about 75 percent of the company's total sales.

The company has continued to increase its profitability not only through expansion to new locations but also by adding to the products and services offered at existing stores. One change has been a greater emphasis on the sale of ready-to-eat delicatessen foods.

The stores have also begun a very successful on-line bill payment service that allows customers to pay their Tokyo Electric bills and Tokyo Gas bills at the stores.

Most Seven-Eleven stores are independently owned, with a franchise fee, based on sales revenues, going to the Seven-Eleven Japan corporation.

Seven-Eleven Japan is a consolidated subsidiary of Ito-Yokado, a major Japanese retailer (and a "Top 100" company also profiled in this book). But while it is part of the Ito-Yokado family, Seven-Eleven is a separate publicly traded company on the Tokyo Stock Exchange.

EARNINGS GROWTH

The company has had solid growth the past few years. Its earnings per share moved up 179 percent over the past five years, 23 percent per year.

Seven-Eleven reported total revenue of 118 billion yen (780 million in U.S. dollars) in fiscal 1990.

STOCK GROWTH

The company's stock price has moved up steadily the past five years, increasing 132 percent for the period—18 percent per year.

Including reinvested dividends, a $10,000 investment in Seven-Eleven Japan stock in 1985 would have grown to about $23,000 five years later. Average annual compounded rate of return (including stock growth and reinvested dividends): about 18 percent.

DIVIDEND YIELD   (no points)

The company generally pays a very modest yield, which has averaged about 0.3 percent over the past five years. During the most recent two-year rating period (1989 and 1990), the stock paid an average annual current return (dividend yield) of 0.35 percent.

DIVIDEND GROWTH

Seven-Eleven traditionally raises its dividend each year. The dividend increased 145 percent (20 percent per year) over the five-year period from 1985 to 1990.

CONSISTENCY

The company has set new records in operating income every year since 1974, and its earnings per share has moved up consistently since 1984. The company's price-earnings ratio of about 50 is normal for a growing Japanese company.

MOMENTUM

Seven-Eleven has had excellent growth in earnings per share, book value and assets the past three years.

SUMMARY

Fiscal year ended: Feb. 28
(Japanese yen; revenue and operating income in billions)

	1990	1989	1988	1987	1986	1985	1984	5-year growth, %† (annual/total)
Revenue	118	102	96	97	85	71	61	11/66
Operating income	—	48	36	33	28	21	14	28/242
Earnings/share	146	127	105	82	67	52	40	23/179
Dividend/share	26	22	18	16	13	11	8	20/145
Dividend yield, %	0.3	0.4	0.3	0.4	0.3	0.3	0.6	—/—
Stock price	7,700	5,317	5,556	4,514	4,132	3,318	1,426	18/132
P/E ratio	52.7	42.0	53.2	55.0	62.0	63.6	35.6	—/—
Book value/share	—	603	403	327	270	187	75	52/701

† 1985–90, except operating income and book value/share, 1984–89
Source: Company sources and Worldscope.

Note: ADR; stock price quoted in the *Wall Street Journal,* the *European Wall Street Journal* and the *Financial Times;* 5-year average annual return in U.S. currency: 32%.

ONO ONO PHARMACEUTICAL CO.,LTD.

ONO PHARMACEUTICAL CO., LTD.

2-1-5 Doshomachi
Chuo-ku
Osaka 541
Japan
Tel: 06 222-5551
Chairman: Junzo Ono
President: Kazuo Sano

EARNINGS GROWTH	★ ★ ★ ★
STOCK GROWTH	**(no points)**
DIVIDEND YIELD	**(no points)**
DIVIDEND GROWTH	★ ★ ★ ★
CONSISTENCY	★ ★ ★ ★
MOMENTUM	★ ★ ★
TYO, OSA	**15 points**

Medical technology consisted of little more than herbs and faith when Ono Pharmaceutical first opened shop. The company traces its roots to 1717, making it one of the oldest pharmaceutical firms in the world.

Ono has had excellent success bringing new drugs to market the past few years—and its fast-rising earnings and revenue reflect that. While Japan is Ono's largest market, the Osaka manufacturer sells its medications around the world.

Some of the company's leading drugs include:

- Kinedak, used for the treatment of diabetes;
- Ronok (developed in conjunction with Upjohn Pharmaceuticals (Japan), a stomach-ulcer treatment;
- Foipan, used for pancreatitis;
- FOY, a prostaglandin used to control blood pressure and as an anticoagulate;
- Opalmon, another leading prostaglandin;
- Prostandin, now being expanded to treat severe hepatitis and skin ulcers.

FOY, Prostandin, Foipan, Opalmon and Cataclot injections have been Ono's biggest revenue generators. The company has also developed medications that relieve bronchial asthma and other respiratory problems, arteriosclerosis, pancreatitis and senile dementia.

Ono is developing new treatments for cancer, emphysema, liver disease, AIDS and other immunological diseases.

EARNINGS GROWTH

The company has had excellent growth the past few years. Its earnings per share increased 270 percent over the past five years, 30 percent per year.

Ono had annual revenue of 70 billion yen (600 million in U.S. dollars) in 1988.

STOCK GROWTH   (no points)

Ono's stock price has been erratic the past five years, but in 1990, when other Japanese stocks were dropping 30 to 50 percent, Ono's stock was moving up. Over the past five years, Ono stock has increased in price 49 percent, 8 percent per year.

Including reinvested dividends, a $10,000 investment in Ono stock in 1984 would have grown to about $15,000 five years later. Average annual compounded rate of return (including stock growth and reinvested dividends): about 8 percent.

DIVIDEND YIELD   (no points)

The company generally pays a meager yield, which has averaged under 0.2 percent over the past five years. During the most recent two-year rating period (1988 and 1989), the stock paid an average annual current return (dividend yield) of 0.2 percent.

DIVIDEND GROWTH

Ono traditionally raises its dividend each year, although the dividend is so small that the 320 percent (33 percent per year) increase during the recent five-year period amounted to only about 9 cents per share.

CONSISTENCY

The company has had very consistent growth in its earnings per share, revenues and book value per share the past five years. Its price-earnings ratio of about 50 is typical of many growing companies.

MOMENTUM

Ono has maintained a solid growth pace. Its stock continued to rise during the down Japanese market in 1990, indicating that the financial community has a high respect for the company's potential.

SUMMARY

Fiscal year ended: Nov. 30
(Japanese yen; revenue and operating income in billions)

	1990*	1989	1988	1987	1986	1985	1984	5-year growth, %† (annual/total)
Revenue	—	—	70	64	55	47	44	11/66
Operating income	—	—	27	21	19	14	14	14/92
Earnings/share	—	—	95	73	51	39	32	30/270
Dividend/share	—	—	12	9	8	7	4	33/320
Dividend yield, %	—	0.2	0.2	0.1	0.1	0.2	0.1	—/—
Stock price	6,060	5,440	5,140	6,255	8,252	3,640	4,951	8/49
P/E ratio	—	50.0	54.0	85.5	161.9	92.8	156.1	—/—
Book value/share	—	—	606	520	455	401	351	20/149

* 5–1–90
† 1983–88, except stock price, 1984–89
Source: Worldscope.

Note: No ADR; stock price quoted in the *Wall Street Journal,* the *European Wall Street Journal* and the *Financial Times;* 5-year average annual return in U.S. currency: 21%.

83

◈ MITSUI & CO., LTD.

MITSUI & CO., LTD.

1-2-1 Ohtemachi
Chiyoda-ku
Tokyo 100
Japan
Tel: 03 285-1111
Chairman: Toshikuni Yahiro

EARNINGS GROWTH	★ ★ ★ ★
STOCK GROWTH	★ ★ ★
DIVIDEND YIELD	★
DIVIDEND GROWTH	**(no points)**
CONSISTENCY	★ ★
MOMENTUM	★ ★ ★ ★
TYO, OSA, OTC, AMS	**14 points**

Mitsui is Japan's oldest trading company, and one of the world's largest. Its annual revenue of $126 billion is about the same as General Motors—America's largest company.

Mitsui's mainstays are mining, machinery and merchandising. Founded in 1876, the Tokyo-based company has entrenched itself around the world, with over 500 separate subsidiaries.

It has 16 offices in the United States, plus offices in Havana, Moscow, Beijing, Warsaw, Prague, Bucharest, Berlin and throughout Europe. It has offices in Istanbul, Baghdad, New Delhi, Beirut, Cairo, Damascus and throughout the Middle East and Africa. It has offices in Central and South America and offices in Manila, Seoul, Shanghai, Sydney and Singapore. As company officials like to put it: "Mitsui is at home everywhere in the world."

The company divides its business into 10 industrial segments:

* Iron, steel and nonferrous metals (70 subsidiaries, 19 percent of revenue). The company produces and trades in a wide range of steel and metal products, including wires, bars, rails, pipes, tubes, plates and

sheets. It mines, produces or trades copper, lead, zinc, tin, uranium, nickel, cobalt, gold, silver, platinum, titanium, aluminum and other metals.

- Machinery (108 subsidiaries, 18 percent of revenue). It sells machinery for electric power plants, iron and steel manufacturing plants, tool manufacturing and factory automation, vehicle parts and other products.
- Energy (40 subsidiaries, 15 percent of revenues). The company is involved in the production and sale of crude oil, petroleum, gas, natural gas, coke and graphite.
- Foodstuffs (73 subsidiaries, 14 percent of revenues). Mitsui sells grains, feed, fats and oils, meat, sugar and other foods throughout the world. It also imports fruits, cheeses and other foods for consumption in Japan.
- Textiles and general merchandise (73 subsidiaries, 9 percent of revenues). The company is a trader of textile raw materials, synthetic fibers, yarn, fabrics, interior and industrial goods, construction materials, lumber, cement, electronics, rubber, paper, medical equipment, light machinery and many other products. It also imports apparel for Japanese consumers.

Mitsui also has divisions involved in transportation and shipping, finance and commodities trading.

EARNINGS GROWTH

Mitsui has had a consistent run of earnings gains the past five years, with an outstanding earnings-per-share gain of 262 percent for the period—29 percent per year. The company has total annual sales of 16.8 trillion yen, about 126 billion in U.S. dollars.

STOCK GROWTH

The company's stock price increased sharply through much of the 1980s, but like most Japanese stocks, it suffered some in the Japanese market crash in the early months of 1990. Over the past five years (through its fiscal 1990), the stock has increased 194 percent (24 percent per year).

Including reinvested dividends, a $10,000 investment in Mitsui stock at its median price in 1985 would have grown to about $30,000 five years later. Average annual compounded rate of return (including stock growth and reinvested dividends): about 25 percent.

DIVIDEND YIELD

The company generally pays a low yield, which has averaged about 1 percent over the past five years. During the most recent two-year rating period (1989 and 1990), the stock paid an average annual current return (dividend yield) of 0.65 percent.

DIVIDEND GROWTH   (no points)

The company has raised its dividend only 25 percent over the past five years, an annual increase of only 5 percent.

CONSISTENCY

Mitsui's growth in earnings per share has been very consistent, but its operating earnings and book value have been somewhat erratic over the past few years. Its total assets declined three years in a row, and its dividend has been raised only twice in the past five years. The company has a very high ratio of long-term-debt-to-capital (80 percent), but its price-earnings ratio of 30 to 35 is very favorable for the Japanese market.

MOMENTUM

The company has had big increases in earnings per share and book value the past two years. And Mitsui reported a strong first half for its fiscal 1990. In fiscal 1989, its earnings per share increased 58 percent.

SUMMARY

Fiscal year ended: Mar. 31
(Japanese yen; revenue and operating income in billions)

	1990	1989	1988	1987	1986	1985	1984	5-year growth, %† (annual/total)
Revenue	—	16,764	15,779	14,168	18,082	17,598	16,181	1/4
Operating income	—	108	84	36	65	90	83	6/30
Earnings/share	—	29	18	12	10	9	8	29/262
Dividend/share	—	6	5	5	4	4	4	5/25
Dividend yield, %	0.7	0.6	0.6	0.8	1.0	1.5	1.4	—/—
Stock price	890	1,000	883	617	437	302	313	24/194
P/E ratio	30.0	35.0	49.0	51.0	45.0	33.4	39.4	—/—
Book value/share	—	278	216	184	172	189	192	9/52

† 1984–89, except stock price, 1985–90
Source: Company sources and Worldscope.

Note: ADR; stock price quoted in *Barron's,* the *Wall Street Journal,* the *European Wall Street Journal* and the *Financial Times;* 5-year average annual return in U.S. currency: 40%.

85

NOMURA

NOMURA SECURITIES CO. LTD.

1-9-1 Nihonbashi
Chuo-ku
Tokyo 103
Japan
Tel: (03) 211-1811
Chairman: Setsuya Tabuchi
President and CEO: Yoshihisa Tabuchi

EARNINGS GROWTH	★ ★ ★ ★
STOCK GROWTH	★ ★
DIVIDEND YIELD	★
DIVIDEND GROWTH	★ ★
CONSISTENCY	★ ★ ★
MOMENTUM	★ ★
TYO, OSA, AMS, OTH	**14 points**

In the gilded halls of trade, where stocks and bonds change hands—in Paris and Rome, London and New York, Sydney, Stockholm, Seoul and Singapore—wherever deals are cut and money rules, Nomura Securities is king.

Nomura has woven a complex web of financial outposts—a trading office in Bangkok, a research center in Washington, a land office in L.A., an affiliate in the People's Republic of China, a fund management group in Hong Kong. Wherever opportunity leads, Nomura follows.

Just how big is Nomura?

Huge. No other brokerage firm compares. In all, it has operations in 46 financial hubs in 22 countries. In 1989 its net earnings (about $2 billion) *far* exceeded the earnings of all 10 of America's largest publicly traded brokerage houses *combined!* (Salomon Brothers, America's most profitable brokerage, earned about $500 million.)

Nomura was founded as a bond sales and underwriting specialty house in 1925 by Tokushichi Nomura II. Two years later, the company established its first foreign office—in New York—and it has been expanding ever since.

The company's bread and butter is still the traditional brokerage trade, although it is steadily branching out into other areas of finance.

The company has built a reputation as a very shrewd, well-managed operation. While other major brokerage firms around the world have struggled financially in recent years as consumer interest in individual stocks subsided, Nomura has been steadily increasing its market share and earnings.

The Tokyo-based company has, however, drawn its share of controversy. A recent book, *The House of Nomura, The Rise to Supremacy of the World's Most Powerful Company,* by Albert J. Alletzhauser depicts Nomura as heavy-handed and, at times, unscrupulous in some of its dealings. The company filed a libel suit against the author in England, claiming, among other things, that the book falsely accuses Nomura of inappropriate dealings with clients, manipulating the Japanese market and engaging in insider trading.

Nomura is a diversified financial operation, offering brokerage and trading services, investment banking, asset management, venture capital and mortgage securities services. In the United States the company has offices in New York, Chicago, Los Angeles, San Francisco, Honolulu and Washington, DC. It has been a registered member of the New York Stock Exchange since 1981 and a primary dealer of U.S. Treasury bonds since 1986.

Worldwide, Nomura draws about 65 percent of its revenues from brokerage commissions and fees, 20 percent from interest and dividends and the balance from gains on trading—although that percentage varies from year to year. The recent decline of the Japanese stock market could have a short-term adverse effect on the company's 1990 earnings. But Nomura's vast global empire—and the diversification it brings—helps minimize the damage from declines in a single regional market.

EARNINGS GROWTH

The company has had excellent growth the past few years, with a gain in earnings per share of 239 percent over the past five years, 28 percent per year.

Nomura reported total revenue of 1.1 trillion yen (8 billion in U.S. dollars) in 1989.

STOCK GROWTH

The company's stock growth had been very strong until the Japanese slump, when it dropped about 30 percent. Over the past five years, the stock has increased 97 percent, 15 percent per year.

Including reinvested dividends, a $10,000 investment in Nomura stock in 1984 would have grown to about $20,000 five years later. Average annual compounded rate of return (including stock growth and reinvested dividends): about 15.5 percent.

DIVIDEND YIELD

The company generally pays a very modest yield, which has averaged about 0.5 percent over the past five years. During the most recent two-year rating period (1989 and 1990), the stock paid an average annual current return (dividend yield) of 0.5 percent.

DIVIDEND GROWTH

Nomura traditionally raises its dividend each year. The dividend increased 114 percent (16 percent per year) over the five-year period from 1984 to 1989.

CONSISTENCY

The company has been fairly consistent, but it did have a drop in earnings per share and total revenues in 1988. Its book value and assets have been moving up steadily.

MOMENTUM

Nomura had a fairly good fiscal 1989 but a weak 1988. The Japanese market crash could also have a temporary negative effect on the company's earnings.

SUMMARY

Fiscal year ended: Mar. 31
(Japanese yen; revenue and operating income in billions)

	1990	1989	1988	1987	1986	1985	1984	5-year growth, %† (annual/total)
Revenue	—	1,064	959	1,073	941	589	437	19/142
Operating income	—	537	470	583	495	249	164	27/227
Earnings/share	—	129	112	142	114	58	38	28/239
Dividend/share	—	14	13	12	10	7	7	16/114
Dividend yield, %	0.6	0.4	0.4	0.3	0.3	0.6	1.0	—/—
Stock price	2,170	3,150	3,270	4,320	3,255	1,097	657	15/97
P/E ratio	18.0	24.0	29.2	30.5	28.4	18.8	17.0	—/—
Book value/share	—	816	684	582	445	334	282	23/189

† 1984–89, except stock price, 1985–90
Source: Company sources and Worldscope.

Note: ADR; stock price quoted in *Barron's,* the *Wall Street Journal,* the *European Wall Street Journal* and the *Financial Times;* 5-year average annual return in U.S. currency: 29%.

86 TOTO LTD.

TOTO LTD.

1-1, Nakashima 2-chome
Kokurakita-ku
Kitakyushu, Fukuoka 802
Japan
Tel: (093) 951-2371
Fax: (093) 922-6789
President: Yoshine Koga

EARNINGS GROWTH	★
STOCK GROWTH	★ ★ ★ ★
DIVIDEND YIELD	★
DIVIDEND GROWTH	**(no points)**
CONSISTENCY	★ ★ ★ ★
MOMENTUM	★ ★ ★
TYO, OSA, OTC	**13 points**

Toto has been turning on faucets and flushing toilets for people all over Japan. The company has helped bring bathrooms into the electronics age through the use of special sensors and other advanced innovations.

One of Toto's newest products is the "Washlet," a sensor-controlled sink with both a faucet and a blow dryer that automatically turns on when users place their hands beneath them. The firm also manufactures sensor-activated toilets and urinals for public restrooms that flush automatically after each use.

Another of Toto's latest innovations is the "Shampoo Dresser," which allows users to wash their hair while fully clothed.

Toto manufactures and markets a wide range of other bathroom and kitchen products for both commercial and home use, including bathtubs, vanities, kitchen tables and chairs, cabinetry and complete "modular kitchens."

While most of its products are bathroom- or kitchen-related, Toto breaks its product line into three segments: sanitary ware (16 percent of sales), metal fittings (17 percent of sales) and "other bathroom and kitchen products" (67 percent of sales).

Toto does the bulk of its business in Japan, where it operates 9 branch offices and more than 50 business outlets. But the company is beginning to expand to other areas in Europe and Asia.

It now has about a dozen affiliate companies and two offices in seven countries, including Hong Kong, Korea, Taiwan, China, Indonesia, France and Germany. Its next target for market expansion, says company president Yoshine Koga, is the United States.

EARNINGS GROWTH

The company has had solid growth the past few years. Its earnings per share increased 95 percent over the past five years, 14 percent per year.

Toto had annual revenue of 293 billion yen in 1988 (2.3 billion in U.S. dollars). The company has 22,000 shareholders of record.

STOCK GROWTH

The company's stock price has moved up very quickly the past five years, increasing 409 percent for the period—38 percent per year.

Including reinvested dividends, a $10,000 investment in Toto stock in 1984 would have grown to about $50,000 five years later. Average annual compounded rate of return (including stock growth and reinvested dividends): about 39 percent.

DIVIDEND YIELD

The company generally pays a modest yield, which has averaged about 0.6 percent over the past five years. During the most recent two-year rating period (1989 and 1990), the stock paid an average annual current return (dividend yield) of 0.5 percent.

DIVIDEND GROWTH (no points)

Toto rarely raises its dividend. The dividend increased only 29 percent over the most recent five years, 5 percent per year.

CONSISTENCY

The company has had very consistent growth in its earnings per share, revenues, operating income and book value per share. Its price-earnings ratio of under 50 is favorable for a growing Japanese company.

MOMENTUM

Toto has continued to maintain solid growth the past couple of years, very much in line with its five-year average.

SUMMARY

Fiscal year ended: Nov. 30
(Japanese yen; revenue and operating income in billions)

	1990*	1989	1988	1987	1986	1985	1984	5-year growth, %†(annual/total)
Revenue	—	—	293	235	203	191	176	13/84
Operating income	—	—	32	22	18	16	15	18/124
Earnings/share	—	—	46	37	32	30	27	14/95
Dividend/share	—	—	9	9	7	7	7	5/29
Dividend yield, %	0.6	0.4	0.5	0.5	0.3	0.9	1.2	—/—
Stock price	2,140	2,880	2,090	1,855	1,836	782	565	38/409
P/E ratio	40.0	50.0	45.4	53.6	63.8	28.9	22.9	—/—
Book value/share	—	—	402	358	333	313	294	8/45

* 5-1-90
† 1983–88, except stock price, 1984–89
Source: CompuStat and Worldscope.

Note: ADR; stock price quoted in the *Wall Street Journal,* the *European Wall Street Journal* and the *Financial Times;* 5-year average annual return in U.S. currency: 56%.

TOYO SEIKAN KAISHA, LTD.

3-1 Uchisaiwaicho 1-chome
Chiyoda-ku, Tokyo 100
Japan
Tel: (03) 508 2111
President: Yoshiro Takasaki

EARNINGS GROWTH	(no points)
STOCK GROWTH	★ ★ ★ ★
DIVIDEND YIELD	(no points)
DIVIDEND GROWTH	(no points)
CONSISTENCY	★ ★ ★
MOMENTUM	★ ★ ★ ★
TYO, OSA	**11 points**

Toyo Seikan may be the world's biggest corporate secret. With annual revenues of $3.5 billion, it leads the world in the production of containers for food and soft drinks. Yet it publishes no annual report—aside from a mandatory balance sheet and a statement of income—and it has no fact sheets and no brochures on its operations, its management or its product lines.

Why keep such a low profile? Perhaps, say some analysts, the company feels it can maintain the upper hand on its international competitors by keeping them in the dark. Or perhaps it shuns exposure to avoid becoming a takeover target by a corporate raider. Or perhaps company officials are perfectly happy to let its statistics do the talking—not a bad strategy when you have the kind of numbers Toyo Seikan has compiled.

The company has a strong balance sheet, a low debt-to-capital ratio, a fairly consistent record of earnings and revenue growth and, by Japanese standards, a very low price-earnings ratio (about 27, compared to P/Es of 50 to 150 for many other Japanese firms).

What little information on Toyo Seikan that is available from other sources portrays the firm as the overwhelming leader in the soft drink and food canning business—particularly in Japan. Food and beverage can production accounts for about 75 percent of its revenue, art cans account for 8 percent, plastic products make up about 15 percent and packing equipment accounts for about 3 percent.

Tin can production is the largest part of the company's operation, although the firm is aggressively adding capacity in the aluminum container segment. While Toyo Seikan dominates the Japanese can market, it is beginning to encounter growing competition within that market from foreign manufacturers.

While Toyo's veil of secrecy may be enough to dissuade some investors from buying its stock, the company's relatively low price-earnings ratio and its strong position in the traditionally stable canning and packaging industry should make Toyo Seikan an alluring prospect for investors with a sense of intrigue.

EARNINGS GROWTH   (no points)

The company has had steady growth the past few years. Its earnings per share increased 48 percent over the past five years, 8 percent per year.

Toyo Seikan reported total revenue of 488 billion yen (3.4 billion in U.S. dollars) in fiscal 1990.

STOCK GROWTH

The company's stock price has moved up very quickly the past five years, increasing 282 percent for the period—31 percent per year.

Including reinvested dividends, a $10,000 investment in Toyo stock in 1985 would have grown to about $40,000 five years later. Average annual compounded rate of return (including stock growth and reinvested dividends): about 32 percent.

DIVIDEND YIELD   (no points)

The company generally pays a very modest yield, which has averaged about 0.5 percent over the past five years. During the most recent two-year rating period (1989 and 1990), the stock paid an average annual current return (dividend yield) of 0.25 percent.

DIVIDEND GROWTH   (no points)

Toyo rarely raises its dividend. In fact, it was the same in 1990 as it was in 1984.

CONSISTENCY

The company has had consistent growth in its revenues, operating income and book value per share, but its earnings per share growth has been a bit inconsistent. Earnings dropped slightly in 1987 and 1989. Its price-earnings ratio of about 27 is very favorable for the Japanese market.

MOMENTUM

Toyo Seikan had a big year in fiscal 1990, increasing its earnings per share 38 percent—its biggest gain in five years.

SUMMARY

Fiscal year ended: Mar. 31
(Japanese yen; revenue and operating income in billions)

	1990	1989	1988	1987	1986	1985	1984	5-year growth, %† (annual/total)
Revenue	488	466	438	386	375	356	330	7/37
Operating income	50	42	42	36	35	33	26	9/51
Earnings/share	124	90	96	82	85	83	60	8/48
Dividend/share	8	8	8	9	8	8	8	0/0
Dividend yield, %	0.2	0.3	0.3	0.4	0.4	0.8	0.9	—/—
Stock price	3,400	2,390	2,870	1,751	1,951	890	805	31/282
P/E ratio	27.5	26.5	30.0	23.8	23.0	10.7	13.5	—/—
Book value/share	1,034	918	835	749	692	613	537	11/68

† 1985–90
Source: Company sources.

Note: No ADR; stock price quoted in the *Wall Street Journal,* the *European Wall Street Journal* and the *Financial Times;* 5-year average annual return in U.S. currency: 48%.

 **ItoYokado**

ITO-YOKADO CO., LTD.

1-4, Shibakoen 4-chome
Minato-ku
Tokyo 105
Japan
Tel: (03) 459 2111
Chairman, President and CEO: Masatoshi Ito

EARNINGS GROWTH	★ ★
STOCK GROWTH	★
DIVIDEND YIELD	★
DIVIDEND GROWTH	**(no points)**
CONSISTENCY	★ ★ ★ ★
MOMENTUM	★ ★ ★
TYO, CIN, PAR, OTH, LUX	**11 points**

Japanese consumers over the years have come to learn one thing about this Tokyo-based retailing giant: if Ito-Yokado doesn't stock it, it probably doesn't exist.

Ito-Yokado is one of the world's largest retailers. Its trail of supermarkets, department stores, discount centers, convenience stores and other retail businesses blankets Japan from one end of the islands to the other.

The company operates about 140 Ito-Yokado Superstores that offer a wide range of products, including clothing, appliances, groceries and housewares. The Superstores are the crown jewel in the Ito-Yokado kingdom.

Ito-Yokado is the parent company of Seven-Eleven Japan, which operates nearly 4,000 convenience stores in Japan. While Seven-Eleven is a consolidated subsidiary of Ito-Yokado—with the same chairman and chief executive officer—it trades independently on the Tokyo Stock Exchange. (Seven-Eleven Japan is also a "Top 100" stock profiled in this book.)

In April, 1990, Ito-Yokado and Seven-Eleven Japan bought a 75 percent share of Southland Corporation, which operates the nationwide chain of Seven-Eleven stores in the United States.

Ito-Yokado has several other wholly owned retail chain subsidiaries. Daikuma discount stores, with about 15 outlets in the Tokyo area, sells TVs, stereos, leisure goods, apparel and appliances. York Mart supermarkets operates about 40 large grocery stores, most of which are also in the Tokyo area.

Ito-Yokado has had great success with one of its newest stores, Robinson's, a massive department store that generates sales of 28 billion yen ($220 million) a year. Because of the success of the first Robinson's store, the company was planning to open a second Robinson's in late 1990.

Denny's Japan, which operates about 350 restaurants in Japan, is a consolidated subsidiary of Ito-Yokado, which, like Seven-Eleven Japan, trades separately on the Tokyo Stock Exchange.

Ito-Yokado also operates about 300 Famil restaurants, several specialty stores and a handful of food processing operations.

EARNINGS GROWTH

The company has had solid growth the past few years. Its earnings per share increased 119 percent over the past five years, 17 percent per year.

Ito-Yokado reported total revenue of 1.5 trillion yen (12 billion in U.S. dollars) in 1989.

STOCK GROWTH

The company's stock price, like all Japanese stocks, was affected by the slumping Japanese market. The stock price moved up 75 percent over the past five years, 12 percent per year.

Including reinvested dividends, a $10,000 investment in Ito-Yokado stock at the end of 1984 would have grown to about $18,000 five years later. Average annual compounded rate of return (including stock growth and reinvested dividends): about 12.5 percent.

DIVIDEND YIELD

The company generally pays a modest yield, which has averaged about 0.6 percent over the past five years. During the most recent two-year rating period (1989 and 1990), the stock paid an average annual current return (dividend yield) of 0.45 percent.

DIVIDEND GROWTH   (no points)

Ito-Yokado has raised its dividend only 54 percent over the past five years, 9 percent per year.

CONSISTENCY

The company has had very consistent growth in its earnings per share, revenues, operating income and book value per share. Its price-earnings ratio of under 30 is high when compared to other companies around the world but low for the Japanese market.

MOMENTUM

Ito-Yokado has continued to post strong earnings and revenue gains the past couple of years. Its stagnant stock price is due not to its own shortcomings but to the slump in the Japanese market.

SUMMARY

Fiscal year ended: Feb. 28
(Japanese yen; revenue and operating income in billions)

	1990*	1989	1988	1987	1986	1985	1984	5-year growth, %† (annual/total)
Revenue	—	1,525	1,372	1,281	1,231	1,057	996	9/53
Operating income	—	141	122	104	93	77	61	18/131
Earnings/share	—	127	108	88	81	68	58	17/119
Dividend/share	—	20	20	18	16	16	13	9/54
Dividend yield, %	0.5	0.4	0.5	0.5	0.5	0.8	0.8	—/—
Stock price	3,620	3,630	3,827	3,473	2,936	2,064	1,545	12/75
P/E ratio	26.0	28.5	35.3	39.4	36.1	30.4	26.7	—/—
Book value/share	—	979	833	727	652	572	506	14/93

* 2–28–90
† 1984–89, except stock price, 1985–90
Source: Company sources and Worldscope.

Note: ADR; stock price quoted in *Barron's,* the *Wall Street Journal,* the *European Wall Street Journal* and the *Financial Times;* 5-year average annual return in U.S. currency: 26%.

▲▲ Yamanouchi Pharmaceutical Co.,Ltd.

YAMANOUCHI PHARMACEUTICAL CO., LTD.

3-11, Nihonbashi-Honcho 2-chome
Chuo-ku, Tokyo 103
Japan
Tel: (03) 244-3000
Chairman, President and CEO: Shigeo Morioka

EARNINGS GROWTH	★ ★ ★ ★
STOCK GROWTH	**(no points)**
DIVIDEND YIELD	**(no points)**
DIVIDEND GROWTH	★
CONSISTENCY	★ ★ ★ ★
MOMENTUM	★ ★
TYO	**11 points**

Yamanouchi Pharmaceutical may have bought itself the proverbial "ground floor opportunity of a lifetime."

Long known in Japan as a developer and producer of life-saving medications, a recent acquisition by Yamanouchi gives the company yet another role: it is the new ground floor of the Shaklee pyramid.

In February, 1989, Yamanouchi purchased Shaklee Japan for $345 million. A month later, it bought out the San Francisco-based parent company, Shaklee Corporation, in a friendly $391-million takeover.

Shaklee had built a thriving grass-roots business, selling vitamins and other nutritional supplements, personal care products and household goods.

The company has been a pioneer in the development of a sales concept often referred to as "multi-level" or "pyramid" marketing. Under the system, Shaklee salespeople recruit friends, relatives and others to work under them—and then encourage their sales recruits to bring yet another layer of salespeople into the fold. Profits from sales of the products flow through the organization, with each layer of the sales force pocketing a percentage of the take. The ground floor was Shaklee itself. Now Yamanouchi has taken its place at the base of the Shaklee profit pyramid.

Yamanouchi's primary business remains the development and marketing of pharmaceuticals. Among its leading drugs are Gaster, a peptic ulcer and gastritis drug; Perdipine, a cardiovascular agent; Elen, a psychoactive drug for the treatment of mental disorders; Josamycin and Yamatetan, both antibiotics; and Lentinan, an anticancer agent.

Two of its newest drugs are Norditropin, a biosynthetic human-growth hormone, and Pronon, an antiarhythmic agent. The company also recently began to market a new insecticide.

Yamanouchi has begun to cultivate an international following for its pharmaceuticals. It has production facilities in Ireland and Taiwan and sales offices in Paris, London and Frankfurt. Its acquisition of Shaklee also gives Yamanouchi an excellent foothold in the United States.

EARNINGS GROWTH

The company has had excellent growth the past few years. Its earnings per share increased 242 percent over the past five years, 28 percent per year.

Yamanouchi reported total revenue of 188 billion yen (1.4 billion in U.S. dollars) in 1989.

STOCK GROWTH   (no points)

The company's stock price has grown steadily through most of the 1980s, but it was devastated by the Japanese market crash. As a result, in 1990 it actually dropped 4 percent from its price of five years earlier.

Including reinvested dividends, a $10,000 investment in Yamanouchi stock in 1985 would have dropped to about $9,700 five years later. Average annual compounded rate of return (including stock growth and reinvested dividends): –0.5 percent.

DIVIDEND YIELD   (no points)

The company generally pays a very modest yield, which has averaged under 0.3 percent over the past five years. During the most recent two-year rating period (1989 and 1990), the stock paid an average annual current return (dividend yield) of 0.35 percent.

DIVIDEND GROWTH

Yamanouchi has had only modest dividend increases the past few years. It rose 66 percent (11 percent per year) over the five-year period from 1984 to 1989.

CONSISTENCY

The company has had very consistent growth in its earnings per share, revenues, operating income and book value per share. Its price-earnings ratio of about 30 is good for a growing Japanese company.

MOMENTUM

Yamanouchi had strong gains in 1988 but only moderate increases in key financial areas in 1989. Its earnings per share rose only 3.6 percent, and its revenue rose only 1.6 percent.

SUMMARY

Fiscal year ended: Mar. 31
(Japanese yen; revenue and operating income in billions)

	1990	1989	1988	1987	1986	1985	1984	5-year growth, %† (annual/total)
Revenue	—	188	185	164	140	117	107	12/75
Operating income	—	54	54	39	29	20	18	25/200
Earnings/share	—	85	82	62	39	25	25	28/242
Dividend/share	—	11	9	8	7	6	6	11/66
Dividend yield, %	0.4	0.3	0.3	0.2	0.2	0.2	0.3	—/—
Stock price	2,620	3,680	3,609	3,491	3,745	2,736	2,298	–1/–4
P/E ratio	30.0	43.2	43.9	56.6	96.6	108.3	92.5	—/—
Book value/share	—	621	590	509	439	401	344	13/80

† 1984–89, except stock price, 1985–90
Source: Company sources and Worldscope.

Note: No ADR; stock price quoted in *Barron's,* the *Wall Street Journal* and the *Financial Times;* 5-year average annual return in U.S. currency: 11½%.

98

✪THE KYOWA BANK, LTD.

THE KYOWA BANK, LTD.

1-2 Otemachi 1-chome
Chiyoda-ku, P.O. Box 800
Tokyo 100
Japan
Tel: (03) 287-2111
Chairman: Tetsuo Yamanaka
President: Kosuke Yokote

EARNINGS GROWTH	★ ★ ★
STOCK GROWTH	★
DIVIDEND YIELD	★
DIVIDEND GROWTH	(no points)
CONSISTENCY	★ ★ ★ ★
MOMENTUM	★
TYO, OSA	**10 points**

Through a series of mergers and acquisitions, Kyowa Bank has expanded rapidly the past few years to become one of Japan's leading banks. But despite its growing prominence in the nation's banking circles, Kyowa has not forgotten the traditional heart and soul of its operation: the little guy.

The company, founded in 1949, has established itself as a leader in the small business market. About two-thirds of Kyowa's loans are made to small companies.

Kyowa breaks its operations into several segments:

- Retail banking. The company has 232 retail bank branches throughout Japan. It offers credit cards, automatic teller machine cards and several types of specialty loan packages. (There's even a special "Resort Loan" for customers who wish to purchase resort properties.)
- International banking. Kyowa is well established abroad, with 17 foreign branches and representative offices and seven overseas subsidiaries. The bank offers a variety of services, including multinational syndicated

loans, project financing, local and offshore loans and merger and acquisition financing.

Kyowa has branches throughout Southeast Asia, Europe and the United States. Its Chicago branch provided much of the financing for Bridgestone's 1988 acquisition of Firestone Tire & Rubber.

- Financial advisory services. The company offers an extensive range of advisory services to both Japanese and foreign clients, including consulting on project planning and financing and funds procurement.
- Capital market activities. The company helps raise financing for corporations through the issuance of corporate bonds. In 1988 Kyowa's London and Zurich subsidiaries acted as managers for 43 corporate bond issues.

Kyowa also offers currency, options and futures exchange services for Japanese investors.

EARNINGS GROWTH

The company has had solid growth the past few years. Its earnings per share increased 144 percent over the past five years, 20 percent per year.

Kyowa reported total revenue of 803 billion yen (6.1 billion in U.S. dollars) in 1989.

STOCK GROWTH

The company's stock price has moved up quickly through the mid- to late 1980s but like most of the Japanese market, has cooled off the past couple of years. The stock price increased 68 percent over the period—11 percent per year.

Including reinvested dividends, a $10,000 investment in Kyowa stock in 1984 would have grown to about $17,000 five years later. Average annual compounded rate of return (including stock growth and reinvested dividends): about 12 percent.

DIVIDEND YIELD

The company generally pays a very modest yield, which has averaged about 0.6 percent over the past five years. During the most recent two-year rating period (1989 and 1990), the stock paid an average annual current return (dividend yield) of 0.55 percent.

DIVIDEND GROWTH   (no points)

Kyowa rarely raises its dividend. The dividend increased only 30 percent (6 percent per year) over the past five-year period from 1984 to 1989.

CONSISTENCY

The company has had very consistent growth in its earnings per share, revenues, operating income and book value per share. Its price-earnings ratio of 35 to 40 is high relative to stocks elsewhere around the world but fairly attractive for the Japanese market.

MOMENTUM

Kyowa's earnings per share increased only 2.8 percent in 1989, and with the recent slump in the Japanese market, the company could face another off year. But its stock price decline during the market crash could make the stock a better value for new investors.

SUMMARY

Fiscal year ended: Mar. 31
(Japanese yen; revenue and operating income in billions)

	1990	1989	1988	1987	1986	1985	1984	5-year growth, %† (annual/total)
Revenue	—	803	708	641	654	646	524	9/53
Operating income	—	76	71	59	44	36	32	19/137
Earnings/share	—	29	28	25	17	13	12	20/144
Dividend/share	—	6	6	6	5	5	5	6/30
Dividend yield, %	0.6	0.5	0.4	0.5	0.6	0.7	1.2	—/—
Stock price	1,120	1,305	1,305	1,181	757	667	399	11/68
P/E ratio	35.0	44.7	46.0	48.2	43.8	51.6	33.4	—/—
Book value/share	—	292	254	197	178	166	157	13/85

† 1984–89, except stock price, 1985–90
Source: Worldscope.

Note: ADR; stock price quoted in the *Financial Times;* 5-year average annual return in U.S. currency: 25%.

THE DAI-ICHI KANGYO BANK, LIMITED

1-5 Uchisaiwaicho 1-chome
Chiyoda-ku
Tokyo 100
Japan
Tel: (03) 596-1111
Chairman: Ichiro Nakamura
President: Kuniji Miyazaki

EARNINGS GROWTH	★ ★ ★ ★
STOCK GROWTH	**(no points)**
DIVIDEND YIELD	**(no points)**
DIVIDEND GROWTH	**(no points)**
CONSISTENCY	★ ★ ★
MOMENTUM	★ ★ ★
TYO, OSA, CIN, AMS, LON, PAR, ZUR	**10 points**

Dai-Ichi Kangyo Bank (DKB) is Japan's oldest savings institution and the world's largest. It has assets of over $400 billion (50 trillion yen)—roughly the size of CitiCorp, BankAmerica and Chase Manhattan combined.

Yet, despite its cumbersome size, DKB's earnings growth has been perking along like a lean machine. From 1985 to 1989, the company doubled its assets and tripled its earnings per share.

Its stock price, on the other hand, was strongly affected by the Japanese market crash early in 1990. Many of its holdings—and its clients' holdings—were battered by the crash. While its share price had grown 275 percent from 1984 to 1989, it dropped 30 percent in the crash. But because of DKB's worldwide diversification, the company is in no serious jeopardy. DKB has offices and subsidiaries in about 30 countries worldwide.

The core of DKB's business is still at home in Japan. Each day, an average of 750,000 customers visit its 370 Japanese branches—180 million customer visits a year. The company lists 40 million individual deposit accounts in Japan. About 2 million people carry DKB's Heart Card credit cards.

Some 7 percent of the companies in Japan—more than 100,000 companies in all—do business with DKB.

In the United States and Europe, DKB has been steadily expanding its role. In the United States it has been underwriting and dealing in Treasury bills, notes and bonds and has begun handling securities brokerage. It is also expanding its other business-related services. The firm has branches in New York, Chicago, Los Angeles, Atlanta and San Francisco and has an office in Houston.

In Europe, DKB underwrote 141 bond issues in 1989. The company has branches and subsidiaries throughout Europe.

With deregulation of the Japanese brokerage market, DKB has moved into the futures, options and bond trading businesses. The company projects trading as an exceptional future growth area since it can draw on its own customer base, which is larger than that of any other bank in Japan.

Founded in 1873, Dai-Ichi Bank was Japan's first bank. In 1971 it merged with Nippon Kangyo Bank to form the Dai-Ichi Kangyo Bank.

EARNINGS GROWTH

The company has had excellent growth the past few years. Its earnings per share increased 227 percent over the past five years, 27 percent per year.

Dai-Ichi reported total revenue of 3.4 trillion yen (26 billion in U.S. dollars) in 1989.

STOCK GROWTH   (no points)

The company's loss in the stock market crash negated an otherwise excellent decade of growth. Over the past five years, the stock price increased 62 percent—about 10 percent per year.

Including reinvested dividends, a $10,000 investment in DKB stock at the end of 1984 would have grown to about $16,500 five years later. Average annual compounded rate of return (including stock growth and reinvested dividends): about 10.5 percent.

DIVIDEND YIELD   (no points)

The company generally pays a very modest dividend, which has averaged about 0.26 percent over the past five years. During the most recent two-year rating period (1989 and 1990), the stock paid an average annual current return (dividend yield) of 0.25 percent.

DIVIDEND GROWTH   (no points)

DKB does not make a habit of raising its dividend every year. The dividend increased only 23 percent (4 percent per year) over the five-year period from 1984 to 1989.

CONSISTENCY

The company has had consistent growth in its key financial areas, with one exception—revenue dipped slightly in 1986 and 1987. Its price-earnings ratio of about 30 is pretty good for the Japanese market, where P/Es can rise to over 100.

MOMENTUM

Prior to the crash, DKB had piled up several years of impressive gains. The crash, however, took some wind out of its sails, but a company this strong should be capable of making a strong rebound.

SUMMARY

Fiscal year ended: Mar. 31
(Japanese yen; revenue and operating income in billions)

	1990	1989	1988	1987	1986	1985	1984	5-year growth, %† (annual/total)
Revenue	—	3,401	2,567	2,102	2,123	2,282	1,827	13/86
Operating income[1]	—	379	316	205	140	132	137	22/176
Earnings/share	—	75	59	43	26	25	23	27/227
Dividend/share	—	8	8	8	7	7	7	4/23
Dividend yield, %	0.3	0.2	0.2	0.2	0.4	0.4	0.7	—/—
Stock price	2,370	3,370	3,095	3,005	1,553	1,454	898	10/62
P/E ratio	30.0	44.7	54.6	81.5	59.5	64.7	42.6	—/—
Book value/share	—	483	387	262	233	202	186	21/160

† 1984–89, except stock price, 1985–90
1. Pre-tax income is given here.
Source: Company sources and Worldscope.

Note: ADR; stock price quoted in *Barron's,* the *Wall Street Journal,* the *European Wall Street Journal* and the *Financial Times;* 5-year average annual return in U.S. currency: 24%.

THE SUMITOMO BANK, LIMITED

6-5, Kitahama 4-chome
Chuo-ku
Osaka 541
Japan
Tel: (06) 227-2111
Chairman: Ichiro Isoda
President: Sotoo Tatsumi

EARNINGS GROWTH	★ ★ ★
STOCK GROWTH	★
DIVIDEND YIELD	**(no points)**
DIVIDEND GROWTH	**(no points)**
CONSISTENCY	★ ★
MOMENTUM	★ ★ ★
TYO, OSA, LON, PAR, OTC, NAG	**9 points**

With financial deregulation sweeping the globe, Sumitomo Bank has positioned itself to make the most of it.

Already ranked as one of the largest banks in the world, with assets of over $400 billion (50 trillion yen), Sumitomo has quietly forged an international financial domain. It has some 60 foreign offices and affiliates in 30 countries. With branches or subsidiaries in London, Paris, Frankfurt, Zurich, Vienna, Brussels, Madrid, Lisbon, Milan and Stockholm, the company hopes to play a key role in helping to underwrite the new era of European development.

Sumitomo also has offices throughout the United States, the Far East and Australia. Despite its international expansion, Sumitomo's Japanese operations still account for about 60 percent of its annual revenue.

Founded in 1895, the Osaka-based institution deals in four primary banking segments:

- Corporate banking. Sumitomo Bank is involved in financing major real estate acquisitions and developments and a variety of special projects primarily in the natural resources development and energy areas. The company also provides loans for a variety of other corporate needs.

- Investment banking. Sumitomo is involved in the underwriting of corporate mergers and acquisitions on an international scale.
- Money and capital markets operations. The company is involved in securities and futures trading operations, foreign currency exchange and commissioned bank advisory services.
- Retail banking. Sumitomo has 365 Japanese offices that offer retail customers the full range of traditional banking services: savings, checking, mortgages, consumer loans, credit cards and electronic banking services.

EARNINGS GROWTH

The company has had excellent growth the past few years. Its earnings per share increased 150 percent over the past five years, 20 percent per year.

Sumitomo reported total revenue of 3.35 trillion yen (25 billion in U.S. dollars) in 1989.

STOCK GROWTH

After several years of excellent growth, Sumitomo's stock price took a 30 percent dive in the Japanese market crash of 1990. Over the past five years, the stock has increased 80 percent, 13 percent per year.

Including reinvested dividends, a $10,000 investment in Sumitomo stock in 1985 would have grown to about $18,000 five years later. Average annual compounded rate of return (including stock growth and reinvested dividends): about 13 percent.

DIVIDEND YIELD   (no points)

The company generally pays a very modest yield, which has averaged less than 0.3 percent over the past five years. During the most recent two-year rating period (1989 and 1990), the stock paid an average annual current return (dividend yield) of 0.25 percent.

DIVIDEND GROWTH   (no points)

Sumitomo has raised its dividend only 44 percent over the past five years, an average of 8 percent per year.

CONSISTENCY

The company has not been particularly consistent lately. Two of the past five years have shown drops in earnings per share and revenues. Its price-earnings ratio of around 40 is pretty good relative to other growing Japanese companies.

MOMENTUM

Sumitomo had phenomenal earnings-per-share gains in its fiscal 1988 (up 162 percent) and 1989 (up 45 percent). But the crash of 1990 could take its toll on Sumitomo, temporarily—as its 30 percent drop in stock price would seem to indicate. The bright side to the price decline, however, is that it makes the stock a better buy for prospective investors.

SUMMARY

Fiscal year ended: Mar. 31
(Japanese yen; revenue and pre-tax income in billions)

	1990	1989	1988	1987	1986	1985	1984	5-year growth, %† (annual/total)
Revenue	—	3,349	2,449	1,957	1,981	2,187	1,722	14/94
Operating income[1]	—	416	300	178	168	159	168	20/147
Earnings/share	—	74	51	19	30	28	30	20/150
Dividend/share	—	7	6	6	6	6	5	8/44
Dividend yield, %	0.3	0.2	0.2	0.2	0.3	0.4	0.5	—/—
Stock price	2,620	3,542	3,444	3,083	1,761	1,448	982	13/80
P/E ratio	35.0	47.9	65.7	108.9	58.7	51.1	33.3	—/—
Book value/share	—	489	371	278	260	233	210	18/132

† 1984–89, except stock price, 1985–90
1. Pre-tax income is given here.
Source: Company sources and Worldscope.

Note: ADR; stock price quoted in *Barron's,* the *Wall Street Journal,* the *European Wall Street Journal* and the *Financial Times;* 5-year average annual return in U.S. currency: 27%.

The Netherlands

Located in northwestern Europe, the Netherlands, population 15 million, has been an international trading power for several hundred years. In terms of foreign investments in the United States, the Dutch rank third behind Great Britain and Japan. The Netherlands has a number of outstanding internationally oriented corporations. The Amsterdam Stock Exchange is the oldest exchange in the world.

Major industries include metals, machinery, chemicals, oil refining, diamond cutting, electronics, publishing and tourism.

The currency is the Dutch guilder (NLG 1.88 = US $1, June, 1990). Its GNP was NLG 448 billion (US $224 billion) in 1988. Its inflation rate the past three years has been under 1 percent. Real economic growth the past several years has averaged about 2.5 percent per year. The market value of all domestic stocks traded on the Amsterdam Exchange was US $104 billion as of January 1, 1989.

In 1989 the Dutch stock market was up 25.3 percent in Dutch currency (31.4 percent in U.S. currency). Through the first six months of 1990, the Dutch market was down about NLG 3.5 percent.

3

KONINKLIJKE NEDERLANDSE PAPIERFABRIEKEN N.V. (KNP)

(Royal Dutch Papermills)
Rijksweg 69, 1411 GE Naarden
P.O. Box 5008
1410 AA Naarden
The Netherlands
Tel: 02159-57222
Chairman: F.J. de Wit

EARNINGS GROWTH	★ ★ ★ ★
STOCK GROWTH	★ ★ ★ ★
DIVIDEND YIELD	★ ★ ★ ★
DIVIDEND GROWTH	★ ★ ★ ★
CONSISTENCY	★ ★ ★ ★
MOMENTUM	★ ★ ★
AMS	**23 points**

Like a sprawling oak, Koninklijke Nederlandse Papierfabrieken (Royal Dutch Papermills) has been branching persistently into the European paper and packaging markets. And with the new territory, KNP's profits have been flourishing, too. The company has had 10 consecutive years of record earnings.

Less than a quarter of KNP's sales (about 23 percent) come from within the borders of its home country, the Netherlands. It sells more of its products in nearby Germany (28 percent) than it does at home. KNP also does a good business in Great Britain (13 percent of net sales), France (10 percent) and Belgium (8 percent). Other European countries account for about 8 percent of sales, and North America accounts for 6 percent. The other 5 percent goes to various countries around the globe.

KNP divides its business into two segments, paper and packaging:

- Paper group. The company produces about 800,000 tons of coated paper and uncoated special printing paper per year. Its papers are used for stationery, greeting cards, books, periodicals, art work and related products. The paper group accounts for about 65 percent of KNP's total revenue and more than 80 percent of its profit.

- Packaging group. The company produces gray board for book binding and folder and puzzle manufacturers, corrugated board, folding board and solid board for packaging. It also has a waste paper division that collects waste paper and converts it to raw materials used by mills for making cardboard and liners. In all, the packaging group produces about 600,000 tons of cardboard and related materials each year.

EARNINGS GROWTH

The company has had excellent, consistent earnings growth the past few years. Its earnings per share increased 269 percent over the past five years, 30 percent per year.

KNP reported total revenue of 2.7 billion guilders (1.4 billion in U.S. dollars) in 1989.

STOCK GROWTH

The company's stock price has soared the past five years, increasing 463 percent for the period—42 percent per year.

Including reinvested dividends, a $10,000 investment in KNP stock in 1984 would have grown to about $67,000 five years later. Average annual compounded rate of return (including stock growth and reinvested dividends): about 46 percent.

DIVIDEND YIELD

The company generally pays a very good yield, which has averaged about 4.5 percent over the past five years. During the most recent two-year rating period (1989 and 1990), the stock paid an average annual current return (dividend yield) of 4.8 percent.

DIVIDEND GROWTH

KNP traditionally raises its dividend each year. The dividend increased 275 percent (30 percent per year) over the five-year period from 1984 to 1989.

CONSISTENCY

The company has had very consistent growth in its key financial categories, including 10 consecutive years of record earnings. Its price-earnings ratio of about 7 is a very attractive level for a growing company.

MOMENTUM

KNP had tremendous growth in its earnings per share in 1988 (55 percent), but it went up only 5 percent in 1989. Operating income and total assets, however, jumped 18 percent and 25 percent, respectively, in 1989.

SUMMARY

Fiscal year ended: Dec. 31
(Dutch guilders; revenue and operating income in millions)

	1990*	1989	1988	1987	1986	1985	1984	5-year growth, %† (annual/total)
Revenue	—	2,710	2,549	2,402	1,601	1,636	1,505	13/80
Operating income	—	295	251	177	148	114	83	29/255
Earnings/share	—	7.05	6.71	4.74	4.05	3.50	2.67	30/269
Dividend/share	—	2.40	2.20	1.55	1.25	1.14	0.64	30/275
Dividend yield, %	5.0	4.6	4.6	5.8	3.4	3.9	6.9	—/—
Stock price	42.40	51.80	47.20	26.45	36.45	29.40	9.20	42/463
P/E ratio	6.5	7.3	7.0	5.6	9.0	8.4	3.4	—/—
Book value/share	—	26.85	27.25	23.84	21.64	16.37	13.74	14/95

* 5–1–90
† 1984–89
Source: Company sources and Worldscope.

Note: No ADR; stock price quoted in *Barron's,* the *European Wall Street Journal* and the *Financial Times;* 5-year average annual return in U.S. currency: 65%.

13

BÜHRMANN-TETTERODE N.V.

Paalbergweg 2
Postbus 4021
1009 AA Amsterdam
The Netherlands
Tel: 31 20 567 2672
Fax: 31 20 977 660
Chairman: H.J. Kruisinga
President: R.F.W. van Oordt

EARNINGS GROWTH	★ ★ ★ ★
STOCK GROWTH	★ ★ ★ ★
DIVIDEND YIELD	★ ★ ★ ★
DIVIDEND GROWTH	★ ★ ★ ★
CONSISTENCY	★ ★ ★
MOMENTUM	★ ★ ★
AMS, LON, OTC (ADR)	**22 points**

In the Netherlands, Buhrmann-Tetterode (BT) has been associated with the graphics and paper business for over 100 years. Its tenure in the United States, though far briefer, has already turned the company into a major distributor in the growing office supplies business.

BT first entered the U.S. office supply market in 1987 with the acquisition of New York-based distributor Summit Office Supply. That was followed quickly by a series of other buy-outs: M.S. Ginn in Washington, DC, Publix Office Supplies in Chicago, E.W. Curry in Pittsburgh and Hillman Company in St. Louis and Kansas City. The acquisitions have helped BT buy its way into a leading share of the office supply business in several key East Coast and Midwest markets.

The company also owns a handful of U.S. printing and graphics equipment manufacturers. Its U.S. sales total about $300 million a year.

In all, BT has about 75 principal companies, with operations in 17 countries. Its products are sold in 70 countries. Foreign sales account for about 60 percent of the company's total sales.

BT divides its operations into three key market areas:

- Graphics and business systems (37 percent of revenues; 55 percent of operating profit). BT is a distributor of some of Europe's finest printing equipment. It has exclusive distribution rights in several European countries for printing presses and equipment manufactured by Heidelberg, Linotype, Polar, Stahl and Muller-Langenfeld.

   The company is also a distributor of office equipment such as fax machines, laser printers, copiers and PC networks. BT has manufacturing operations that design and produce collating equipment, dispatch lines and other equipment for the printing industry.
- Graphic paper and office supplies (33 percent of revenue; 10 percent of operating profit). The company sells a wide selection of graphics and printing papers, stationery and other office supplies.
- Packaging (30 percent of revenue; 36 percent of operating profit). BT is a major producer and distributor of solid board and corrugated board packaging and a producer of flexible and protective packaging for a wide range of products.

Buhrmann-Tetterode was created in 1963 as a result of the merger of two century-old Dutch companies—a paper wholesaler and a graphics equipment distributor.

EARNINGS GROWTH

BT has had seven consecutive years of increased earnings. Its record the past five years has been exceptional: earnings per share up 29 percent per year, on average, 256 percent total over the past five years.

With total annual revenues of $2.67 billion (5.1 billion guilders), BT has about 12,000 employees.

STOCK GROWTH

The company's stock has risen quickly over the past five years, declining only in 1987 (as part of the market crash). Total stock growth during the period equaled 276 percent (30 percent per year).

Including reinvested dividends, a $10,000 investment in BT stock in 1984 would have grown to about $43,000 five years later. Average annual compounded rate of return (including stock growth and reinvested dividends): about 34 percent.

DIVIDEND YIELD

The company generally pays a very good yield, which has averaged about 4 percent over the past five years. During the most recent two-year rating period (1989 and 1990), the stock paid an average annual current return (dividend yield) of 4.2 percent.

DIVIDEND GROWTH

BT has raised its dividend nine consecutive years. The dividend increased 205 percent (25 percent per year) over the five-year period from 1984 to 1989.

CONSISTENCY

The company has had very consistent growth in its earnings per share and revenues, but its operating income had a couple of negative years in the past five. The company has a moderately high, but manageable, long-term-debt-to-capital ratio of 26 percent and a very attractive price-earnings ratio of about 8.0.

MOMENTUM

BT has had nice gains the past couple of years in earnings and revenues. Its 25.5 percent increase in earnings per share in 1989 was about in line with its excellent performance over the past five years.

SUMMARY

Fiscal year ended: Dec. 31
(Dutch guilders; revenue and operating income in millions)

	1990*	1989	1988	1987	1986	1985	1984	5-year growth, %† (annual/total)
Revenue	—	5,097	4,520	3,779	3,396	3,253	3,180	10/60
Operating income	—	320	232	236	167	138	394	−4/−23
Earnings/share	—	7.71	6.14	5.32	3.92	3.17	2.16	29/256
Dividend/share	—	2.75	2.45	2.10	1.55	1.26	0.90	25/205
Dividend yield, %	4.3	4.1	4.3	4.9	2.6	3.8	5.1	—/—
Stock price	63.40	66.40	57.23	43.15	60.67	32.82	17.63	30/276
P/E ratio	8.0	8.6	9.3	8.1	15.5	10.3	8.2	—/—
Book value/share	—	40.46	38.46	35.97	35.30	32.21	32.46	4/24

* 5–1–90
† 1984–89
Source: Company sources and Worldscope.
Note: ADR; stock price quoted in *Barron's,* the *Wall Street Journal,* the *European Wall Street Journal* and the *Financial Times;* 5-year average annual return in U.S. currency: 51%.

31

ELSEVIER

P.O. Box 470
1000 AL
Amsterdam
The Netherlands
Tel: (020) 515 9111
Chairman: P.J. Vinken

EARNINGS GROWTH	★ ★ ★
STOCK GROWTH	★ ★ ★ ★
DIVIDEND YIELD	★ ★
DIVIDEND GROWTH	★ ★ ★ ★
CONSISTENCY	★ ★ ★
MOMENTUM	★ ★ ★ ★
AMS	**20 points**

Elsevier has been a big name in the Dutch publishing industry for more than 300 years. Now, the Amsterdam-based firm is slowly expanding its publishing empire to markets well beyond the Netherlands.

The company, which draws the bulk of its revenue from newspapers and scientific publishing enterprises, has established a growing presence in the United States. About 29 percent of its total sales come from the U.S. market.

About 50 percent of its revenue still comes from sales within the Netherlands while sales elsewhere in Europe account for about 12 percent. Elsevier has also tapped into the Japanese market, which accounts for about 4 percent of its revenue. Another 4 percent of its sales come from various markets throughout the world.

The company breaks its business into five key sectors:

- Scientific information (27 percent of sales). The company releases about 700 new science-related books each year (although books account for only about one-fifth of the sector's total sales). The bulk of its revenue in the scientific information sector comes from scientific journals and specialized research information.

- Newspapers (27 percent of sales). Elsevier owns several Dutch newspapers, including *Algemeen Dagblad* (circulation 400,000) and *NRC Handelsblad* (circulation 220,000).
- American publishing activities (22 percent of sales is attributed to this sector, although sales in the United States from some of the company's other sectors boost total U.S. sales to about 29 percent of Elsevier's revenue). In the United States, Elsevier owns several publishing establishments, including Congressional Information Service, Greenwood Press, Real Estate Data and Damar and several small, business-related firms.
- Business information (14 percent). The sector includes Misset Publishers, which publishes a variety of business titles in the Netherlands, and Pan European Publishing, which publishes product information journals for several markets outside the Netherlands. The company also offers a variety of business courses and seminars.
- Consumer publications (7 percent). Elsevier puts out consumer publications, including *Elsevier* magazine, *Grote Winkler Prins* encyclopedias and *Kramer* dictionaries.

In 1988 the company executed a stock swap with Pearson Plc., the large British publisher. Pearson has purchased a 22 percent stake in Elsevier, while Elsevier owns about 8 percent of Pearson stock.

EARNINGS GROWTH

The company has had excellent growth the past few years. Its earnings per share increased 186 percent over the past five years, 23 percent per year.

Elsevier reported total revenue of 1.95 billion guilders (810 million in U.S. dollars) in 1989.

STOCK GROWTH

The company's stock price has increased rapidly the past five years, climbing 259 percent for the period—29 percent per year.

Including reinvested dividends, a $10,000 investment in Elsevier stock in 1984 would have grown to about $39,000 five years later. Average annual compounded rate of return (including stock growth and reinvested dividends): about 31 percent.

DIVIDEND YIELD

The company generally pays a fairly good yield, which has averaged about 2 percent over the past five years. During the most recent two-year rating period (1989 and 1990), the stock paid an average annual current return (dividend yield) of 2.3 percent.

DIVIDEND GROWTH

Elsevier has raised its dividend five consecutive years. The dividend increased 200 percent (25 percent per year) over the five-year period from 1984 to 1989.

CONSISTENCY

The company has had very consistent growth in most of its key areas although in 1987 revenues and book value declined. Its price-earnings ratio of about 15 is about normal for a growing company.

MOMENTUM

Elsevier has had excellent growth the past two years. Its earnings per share increased 21 percent in 1988 and 34 percent in 1989.

SUMMARY

Fiscal year ended: Dec. 31
(Dutch guilders; revenue and operating income in millions)

	1990*	1989	1988	1987	1986	1985	1984	5-year growth, %† (annual/total)
Revenue	—	1,955	1,625	1,469	1,568	1,525	1,429	6/36
Operating income	—	328	280	239	206	181	148	17/121
Earnings/share	—	4.95	3.70	3.05	2.51	2.09	1.73	23/186
Dividend/share	—	1.80	1.40	1.15	1.00	0.72	0.60	25/200
Dividend yield, %	2.3	2.2	2.2	2.7	1.6	1.8	2.7	—/—
Stock price	88.00	80.80	62.90	42.00	50.20	39.10	22.50	29/259
P/E ratio	15.0	16.3	17.0	13.8	20.0	18.7	13.0	—/—
Book value/share	—	8.07	7.66	6.61	7.96	6.68	7.60	2/6

* 6–1–90
† 1984–89
Source: Company sources and Worldscope.

Note: No ADR; stock price quoted in *Barron's,* the *Wall Street Journal,* the *European Wall Street Journal* and the *Financial Times;* 5-year average annual return in U.S. currency: 48%.

76

VERENIGDE NEDERLANDSE UITGEVERSBEDRIJVEN (VNU)

Postbus 4028
2003 EA Haarlem
Netherlands
Tel: 023-304 304
Chairman, Supervisory Board: G. van den Brink
Chairman, Executive Board: J.L. Brentjens

EARNINGS GROWTH	★ ★
STOCK GROWTH	★ ★
DIVIDEND YIELD	★ ★ ★
DIVIDEND GROWTH	★
CONSISTENCY	★ ★ ★ ★
MOMENTUM	★ ★ ★ ★
AMS	**16 points**

From *Popular Crosswords* to *Personal Computing* to the saucy *Panorama,* VNU puts out dozens of publications—newspapers as well as magazines—making it the Netherlands's largest publisher and one of the biggest in Europe.

Formed in 1964 through the merger of two of the Netherlands's largest publishers (Cebema and Spaarnestad), VNU has been growing quickly the past few years through a series of acquisitions. Its primary markets outside the Netherlands are Belgium, the United Kingdom and the United States.

The company's principal business segments include:

- Magazines (25 percent of revenues). The company publishes a wide range of consumer magazines for the European market, including women's *(Nouveau, Flair, Avenue),* children's *(Junior Puzzler, Word Search),* teens *(Muziek Expres, Foto)* and general interest magazines *(TeleVizier, Panorama, Revu).* It also publishes European editions of some of the better-known American publications such as *Playboy, Cosmopolitan* and *Disneyland Monthly.*

- Newspapers (21 percent of revenues). The company operates a network of regional newspapers in the Netherlands, with a combined circulation of 750,000.
- Business publications (15 percent of revenues). VNU publishes a number of business magazines, most of which are geared to the computer trade, including *Computing, Personal Computer, PC Magazine, Micros, Computable* and *Network*.
- Business information services (9 percent of revenues). Formerly Amvest (a U.S.-based operation), VNU Business Information Services provides computer-based marketing, financial and health-care industry information services for businesses.
- Printing (21 percent of revenues). The company operates a thriving printing operation that not only prints VNU's company-owned publications but also handles a large volume of outside projects.
- Educational publishing (2 percent of revenues). The firm publishes a range of children's books through its Malmberg subsidiary.

EARNINGS GROWTH

The company has had steady earnings growth the past few years. Its earnings per share increased 98 percent over the past five years, 15 percent per year.

VNU reported total revenue of 2.6 billion guilders (1.3 billion in U.S. dollars) in 1989.

STOCK GROWTH

The company's stock price has increased 113 percent over the past five years, 16 percent per year.

Including reinvested dividends, a $10,000 investment in VNU stock in 1984 would have grown to about $24,000 five years later. Average annual compounded rate of return (including stock growth and reinvested dividends): about 19 percent.

DIVIDEND YIELD

The company generally pays a good yield, which has averaged about 3 percent over the past five years. During the most recent two-year rating period (1989 and 1990), the stock paid an average annual current return (dividend yield) of 3.7 percent.

DIVIDEND GROWTH

VNU traditionally raises its dividend every year. The dividend increased 84 percent (13 percent per year) over the five-year period from 1984 to 1989.

CONSISTENCY

The company has had very consistent growth in its earnings per share, revenues and operating income. Its price-earnings ratio of under 10 is very favorable for a growing company.

MOMENTUM

VNU has had excellent growth the past two years. Its earnings per share increased 19 percent in 1988 and 18 percent in 1989, and its book value per share rose 73 percent in 1989.

SUMMARY

Fiscal year ended: Dec. 31
(Dutch guilders; revenue and operating income in millions)

	1990*	1989	1988	1987	1986	1985	1984	5-year growth, %† (annual/total)
Revenue	—	2,612	2,503	1,971	1,735	1,590	1,524	11/71
Operating income	—	237	222	154	130	108	98	19/141
Earnings/share	—	11.11	9.41	7.88	6.41	6.04	5.59	15/98
Dividend/share	—	3.60	3.20	2.75	2.31	2.13	1.95	13/84
Dividend yield, %	4.0	3.3	3.1	4.3	2.4	2.5	1.0	—/—
Stock price	93.70	108.70	94.80	56.00	87.50	81.75	50.95	16/113
P/E ratio	8.0	9.0	10.0	6.5	13.1	13.4	8.3	—/—
Book value/share	—	45.21	25.77	25.25	21.28	28.84	24.26	13/86

* 5–1–90
† 1984–89
Source: Company sources and CompStat.

Note: No ADR; stock price quoted in *Barron's,* the *Wall Street Journal,* the *European Wall Street Journal* and the *Financial Times;* 5-year average annual return in U.S. currency: 34%.

87 HunterDouglas

THE HUNTER DOUGLAS GROUP

2 Piekstraat
3071 EL Rotterdam
The Netherlands
Tel: 010-486 9911
President: Ralph Sonnenberg

EARNINGS GROWTH	★
STOCK GROWTH	★ ★ ★ ★
DIVIDEND YIELD	★ ★
DIVIDEND GROWTH	**(no points)**
CONSISTENCY	★ ★
MOMENTUM	★ ★ ★ ★
AMS	**13 points**

Hunter Douglas has turned the business of blinds, drapes, shades and curtains into its own window of opportunity into the global marketplace. The Rotterdam-based manufacturer owns over 100 companies and has marketing operations in more than 80 countries worldwide.

If it covers a window, Hunter Douglas probably makes it. The company manufactures all types of window coverings—residential as well as commercial—including roller shades, pleated shades, venetian blinds, horizontal blinds, vertical drapes, roll-up shutters, louvers, screens and awnings. Among its leading brands are Luxaflex, Flexalum and Sunflex.

The company does the bulk of its business in North America (40 percent of sales), Europe (about 39 percent of sales) and the Asia-Pacific area (17 percent). It also has sales operations in Latin America (4 percent) and Africa.

In addition to window coverings, Hunter Douglas is a leading manufacturer of siding and roofing and produces a line of commercially oriented architectural products such as metal ceilings, building facades, special walls and aluminum poles.

The company's window covering, home improvement and architectural products segments account for about 84 percent of its gross profit.

Hunter Douglas also does a brisk business in the scrap aluminum trade, processing and recycling tons of aluminum for its own manufacturing operations and actively trading in aluminum on the world metals market. The metals segment runs on a tight margin. While its metals trading segment accounts for about 40 percent of the company's net sales, it contributes only 4 percent of gross profit.

The company's third segment is its precision machinery operation that manufactures milling, grinding and boring machines for manufacturing companies throughout the world. The precision machinery segment accounts for about 11 percent of the company's gross profit.

EARNINGS GROWTH

The company has grown steadily the past few years. Its earnings per share increased 90 percent over the past five years, 14 percent per year.

Hunter reported total revenue of 1.7 billion guilders (860 billion in U.S. dollars) in 1989. The company has about 8,000 employees worldwide.

STOCK GROWTH

The company's stock price has increased rapidly the past five years, climbing 302 percent for the period—32 percent per year.

Including reinvested dividends, a $10,000 investment in Hunter Douglas stock in 1984 would have grown to about $45,000 five years later. Average annual compounded rate of return (including stock growth and reinvested dividends): about 35 percent.

DIVIDEND YIELD

The company generally pays a fairly good yield, which has averaged about 2.5 percent over the past five years. During the most recent two-year rating period (1989 and 1990), the stock paid an average annual current return (dividend yield) of 2.0 percent.

DIVIDEND GROWTH (no points)

Hunter raises its dividend most years—but not by much. The dividend increased 60 percent (10 percent per year) over the five-year period from 1984 to 1989.

CONSISTENCY

The company has been fairly consistent in most key financial categories—with some exceptions. The earnings per share and operating income declined in 1986. Book value declined in 1986 and 1987. Revenues declined in 1985. Its price-earnings ratio of about 9 to 10 is a very attractive level for a growing company.

MOMENTUM

Hunter Douglas has had excellent growth the past two years. Its earnings per share increased 43 percent in 1988 and 20 percent in 1989.

SUMMARY

Fiscal year ended: Dec. 31
(Dutch guilders; revenue and operating income in millions)

	1990*	1989	1988	1987	1986	1985	1984	5-year growth, %† (annual/total)
Revenue[1]	—	1,713	2,783	2,041	1,736	1,685	1,922	—/—
Operating income	—	276	252	184	131	157	138	15/100
Earnings/share	—	11.52	9.57	6.68	6.09	7.57	6.05	14/90
Dividend/share	—	2.00	1.80	1.50	1.40	1.40	1.25	10/60
Dividend yield, %	2.2	1.8	2.2	4.1	2.3	2.0	4.5	—/—
Stock price	105.00	111.00	81.40	36.50	60.60	72.00	27.60	32/302
P/E ratio	9.0	9.6	8.5	5.5	10.0	9.5	4.6	—/—
Book value/share	—	32.65	24.68	17.76	19.04	19.34	18.33	12/78

* 5–1–90
† 1984–89
1. Metals trading is reported separately from other revenue beginning in 1989.
Source: Company sources and Worldscope.

Note: No ADR; stock price quoted in *Barron's,* the *European Wall Street Journal* and the *Financial Times;* 5-year average annual return in U.S. currency: 53%.

Unilever

UNILEVER N.V.

Postbus 760
3000 DK, Rotterdam
The Netherlands
Chairman (Netherlands): Floris A. Maljers

U.K. address:	New York office:
Unilever PLC	390 Park Ave.
Unilever House	New York, NY 10022
London EC4P 4BQ	Tel: (212) 888-1260

Chairman (U.K.): Sir Michael Angus

EARNINGS GROWTH	(no points)
STOCK GROWTH	★ ★ ★
DIVIDEND YIELD	★ ★ ★ ★
DIVIDEND GROWTH	★
CONSISTENCY	★ ★ ★
MOMENTUM	★ ★
AMS, LON, NYSE	**13 points**

Two heads, one heart, Unilever, the mammoth consumer-products conglomerate, is the Siamese twin of the international corporate community.

There are actually two Unilevers, Unilever N.V. of Rotterdam, the Netherlands, and Unilever PLC of London, England. They are not clones of one another nor is one a subsidiary or a spin-off of the other. Rather, they are twins, attached at the balance sheet.

They have separate chairmen, their stock trades separately and they operate out of separate home offices. Yet they report the same earnings and revenues, pay shareholders the same dividend, have the same directors and mail out the same annual report.

The company(ies) explains it this way: "There are two parent companies: Unilever PLC and Unilever N.V. The two companies operate as nearly as is practical as a single entity...and are linked by a series of agreements of which the principal is the Equalization Agreement. This agreement equalizes the dividends payable on the ordinary capitals of PLC and N.V., with the result that all shareholders participate in the prosperity of the whole business."

In other words, whether you invest in the British version or the Dutch version (or the U.S. ADR of the British Unilever or the Dutch Unilever—and there is an ADR for both), you are essentially investing in the same company and can anticipate basically the same results.

The company has enormous revenues—$35 billion a year—and operates in several different food and consumer-goods-related areas, including:

- Margarine, edible fats and oils, dairy products (21 percent of revenue). The company offers a variety of products in this category, including Delight, Du darfst, Effi and "I Can't Believe It's Not Butter" margarines and Country Crock cheese spread.
- Frozen foods and ice cream (12 percent). The company owns several brands of frozen desserts, including Gold Bond Ice Cream, and a variety of frozen entrees.
- Food and drinks (16 percent of revenue). Unilever owns Lipton Tea, Pronto pizza, Ragu spaghetti sauce and a variety of other food and drink products.
- Detergents (21 percent of revenue). Unilever makes Wisk laundry detergent, Dove soap, Lux soap and several European brands, including Svelto dishwashing formula, USA and Radion laundry detergents.
- Personal products (11 percent of revenue). The company owns Fabergé in the United States, Vaseline products, Obsession for Men and other cosmetic and beauty products.

Unilever also has a specialty chemicals division (8 percent of revenue) and an agribusiness segment (3 percent of sales).

EARNINGS GROWTH   (no points)

The company has had slow growth in earnings per share the past few years, with an increase of 56 percent for the period, 9 percent per year.

Unilever reported total revenue of 66 billion guilders (35 billion in U.S. dollars) in 1989.

STOCK GROWTH

The company's stock price has moved up quickly the past five years, increasing 159 percent for the period—21 percent per year.

Including reinvested dividends, a $10,000 investment in Unilever stock in 1984 would have grown to about $30,000 five years later. Average annual compounded rate of return (including stock growth and reinvested dividends): about 25 percent.

DIVIDEND YIELD

The company generally pays a good yield, which has averaged about 4 percent over the past five years. During the most recent two-year rating period (1989 and 1990), the stock paid an average annual current return (dividend yield) of 3.4 percent.

DIVIDEND GROWTH

Unilever traditionally raises its dividend each year. The dividend increased 67 percent (11 percent per year) over the five-year period from 1984 to 1989.

CONSISTENCY

The company has had fairly steady growth in its key financial areas although it did have a dip in earnings per share in 1985 and a drop in revenue in 1987. Its operating profit has climbed steadily the past five years.

MOMENTUM

Unilever had a 20 percent gain in earnings per share in 1988—one of its best increases in years, but in 1989 earnings climbed only 7.5 percent.

SUMMARY

Fiscal year ended: Dec. 31
(Dutch guilders; revenue and operating profit in millions)

	1990*	1989	1988	1987	1986	1985	1984	5-year growth, %† (annual/total)
Revenue	—	66,285	61,961	60,103	63,206	60,490	58,615	4/13
Operating income[1]	—	6,091	5,486	4,971	4,077	3,466	3,397	13/79
Earnings/share	—	11.59	10.78	8.97	7.64	7.36	7.40	9/56
Dividend/share	—	4.72	4.29	3.62	3.07	2.96	2.82	11/67
Dividend yield, %	3.5	3.3	3.8	2.9	3.6	4.1	5.2	—/—
Stock price	139.50	140.00	111.00	123.00	84.00	72.00	54.00	21/159
P/E ratio	11.0	12.0	10.0	12.0	11.0	9.0	8.0	—/—
Book value/share	—	—	—	—	—	—	—	—/—

* 5-1-90
† 1984-89
1. Operating profit is given here.
Source: Company sources.

Note: ADR; stock price quoted in *Barron's,* the *Wall Street Journal,* the *European Wall Street Journal* and the *Financial Times;* 5-year average annual return in U.S. currency: 41%.

New Zealand

Located near Australia on two islands in the southwest Pacific, New Zealand is a country of only 3.4 million people. Its major industries include food processing, fishing, textiles, forest products and machinery.

The currency is the New Zealand dollar (NZD 1.70 = US $1, June, 1990). Its GNP was NZD 57 billion (US $33 billion) in 1988. Its inflation rate the past three years has been about 11 percent. Real economic growth the past several years has actually gone in reverse—averaging –2 percent. The market value of all domestic stocks traded on the New Zealand Exchange was US $16 billion as of September 1, 1989.

The New Zealand market has been in a slump recently. Although it was up NZD 13.5 percent (7.5 percent in U.S. currency) in 1989, it was down about 7 percent through the first six months of 1990.

FLETCHER CHALLENGE LIMITED

Fletcher Challenge House
810 Great South Road
Penrose, Auckland
New Zealand
Tel: (64) 9 590-000
Fax: (64) 9 525-0559
Chairman: Sir Ronald Trotter
CEO: Hugh A. Fletcher

EARNINGS GROWTH	★ ★ ★
STOCK GROWTH	★ ★ ★ ★
DIVIDEND YIELD	★ ★ ★ ★
DIVIDEND GROWTH	★ ★ ★
CONSISTENCY	★ ★ ★
MOMENTUM	★
LON, NZ, AUS, TOR, MONT, VIE, FRA, OTC (ADR)	**18 points**

Fletcher Challenge first took root in the forests of New Zealand. Now its creations spire high over the Seattle skyline and sprout up all along the California coast.

The New Zealand lumber and building giant has blossomed into a major international force in the lumber and construction industries. It owns close to 10 million acres of woodlands in six countries (New Zealand, Australia, Canada, the United States, Chile and Brazil) and counts among its subsidiaries two of the U.S. West Coast's largest construction firms.

Wright Schuchart, a wholly owned subsidiary of Fletcher Challenge, built eight of Seattle's tallest structures, including the Space Needle and the 76-story Columbia Seafirst Center. Fletcher also recently acquired Dinwiddie Construction, one of California's largest construction firms.

The company divides its operations into three primary segments:

- Forestry and forest products (46 percent of revenues). The company is the world's second largest producer of newsprint. It is also a major producer of lightweight coated paper and other paper products, market pulp (for the production of paper), wood fiber and chips, sawlogs, lumber, wood panel products, plywood and fiberboard. The company sells its products in more than 50 countries around the world.
- Building products and services (37 percent of revenues). The firm offers a range of building services, including construction of commercial and residential properties, civil engineering and property management and development. It has operations in New Zealand, Australia and the United States. Fletcher also sells a variety of building materials, including cement and concrete products, aggregates, gypsum wallboard, steel rod and bar products, aluminum joinery and insulation.
- Primary industries and energy (17 percent of revenues). Fletcher's energy-related holdings account for only about 6 percent of the company's revenue, but it brings in 29 percent of the earnings. Fletcher produces and distributes oil, gas and petrochemical products for the New Zealand market.

The company offers a number of agribusiness services through its Wrightson subsidiary, including rural financing, livestock and wool services, rural real estate, merchandise, seeds and agricultural and horticultural chemicals. Fletcher Fishing is New Zealand's largest fish-catching and processing company.

EARNINGS GROWTH

The company has had very good growth the past few years. Its earnings per share increased 150 percent over the past five years, 20 percent per year.

Fletcher reported total revenue of 11.5 billion New Zealand dollars (6.5 billion in U.S. dollars) in 1989.

STOCK GROWTH

The company's stock price moved up rapidly through the mid-1980s, although it has declined since its 1987 high. For the five-year period, the stock price increased 278 percent, 30 percent per year.

Including reinvested dividends, a $10,000 investment in Fletcher stock at the end of 1984 would have grown to about $47,000 five years later. Average annual compounded rate of return (including stock growth and reinvested dividends): about 36 percent.

DIVIDEND YIELD

The company generally pays an excellent dividend, which has averaged about 5.5 percent over the past five years. During the most recent two-year rating period (1989 and 1990), the stock paid an average annual current return (dividend yield) of 5.75 percent.

DIVIDEND GROWTH

Fletcher traditionally raises its dividend each year. The dividend increased 150 percent (20 percent per year) over the five-year period from 1984 to 1989.

CONSISTENCY

The company has had consistent growth in its key financial areas through most of the past several years although in 1986 it had a slight dip in revenues and total assets and in fiscal 1990 it had a slight drop in earnings per share.

MOMENTUM

Fletcher's growth has slowed considerably the past couple of years, due in large measure to New Zealand's depressed condition. Although the company has maintained its excellent dividend, its stock price mid-way through 1990 was 36 percent lower than its price of three years earlier. But when the New Zealand economy turns around, Fletcher Challenge is poised to move with it. And with a price-earnings ratio hovering between 6 and 8, the stock could be an excellent value.

SUMMARY

Fiscal year ended: June 30
(New Zealand dollar; revenue and operating income in millions)

	1990*	1989	1988	1987	1986	1985	1984	5-year growth, %† (annual/total)
Revenue	—	11,509	9,174	5,822	4,268	4,412	3,460	27/232
Operating income	—	1,499	1,088	681	419	515	310	37/383
Earnings/share	0.58**	0.60	0.56	0.46	0.36	0.30	0.24	20/150
Dividend/share	—	0.25	0.24	0.21	0.17	0.13	0.10	20/150
Dividend yield, %	6.0	5.5	5.6	4.2	5.8	6.7	8.3	—/—
Stock price	3.20	4.54	4.32	5.01	2.95	1.95	1.20	30/278
P/E ratio	6.5	7.6	7.7	10.9	8.2	6.5	5.0	—/—
Book value/share	—	3.39	3.01	2.83	1.90	1.65	1.55	17/118

* 5–1–90
** Estimate
† 1984–89
Source: Company sources and Worldscope.

Note: ADR; stock price quoted in *Barron's* and the *Financial Times;* 5-year average annual return in U.S. currency: 43%.

Singapore

Located off the tip of the Malaysian Peninsula in southeast Asia, Singapore is a thriving nation of 2.7 million people. The name Singapore can refer to either the country or its major city, which is the world's second-busiest seaport.

Singapore's major industries include shipbuilding, oil refining, electronics, banking, textiles, food, rubber, lumber, processing and tourism.

The currency is the Singapore dollar (SGD 1.84 = US $1, June, 1990). Singapore's GNP was SGD 43 billion (US $22 billion) in 1987. Its inflation rate the past three years has been under 1 percent. Real economic growth the past several years is estimated at about 5 to 8 percent. The market value of all domestic stocks traded on the Singapore Exchange was US $24 billion as of January 1, 1989.

In 1989 the Singapore and Malaysian markets—which are closely linked—were up 40 percent. The Singapore market was up about 1 percent through the first six months of 1990. The Singapore market has proven to be somewhat volatile and unstable in the past, but the region's rapid growth offers exceptional potential for stock market investors.

56

SINGAPORE AIRLINES LIMITED

Airline House
Airline Road
Singapore 1781
Tel: 542 3333
Chairman: J. Y. Pillay

EARNINGS GROWTH	★ ★ ★
STOCK GROWTH	★ ★ ★
DIVIDEND YIELD	★
DIVIDEND GROWTH	★ ★ ★ ★
CONSISTENCY	★ ★ ★
MOMENTUM	★ ★ ★ ★
SIN	**18 points**

With a growing stable of new Boeing "Megatops"—and the multi-billion dollar mega-price tag that comes with it—fast-rising Singapore Airlines has taken a global gamble.

The Megatop, a huge double-decker 747 high-speed jet, has 386 seats (complete with footrests) and a flying range of 8,000 nautical miles (13,100 kilometers). It can fly from Singapore to London or San Francisco to Singapore non-stop at supersonic speeds.

But can the company pay the freight? Each Megatop costs almost $300 million, and Singapore Air has ordered a total of 29 of the winged wonders. The projected $7 billion (U.S.) cost of the new fleet far exceeds the company's total assets (about $3.2 billion) as well as its total annual revenue ($2.1 billion).

But the company, which has been aggressively negotiating for new destinations around the world, is gambling that its mega-fleet of Megatops will bring in mega-bucks.

Singapore Air already flys to 57 cities in 37 countries, including most of the major hubs in Europe, Asia and Australia. Its U.S. stops include Honolulu, Los Angeles and San Francisco.

The company is adding more flights and more destinations worldwide. Beginning in 1990, it was cleared to begin Europe to North America flights for the first time ever—thanks, in part, to its Megatops. Tentative plans call for a flight pattern that could send the Megatop around the world in just two stops—from Singapore to the Netherlands, from the Netherlands over the Atlantic to Canada and from Canada over the Pacific back to Singapore.

In addition to its 14 Megatops, Singapore Airlines operates 35 other commercial aircraft. It carries about 6.2 million passengers a year and has reported an increase in passenger load every year for the past decade. The airline also operates a cargo service that moves millions of tons of goods a year to worldwide destinations.

EARNINGS GROWTH

The company has had solid growth the past few years. Its earnings per share increased 174 percent over the past five years, 22 percent per year. It reported total revenue of 4.5 billion Singapore dollars (1.2 billion in U.S. dollars) in 1989.

STOCK GROWTH

The company's stock has been publicly traded only since 1986, but in its first four years, it has climbed 104 percent, 20 percent per year.

Including reinvested dividends, a $10,000 investment in Singapore Air stock in 1986 would have grown to about $21,000 four years later. Average annual compounded rate of return (including stock growth and reinvested dividends): about 21 percent.

DIVIDEND YIELD

The company generally pays a modest yield, which has averaged about 1 percent over the past four years. During the most recent two-year rating period, the stock paid an average annual return (dividend yield) of 1.3 percent.

DIVIDEND GROWTH

Singapore Air has raised its dividend rapidly since going public in 1986. The dividend increased 267 percent (55 percent per year) over the three-year period from 1986 to 1989.

CONSISTENCY

Like the rest of the airline industry, Singapore Air's ascent has not come without some turbulence. Its earnings per share has dropped once in the past six years, and its operating income and book value took large tumbles in 1986. But revenues have increased for at least seven consecutive years. Its price-earnings ratio of about 10 is very favorable for a fast-rising company.

MOMENTUM

Singapore Airlines is the fastest-growing publicly traded airline company in the world's fastest-growing region for air travel. Its earnings per share jumped 33 percent in 1988 and 63 percent in 1989. Fasten your seat belt.

SUMMARY

Fiscal year ended: Mar. 31
(Singapore dollars; revenue and operating income in millions)

	1990	1989	1988	1987	1986	1985	1984	5-year growth, %† (annual/total)
Revenue	—	4,572	4,010	3,483	3,174	3,165	2,943	9/55
Operating income	—	—	723	674	190	399	357	17/123
Earnings/share	—	1.59	0.97	0.73	0.50	0.71	0.58	22/174
Dividend/share	—	0.22	0.15	0.08	0.06	NL	NL	55/267
Dividend yield, %	—	1.6	0.9	0.7	0.7	NL	NL	—/—
Stock price	18.80	13.60	11.00	11.30	9.20	NL	NL	20/104
P/E ratio	10.0	8.55	11.3	15.5	18.3	NL	NL	—/—
Book value/share	—	6.49	5.18	4.30	3.66	5.93	4.63	7/40

† 1984–89, except operating income, 1983–88; stock price, 1986–90; and dividend/share, 1986–89
NL = Not listed on stock exchange
Source: Company sources and Worldscope.

Note: No ADR; stock price quoted in the *European Wall Street Journal* and the *Financial Times;* 5-year average annual return in U.S. currency: 25%.

South Africa

Under present conditions, South Africa is no place to invest your money. Its racist apartheid policies have appalled the world, and the world's investment community has responded by pulling much of its money out of the South African market.

As long as racism haunts this nation of 36 million people, many investors will continue to shun investment in the country's stock market.

But the winds of change are blowing in South Africa. If the country is able to bring about reform and grant its black population basic human rights, the outside world will take a whole new view of South Africa.

For South Africa, the challenge is immense: to forge a policy that would bring its black majority into the fold without jeopardizing the country's governmental and industrial stability. But if it is successful in bringing about reform while maintaining a stable economic system, South Africa could become one of the most fertile investment markets in the world.

The reforms would mean an avalanche of new business from companies and countries that have been avoiding ties with South Africa. It would also bring in a flood of stock market investors who would hope to profit from the undervalued South African stock market.

South African stocks are not presently recommended—particularly for those who consider themselves ethically responsible. But if acceptable reforms are instituted in South Africa, these stocks could hold great promise.

The country's currency is the South African rand (ZAR 2.66 = US $1, June, 1990).

8

IRVIN & JOHNSON LIMITED

20th Floor, Cape Town Centre
Heerengracht, Cape Town 8001
South Africa
Tel: 21 21 6400
Chairman: J.C. Robbertze

EARNINGS GROWTH	★ ★ ★ ★
STOCK GROWTH	★ ★ ★ ★
DIVIDEND YIELD	★ ★ ★
DIVIDEND GROWTH	★ ★ ★ ★
CONSISTENCY	★ ★ ★ ★
MOMENTUM	★ ★ ★
JNB	**22 points**

Each afternoon, a fleet of Irvin & Johnson trawlers motors in from sea with a full haul of what looks, smells and feels like freshly caught cod (or hake, as it's also known). But from the look of I&J's balance sheet, you'd swear the catch was gold, not cod.

Over the past 10 years, I&J has netted one of the most enviable growth records in the world: 10 consecutive years of record earnings, with average annual compounded sales growth of 21 percent, annual average pre-tax profit growth of 31 percent, earnings per share growth of 30 percent and annual stock price appreciation of 39 percent.

The company's bulging profit growth coincides with the worldwide increase in fish consumption. It's a trend that should continue as health-conscious consumers continue to cut back on red meat in favor of fish.

The Cape Town-based operation owns one of the largest fishing fleets in the Southern Hemisphere. Its fleets work out of several bases of operation, including Cape Town, Mossel Bay, Port Elizabeth and Durban. I&J concentrates on deep-sea white fish, of which hake (a form of cod) is most abundant.

I&J not only owns its own fleet of fishing trawlers, it also cleans and prepares the fish, then markets it (primarily in the local South African market) under a number of brand names, including Deep Water Hake, Light 'n Crispy, Battercrisp, Fish Braai, Clipper Kings and Crumbles.

In addition to its seafood division, the company also produces and markets a wide range of frozen vegetables. I&J contracts with local farmers to grow the crops, then it harvests them mechanically with its own I&J harvesting team. The company also produces and sells pastry products, burgers, pizzas, pickles and other condiments.

In all, I&J claims to have more than 20,000 customers in the retail, wholesale, catering and institutional food service businesses. The company has a fleet of about 200 refrigerated trucks that handles the distribution from 20 distribution centers throughout South Africa.

EARNINGS GROWTH

The company has had outstanding growth the past few years. Its earnings per share increased 404 percent over the past five years, 38 percent per year.

I&J reported total revenue of 1.1 billion rands (320 million in U.S. dollars) in 1989.

STOCK GROWTH

The company's stock price has exploded the past five years, climbing 630 percent for the period—49 percent per year.

Including reinvested dividends, a $10,000 investment in I&J stock at the end of 1984 would have grown to about $85,000 five years later. Average annual compounded rate of return (including stock growth and reinvested dividends): about 53 percent.

DIVIDEND YIELD

The company generally pays a good yield, which has averaged about 3.2 percent over the past five years. During the most recent two-year rating period (1989 and 1990), the stock paid an average annual current return (dividend yield) of about 3 percent.

DIVIDEND GROWTH

I&J traditionally raises its dividend every year. The dividend increased 268 percent (30 percent per year) over the five-year period from 1984 to 1989.

CONSISTENCY

The company has had a flawless record of growth in its earnings per share, revenues, operating income and book value per share. Its price-earnings ratio of about 10 is a very attractive level for a growing company.

MOMENTUM

The company's earnings continue to move up well although its stock price growth has flattened out over the past year. Socially conscious investors will shun this stock—and all South African stocks—as long as the country's racist policies continue. But if South Africa ever does resolve its racial problems, watch for this stock to be among many South African issues to move up quickly.

SUMMARY

Fiscal year ended: June 30
(South African rands; revenue and operating income in millions)

	1990*	1989	1988	1987	1986	1985	1984	5-year growth, %† (annual/total)
Revenue	—	1,094	890	736	612	518	405	22/170
Operating income	—	101	81	58	38	34	24	34/339
Earnings/share	—	2.32	1.79	1.22	0.72	0.67	0.46	38/404
Dividend/share	—	0.70	0.55	0.38	0.26	0.25	0.19	30/268
Dividend yield, %	3.0	2.9	3.8	3.2	3.1	4.8	5.8	—/—
Stock price	26.00	23.75	14.50	12.00	8.50	5.20	3.25	49/630
P/E ratio	10.0	10.2	8.1	9. .8	11.8	7.7	7.0	—/—
Book value/share	—	7.72	5.94	4.29	3.87	3.25	2.79	23/176

*5–1–90
† 1984–89
Source: Company sources, CompuStat and Worldscope.
Note: No ADR; 5-year average annual return in U.S. currency: 61%.

Spain

This southwestern European nation has a population of 40 million. Its major industries include machinery, steel, textiles, shoes, autos and processed foods.

The currency is the peseta (ESP 103 = US $1, June, 1990). Its GNP was ESP 32 trillion (US $255 billion) in 1986. Its inflation rate the past three years has been about 6 percent. Real industrial growth the past several years has averaged about 3 percent per year. The market value of all domestic stocks traded on the Madrid Exchange was US $91 billion as of January 1, 1989.

In 1989 the Spanish market was up 2.8 percent in Spanish currency (6.5 percent in U.S. currency). Through the first six months of 1990, it was down about 4 percent.

1

BANCO POPULAR ESPAÑOL

34 Velazquez Street
28001 Madrid
Tel: 435 36 20
Fax: 402 94 66
Co-chairmen: Javier Valls, Luis Valls
CEO: Ildefondo Ayala

EARNINGS GROWTH	★ ★ ★ ★
STOCK GROWTH	★ ★ ★ ★
DIVIDEND YIELD	★ ★ ★ ★
DIVIDEND GROWTH	★ ★ ★ ★
CONSISTENCY	★ ★ ★ ★
MOMENTUM	★ ★ ★ ★
MAD	**24 points**

In an imperfect world, Banco Popular Espanol has been one of the world's most perfect stocks. The Madrid-based banking organization has rung up impressive figures in every key category—stock growth, earnings growth, dividend yield, consistency and momentum. Even its price-earnings ratio (about 7.0) is very appealing for a growing company.

Founded in 1926, Banco Popular has become a leading force in Spain's financial community by acquiring controlling interest in more than 30 other banks and financially related institutions.

In addition to its flagship bank in Madrid, Banco Popular Espanol operates a core banking group that includes Banco de Andalucia, Banco de Castilla, Banco de Credito Balear, Eurobanco, Banco de Galicia and Banco de Vasconia. The company also holds controlling interest in a dozen real estate companies, a dozen investment companies and five finance companies. Outside of Spain, Banco Popular holds controlling interest in two banks—one in Grand Cayman and one in Paris, France.

The Banco Popular organization includes more than 2,600 managers and officers.

The company has managed to turn a consistent growth profit over the years by adhering to a fairly conservative lending and management philosophy. As part of its corporate strategy, the company maintains that it will always opt for "profitability rather than growth. [The bank's] aim is to maintain regularity—the proper cruising speed, with no sudden accelerations or brusque braking—in the conduct of its banking business."

While other major banks around the world have lost billions to speculation in recent years, Banco Popular has managed to keep its profits growing consistently by maintaining its focus. According to the bank management, "Since its foundation, Banco Popular has traditionally been an exclusively commercial bank, that is, it uses its funds to service its customers' financial needs. The bank has shunned the trend to acquire shareholdings in companies whose business activities were not complementary to its own banking business."

EARNINGS GROWTH

The company has had strong, consistent earnings growth for many years. Over the past five years, its earnings per share has increased 289 percent—31 percent per year.

It has annual revenue of 250 billion pesetas (about 2.3 billion in U.S. dollars).

STOCK GROWTH

The company's stock price has moved up very quickly the past five years, increasing 417 percent (39 percent per year) during the period.

Including reinvested dividends, a $10,000 investment in Banco Popular stock in 1984 would have grown to about $66,000 five years later. Average annual compounded rate of return (including stock growth and reinvested dividends): about 46 percent.

DIVIDEND YIELD

The company generally pays an excellent yield, which has averaged nearly 7 percent over the past five years. During the most recent two-year rating period (1988 and 1989), the stock paid an average annual current return (dividend yield) of 5.0 percent.

DIVIDEND GROWTH

The company's dividend has risen sharply the past few years, climbing 240 percent (28 percent per year) over the five-year period from 1984 to 1989.

CONSISTENCY

The company has consistently increased its revenue and earnings per share for many years. Its price-earnings ratio of about 7.0 is very attractive.

MOMENTUM

Banco Popular has had sustained growth in the key areas of earnings, revenues, net income and book value. Its most recent reported increase in earnings per share (33 percent in fiscal 1989) was even higher than its five-year average.

SUMMARY

Fiscal year ended: Dec. 31
(Spanish pesetas; revenue and operating income in billions)

	1990*	1989	1988	1987	1986	1985	1984	5-year growth, %†(annual/total)
Revenue	—	—	240.6	212.6	188.5	131.1	126.9	16/118
Operating income[1]	—	—	48.0	38.1	33.6	18.6	12.1	32/296
Earnings/share	—	1,294.00	971.00	746.23	564.98	491.59	332.26	31/289
Dividend/share	—	500.00	400.00	280.00	243.00	212.00	147.00	28/240
Dividend yield, %	6.0	5.5	4.5	3.9	3.4	9.7	8.4	—/—
Stock price	8,300	9,025	8,900	7,225	7,200	2,195	1,745	39/417
P/E ratio	6.5	7.0	9.2	9.7	12.7	4.5	5.3	—/—
Book value/share	—	5,179	4,829	3,757	3,759	3,395	2,987	12/73

*5–1–90
† 1984–89, except revenue and pre-tax income, 1983–88
1. Pre-tax income is given here.
Source: Worldscope.

Note: No ADR; stock price quoted in the *Financial Times;* 5-year average annual return in U.S. currency: 60%.

Sweden

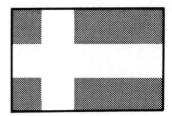

This Scandinavian nation of about 8.5 million people has a well-developed industrial core. Its major industries include machinery, steel, instruments, autos, shipbuilding, shipping and paper.

The currency is the Swedish krona (SEK 6.07 = $1 US, June 1990). Its GNP was SEK 989 billion (US $149 billion) in 1987. Its inflation rate the past three years has been about 5 percent. Real economic growth has averaged about 1.5 percent per year over the past several years. The market value of all domestic stocks traded on the Stockholm Exchange was US $99.7 billion as of January 1, 1989.

In 1989, the Swedish market was up 32 percent in local currency, 30 percent in U.S. currency. Through the first six months of 1990, it was up about 2 percent.

25
TRELLEBORG ▽

TRELLEBORG AB

Nygatan 102
S-231 81 Trelleborg
Sweden
Tel: 46 410 51 000
Chairman: Ernst Herslow

EARNINGS GROWTH	★	★	★	★
STOCK GROWTH	★	★	★	★
DIVIDEND YIELD	★	★	★	
DIVIDEND GROWTH	★	★	★	★
CONSISTENCY	★	★	★	★
MOMENTUM	★			
STO	**20 points**			

To say the least, the business of mining and metals has been very, very good to Trelleborg; the company's earnings have rocketed 20-fold in just five years. A $10,000 investment in Trelleborg stock in 1984 would have grown to $150,000 by 1990.

But this Swedish conglomerate is not content to rest its fate strictly on the often-volatile metals trade. It has been using the cash flow from its mining (and other) operations to bankroll a serious corporate buying binge. In 1988 alone, Trelleborg acquired some 30 new subsidiaries.

It now has operations in nearly 30 countries around the world. And, unlike many other corporations that have incurred heavy debt to finance their takeovers, Trelleborg has managed to maintain a very modest debt level—thanks primarily to the piles of cash generated by its mining division.

While Trelleborg's mining operations account for only about a third of the company's total revenue, it has been generating more than 50 percent of Trelleborg's profits the past two years. The firm mines copper, lead, zinc, gold and silver. Its largest mining division is Boliden Mineral, which has operations throughout the world, including the United States.

Trelleborg's other business segments include:

- Building and distribution (36 percent of sales). The company is involved in the manufacture and wholesale distribution of heating, ventilation, plumbing, roofing, electrical, air conditioning and refrigeration products. It also sells steel, aluminum, wire products and pipes.
- Rubber and plastics (13 percent of sales). The company manufactures a variety of rubber and plastic products, including tires, hose lines, molded products, sealing strips, rubber sheeting and rubber mats.
- Mineral processing systems (16 percent of sales). Trelleborg manufactures large mechanized systems for mining, crushing, milling and processing stone and minerals.

EARNINGS GROWTH

The company has had sensational growth the past few years. Its earnings per share increased 1,775 percent over the past five years, 80 percent per year.

Trelleborg reported total revenue of 26 billion kronor (4 billion in U.S. dollars) in 1989.

STOCK GROWTH

The company's stock price has also soared the past five years, increasing 1,367 percent—71 percent per year.

Including reinvested dividends, a $10,000 investment in Trelleborg stock in 1984 would have grown to about $150,000 five years later. Average annual compounded rate of return (including stock growth and reinvested dividends): about 73 percent.

DIVIDEND YIELD

The company generally pays a fairly good yield, which has averaged about 2.5 percent over the past five years. During the most recent two-year rating period (1988 and 1989), the stock paid an average annual current return (dividend yield) of 3.0 percent.

DIVIDEND GROWTH

Trelleborg has been hiking its dividend dramatically the past few years. The dividend jumped 1,614 percent (76 percent per year) over the five-year period from 1984 to 1989.

CONSISTENCY

The company has had very consistent growth in its earnings per share, revenues, operating income and book value per share. Its price-earnings ratio of about 6 is very favorable for a fast-growing company—as long as the metals market holds up.

MOMENTUM

Trelleborg's 1989 earnings per share gain of 9 percent was a decided step back from the 223 percent increase it enjoyed in 1988 and the 111 percent increase in 1987. And in 1990, its earnings are expected to drop below 1989 earnings.

SUMMARY

Fiscal year ended: Dec. 31
(Swedish kronor; revenue and operating income in millions)

	1990*	1989	1988	1987	1986	1985	1984	5-year growth, %† (annual/total)
Revenue	—	26,485	21,523	17,094	2,842	2,132	1,861	70/1,323
Operating income	—	—	1,431	562	235	143	127	71/1,357
Earnings/share	—	30.00	27.50	8.53	4.04	2.50	1.60	80/1,775
Dividend/share	—	6.00	4.00	2.00	1.00	0.63	0.35	76/1,614
Dividend yield, %	3.3	3.1	2.9	2.2	1.8	2.6	3.4	—/—
Stock price	173.00	189.00	139.00	88.00	62.50	30.25	12.88	71/1,367
P/E ratio	6.0	6.3	5.1	16.1	20.1	11.7	16.9	—/—
Book value/share	—	—	65.87	30.57	28.40	15.27	12.54	42/494

*6–1–90
† 1984–89, except operating income and book value/share, 1983–88
Source: Company sources and Worldscope.
Note: No ADR; stock price quoted in *Barron's,* the *European Wall Street Journal* and the *Financial Times;* 5-year average annual return in U.S. currency: 87%.

ASTRA

ASTRA

S-15185 Södertälje
Sweden
Tel: 46 755-260 00
Chairman: Sten Gustafsson
President and CEO: Håkan Mogren

EARNINGS GROWTH	★ ★ ★		
STOCK GROWTH	★ ★ ★ ★		
DIVIDEND YIELD	★		
DIVIDEND GROWTH	★ ★ ★ ★		
CONSISTENCY	★ ★ ★ ★		
MOMENTUM	★ ★ ★ ★		
STO, LON	**20 points**		

For 40 years, Astra's Xylocaine anesthetic has been killing pain and reaping profits. Even today, more than 40 years after its introduction, Xylocaine's market shows no signs of decline.

Xylocaine's success has helped propel Astra to world-class status among the major pharmaceutical concerns. Its medications are sold in more than 100 countries throughout the world. About 90 percent of Astra's sales come from outside of Sweden.

The company, which was founded in 1913, produces dozens of medications, primarily related to the heart, lungs and stomach, including:

- Cardiovascular medications (28 percent of revenues). Astra's leading cardiovascular drug is Seloken, which is used for the treatment of hypertension, myocardial infarction and angina pectoris. Seloken is one of the largest-selling pharmaceuticals in the world. Astra has also enjoyed wide success with one of its newest drugs, Plendil, which is used as a "calcium antagonist" in combating hypertension.
- Respiratory medications (25 percent of revenues). Astra's largest-selling respiratory medication is Bricanyl, a bronchodilatory agent for relaxing

airway spasms. Launched in 1970, Bricanyl remains a major seller in the world market. Astra also produces two other major antiasthma medications, Theo-Dur and Pulmicort (an anti-inflammatory agent).

- Local anesthetics (22 percent of revenues). Xylocaine continues to be Astra's leading local anesthetic, but the company also produces a number of other similar medications—both injectable and topical. It also has a line of anesthetics used strictly for dental applications.
- Anti-infective agents (8 percent of revenues). Astra is the leading penicillin company in the Nordic market and has cultivated a strong market for its anti-infective preparations elsewhere in Europe and Southeast Asia.
- Astra has also developed medications for the treatment of gastrointestinal diseases (including Losec, a popular new peptic ulcer medication) and central nervous system disorders.
- Astra's medical care equipment division (3 percent of revenues) manufactures products for surgery, radiography, urology and diagnostics.

EARNINGS GROWTH

The company has had eight consecutive years of earnings increases. Its earnings per share has grown 159 percent the past five years (21 percent per year).

Astra reported total revenue in 1989 of 7.8 billion Swedish kronor (1.2 billion in U.S. dollars). It has about 7,000 employees and 27,000 shareholders.

STOCK GROWTH

After some fairly consistent growth through much of the decade, the company's stock price exploded in 1989, going from 184 kronor to 420 kronor. Over the five-year rating period, Astra's stock price increased 418 percent (39 percent per year).

Including reinvested dividends, a $10,000 investment in Astra stock in 1984 would have grown to about $54,000 five years later. Average annual compounded rate of return (including stock growth and reinvested dividends): about 40 percent.

DIVIDEND YIELD

The company generally pays a fairly low yield, which has averaged about 1 percent over the past five years. During the most recent two-year rating period (1988 and 1989), the stock paid an average annual current return (dividend yield) of 0.9 percent.

DIVIDEND GROWTH

Astra increases its dividend most years. The dividend increased 257 percent (29 percent per year) over the five-year period from 1984 to 1989.

CONSISTENCY

The company has had very consistent growth in the key areas of earnings per share, revenues, operating income and book value per share. But its recent price-earnings ratio of 36 to 38 is perilously high.

MOMENTUM

Astra has experienced exceptional growth the past couple of years. Its earnings per share increased 33 percent in 1989.

SUMMARY

Fiscal year ended: Dec. 31
(Swedish kronor; revenue and operating income in millions)

	1990*	1989	1988	1987	1986	1985	1984	5-year growth, %† (annual/total)
Revenue	—	7,822	6,632	5,802	5,349	4,819	4,223	13/85
Operating income	—	1,708	1,395	1,231	1,067	966	769	17/121
Earnings/share	—	11.00	8.28	7.04	6.62	6.14	4.24	21/159
Dividend/share	—	2.50	2.00	1.60	1.25	1.00	0.70	29/257
Dividend yield, %	0.8	0.6	1.1	1.1	0.8	1.0	1.1	—/—
Stock price	402.00	420.00	184.00	152.00	166.00	126.00	81.00	39/418
P/E ratio	36.0	38.0	22.0	22.0	24.0	16.0	13.0	—/—
Book value/share	—	56.00	44.14	37.17	31.67	16.26	12.45	35/349

* 5–1–90
† 1984–89
Source: Company sources and Worldscope.
Note: No ADR; stock price quoted in *Barron's,* the *European Wall Street Journal* and the *Financial Times;* 5-year average annual return in U.S. currency: 54%.

35

ATLAS COPCO

Sickla Industrivag 3
S-105 23 Stockholm
Sweden
Tel: 46 8 743 80 00
Chairman: Peter Wallenberg
President and CEO: Tom Wachtmeister

EARNINGS GROWTH	★ ★ ★ ★
STOCK GROWTH	★ ★ ★ ★
DIVIDEND YIELD	★ ★ ★
DIVIDEND GROWTH	★ ★
CONSISTENCY	★ ★ ★
MOMENTUM	★ ★ ★ ★
STO, FRA, DUS, HAM	**20 points**

Atlas Copco has built a multinational conglomerate out of thin air. Its air compressors and compressor-powered tools—industrial drills, jack hammers and other construction and mining equipment—rank among the top selling compression equipment in the world.

The company is also a leader in the production of hand-held power tools, assembly systems and hydraulic and pneumatic systems. In all, Atlas Copco markets 3,000 products and services to some 250,000 customers around the world. It has 43 manufacturing plants in 17 countries, sales companies in 50 countries and independent distributors in another 85 countries.

Atlas Copco's leading business segment is the manufacture and marketing of air compressors. The division generates 45 percent of the company's sales revenue and nearly 50 percent of its earnings.

The company manufactures turbo-powered air and gas industrial compressors, air dryers and portable compressors and generators (for water pumps, jackhammers and other construction and drilling equipment).

Atlas Copco's other primary segments include:

- Construction and mining equipment (33 percent of sales; 26 percent of earnings). The firm manufactures rock-drilling and demolition equipment for the construction and mining industries.
- Industrial equipment (22 percent of sales; 25 percent of earnings). Atlas manufactures hand-held power drills, screwdrivers and other tools. It also produces automated assembly equipment for manufacturing plants, and it builds hydraulic valves for heavy equipment as well as other pneumatic and hydraulic components.

EARNINGS GROWTH

Atlas has had some very strong earnings growth the past five years. Its earnings per share has increased 217 percent for the period, an average of 26 percent per year.

The company reported 1989 revenues of 15 billion Swedish kronor (2.4 billion in U.S. dollars). It has about 17,000 employees.

STOCK GROWTH

The company's stock has had its ups and downs but over the recent five-year rating period has done very well—a 201 percent total increase, 25 percent per year.

Including reinvested dividends, a $10,000 investment in Atlas stock in 1984 would have grown to about $36,000 five years later. Average annual compounded rate of return (including stock growth and reinvested dividends): about 29 percent.

DIVIDEND YIELD

The company generally pays a pretty good yield, which has averaged about 4 percent over the past five years. During the most recent two-year rating period (1989 and 1990), the stock paid an average annual current return (dividend yield) of 2.6 percent.

DIVIDEND GROWTH

Atlas increases its dividend most years. The dividend rose 137 percent (19 percent per year) over the five-year period from 1984 to 1989.

CONSISTENCY

The company has had very consistent growth in the key categories of earnings per share, revenues, operating income and book value per share. It did, however, have an earnings per share and operating income decline in 1986. Its price-earnings ratio of about 11 is very attractive for a growing company.

MOMENTUM

Atlas has had exceptional earnings and revenue growth the past two years. Its earnings per share climbed 70 percent in 1988 and 37 percent in 1989.

SUMMARY

Fiscal year ended: Dec. 31
(Swedish kronor; revenue and operating income in millions)

	1990*	1989	1988	1987	1986	1985	1984	5-year growth, %† (annual/total)
Revenue	—	15,035	12,812	11,520	10,351	10,062	9,099	11/65
Operating income	—	1,726	1,169	893	844	1,024	845	15/104
Earnings/share	—	26.75	19.60	11.55	11.06	12.79	8.44	26/217
Dividend/share	—	8.00	6.38	5.63	5.25	4.88	3.38	19/137
Dividend yield, %	2.5	2.7	3.0	4.8	4.2	3.4	4.7	—/—
Stock price	305.00	289.00	276.00	155.00	168.00	190.00	96.00	25/201
P/E ratio	11.0	10.8	10.5	9.7	10.4	10.9	7.6	—/—
Book value/share	—	152.00	120.00	119.00	106.00	96.00	85.00	13/79

* 5–1–90
† 1984–89
Source: Worldscope and company sources.
Note: ADR; stock price quoted in *Barron's,* the *European Wall Street Journal* and the *Financial Times;* 5-year average annual return in U.S. currency: 39%.

90
VOLVO

VOLVO

S-405 08 Goteborg
Sweden
Tel: 46 31 59 0000
U.S. address: 535 Madison Ave.
New York, NY 10022
(212) 754-3300
Chairman and CEO: Pehr G. Gyllenhammar

EARNINGS GROWTH	(no points)
STOCK GROWTH	★ ★
DIVIDEND YIELD	★ ★ ★ ★
DIVIDEND GROWTH	★ ★ ★ ★
CONSISTENCY	★ ★
MOMENTUM	(no points)
STO, LON, TYO, OTC	**12 points**

Volvo is well known for its durable, high-end automobiles, but its operations go well beyond the auto industry. If it rolls, flies or floats, Volvo probably makes a market in it. The Swedish manufacturer builds buses and trucks, engines for boats and jets and components for Ariane space rockets.

The company puts out a line of Volvo luxury cars that has become particularly popular in the United States, where it sells about 100,000 cars a year. Its other major markets are Great Britain (80,000 cars a year) and Sweden (75,000 cars a year).

Car sales comprise about 40 percent of the company's annual revenue. In 1990 the company sank a considerable amount of money into research and development of a line of cars that could replace its popular, 20-year-old 200 series. The expense, along with stiff competition in the auto industry and rising costs in Sweden, was expected to cause a steep drop in the company's 1990 earnings.

Volvo's other primary segments include:

244

- Trucks (24 percent of revenues). Volvo is the second largest manufacturer of heavy trucks in the world. It sells about 60,000 trucks a year, nearly a third in the United States. The company's U.S. plants also produce more Volvo trucks—about 20,000 a year—than any other country, including Sweden (which produces about 15,000 trucks a year).
- Buses (4 percent of sales). The company is the second largest bus manufacturer in Europe. Outside of Sweden, Volvo also has production operations in Brazil, Peru, Australia and Great Britain. The company sells about 5,500 buses a year.
- Marine and industrial engines (3 percent of sales). The company makes diesel and gas engines for leisure and commercial boats. The company's Volvo Penta engines are sold in 130 markets worldwide.
- Aerospace (2 percent of sales). Volvo manufactures jet engines for the Swedish Air Force and has recently begun manufacturing engines for commercial jets. It also produces vital components for the Ariane space rocket.
- Food (11 percent of sales). The company produces a wide range of foods through several subsidiaries. Its leading subsidiary is Abba, which concentrates on the fish and shellfish market. Other leading food subsidiaries include Felix (a frozen foods and preserved foods specialist), Sockerbolaget (Sweden's only sugar production company) and Lithells (a meat production company).
- Trading (12 percent of sales). The company is an active trader in several commodities, including oil and fruit.

EARNINGS GROWTH   (no points)

The company has had slow earnings growth the past few years. Its earnings per share increased only 13 percent over the past five years—2 percent per year. But on the bright side, its book value more than doubled during the period.

Volvo reported total revenue of 91 billion kronor (15 billion in U.S. dollars) in 1989.

STOCK GROWTH

The company's stock price has moved up steadily the past five years, increasing 116 percent for the period—17 percent per year.

Including reinvested dividends, a $10,000 investment in Volvo stock in 1984 would have grown to about $25,000 five years later. Average annual compounded rate of return (including stock growth and reinvested dividends): about 20 percent.

DIVIDEND YIELD

The company generally pays a good yield, which has averaged about 3.5 percent over the past five years. During the most recent two-year rating period (1988 and 1989), the stock paid an average annual current return (dividend yield) of 3.7 percent.

DIVIDEND GROWTH

Volvo traditionally raises its dividend nearly every year. The dividend increased 220 percent (27 percent per year) over the five-year period from 1984 to 1989.

CONSISTENCY

The company has been hanging around the same level of revenue and earnings per share—with slight movements one way or the other—for the past five years. Before that, Volvo had earnings-per-share increases of 73 percent and 92 percent (in 1983 and 1984, respectively), so the company is capable of explosive growth in a healthy market. The company's book value per share has gone up for seven consecutive years.

MOMENTUM   (no points)

Volvo's revenue and earnings have gone nowhere for the past three years and appear to be headed down about 20 percent in 1990. But prospective investors could take heart in the fact that the stock price also declined about 25 percent in the first half of 1990, making it a much better value.

SUMMARY

Fiscal year ended: Dec. 31
(Swedish kronor; revenue and operating income in millions)

	1990*	1989	1988	1987	1986	1985	1984	5-year growth, %† (annual/total)
Revenue	—	90,824	96,639	92,520	84,090	86,196	87,052	1/4
Operating income	—	—	7,208	6,722	6,494	6,475	6,628	10/60
Earnings/share	—	52.85	52.80	57.80	48.20	49.20	46.50	2/13
Dividend/share	—	17.00	14.00	10.50	9.25	8.50	5.30	27/220
Dividend yield, %	—	3.8	3.6	3.9	2.7	2.9	2.6	—/—
Stock price	328.00	445.00	385.00	274.00	344.00	314.00	206.00	17/116
P/E ratio	—	8.4	7.3	6.4	10.4	8.8	10.1	—/—
Book value/share	—	217.54	191.50	158.03	130.46	113.37	94.79	18/129

* 5-1-90
† 1984–89, except operating income, 1983–88
Source: Company sources and Worldscope.

Note: ADR; stock price quoted in *Barron's,* the *European Wall Street Journal* and the *Financial Times;* 5-year average annual return in U.S. currency: 30%.

United Kingdom

The British have been among the world's most ambitious and successful international traders for centuries, and they still exhibit great expertise in the international market. Many of the top corporations of Great Britain have been in business for well over a century. The British equity markets are considered to be the most highly developed in the world.

The United Kingdom's industries include steel, metals, building materials, vehicles, shipbuilding, shipping, banking, insurance, textiles, chemicals, electronics, aircraft, machinery and distilling.

The currency is the British pound (GBP 1 = US $1.73, June, 1990). Its gross domestic product was GBP 454 billion (US $702 billion) in 1988. Its inflation rate the past three years has been about 5 percent. Real economic growth the past several years has also averaged about 5 percent per year. The market value of all domestic stocks traded on the London Exchange was US $712 billion as of January 1, 1989.

In 1989 the British market was up 32 percent in local currency, 18 percent in U.S. currency. Through the first four months of 1990, the British market dropped 13 percent, then rallied back to only a 2 percent deficit by the end of June.

14
WOLSELEY ▬

WOLSELEY PLC

Vines Lane, Droitwich
Worcestershire WR9 8ND
United Kingdom
Tel: 0905 794444
Chairman and Managing Director: Jeremy Lancaster

EARNINGS GROWTH	★	★	★	
STOCK GROWTH	★	★	★	★
DIVIDEND YIELD	★	★	★	★
DIVIDEND GROWTH	★	★	★	★
CONSISTENCY	★	★	★	★
MOMENTUM	★	★	★	
LON	**22 points**			

It got its start as the Wolseley Sheep Shearing Machine Company in 1889, but popular as its mechanical clippers became, living on the lamb proved increasingly difficult for Wolseley. The company began to diversify into other ventures, including the manufacture of a Wolseley automobile that was the forerunner of the Austin-Healy.

Today, Wolseley's wool-trimmer trade is history—and so is its automobile business. Instead, the company has tapped into the lucrative plumbing supplies business. As the world's leading supplier of plumbing and heating materials, Wolseley has been enjoying a growing stream of sales and profits for many years.

In the United Kingdom the company operates about 230 Plumb Centers and 20 Pipeline Centers that sell heating equipment and pipes, sinks and other plumbing supplies primarily to the construction trade. Wolseley's subsidiaries account for about 20 percent of all the central heating materials and 10 percent of the bathroom and plumbing supplies sold each year in the United Kingdom.

Wolseley also operates 44 Builder Centers and 51 Plant & Tools outlets that sell a variety of building supplies to the construction trade. The compa-

251

ny's U.K. plumbing, heating and building supply segment accounts for about 37 percent of its annual earnings.

The company also has several subsidiaries in the United States, including Ferguson Enterprises, Familian Corp, Familian Northwest and Carolina Builders. Together, Wolseley's U.S. operations comprise the largest plumbing wholesale business in the United States. Its U.S. businesses contribute about 37 percent of Wolseley's earnings.

The company's other operations (which account for about 26 percent of its earnings) consist of a group of British manufacturing concerns that produce electrical components and plastic products. It also operates a handful of Keith Johnson & Pelling photographic equipment centers.

EARNINGS GROWTH

The company has had excellent growth the past few years. Its earnings per share increased 164 percent over the past five years, 21 percent per year.

Wolseley reported total revenue of 1.6 billion pounds (2.7 billion in U.S. dollars) in 1989.

STOCK GROWTH

The company's stock price has climbed quickly the past five years, increasing 225 percent for the period—27 percent per year.

Including reinvested dividends, a $10,000 investment in Wolseley stock in 1984 would have grown to about $37,000 five years later. Average annual compounded rate of return (including stock growth and reinvested dividends): about 30 percent.

DIVIDEND YIELD

The company generally pays a good yield, which has averaged about 3 percent over the past five years. During the most recent two-year rating period (1988 and 1989), the stock paid an average annual current return (dividend yield) of 3.6 percent.

DIVIDEND GROWTH

Wolseley traditionally raises its dividend every year. The dividend increased 266 percent (30 percent per year) over the five-year period from 1984 to 1989.

CONSISTENCY

The company has had many years of flawless growth in its earnings per share, revenues, operating income and book value per share. Its price-earnings ratio of under 9 is very favorable for a growing company.

MOMENTUM

Wolseley has had excellent growth the past two years, well in line with its growth over the past five years. Its earnings per share increased 24 percent in 1988 and 19 percent in 1989.

SUMMARY

Fiscal year ended: July 31
(British pounds; revenue and operating income in millions)

	1990*	1989	1988	1987	1986	1985	1984	5-year growth, %† (annual/total)
Revenue	—	1,644	1,280	977	739	527	445	30/269
Operating income	—	127	74	67	46	29	24	40/429
Earnings/share	—	0.37	0.31	0.25	0.21	0.16	0.14	21/164
Dividend/share	—	0.11	0.09	0.07	0.06	0.04	0.03	30/266
Dividend yield, %	4.7	3.8	3.4	2.0	2.2	3.2	3.7	—/—
Stock price	3.13	2.90	2.64	3.43	2.61	1.27	0.89	27/225
P/E ratio	8.5	7.9	8.6	13.9	12.6	7.9	6.3	—/—
Book value/share	—	1.43	1.23	1.17	1.06	0.88	0.79	13/81

* 6–1–90
† 1984–89
Source: Company sources and Worldscope.
Note: No ADR; stock price quoted in the *European Wall Street Journal* and the *Financial Times;* 5-year average annual return in U.S. currency: 39%.

15

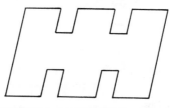

HIGGS AND HILL PLC

Crown House
Kingston Road
New Malden, Surrey KT3 3ST
United Kingdom
Tel: 01-942 8921
Chairman and Chief Executive: Sir Brian Hill

EARNINGS GROWTH	★ ★ ★
STOCK GROWTH	★ ★ ★ ★
DIVIDEND YIELD	★ ★ ★ ★
DIVIDEND GROWTH	★ ★ ★ ★
CONSISTENCY	★ ★ ★ ★
MOMENTUM	★ ★ ★
LON	**22 points**

Since 1874, when Higgs merged with Hill, this British construction firm has been erecting some of England's most familiar landmarks. It built the main structure at the Royal Naval College in Dartmouth in 1905, London's Libertys Department Store in 1924, the BBC Television Centre in 1960 and the British Telecom Headquarters in 1985.

But its architectural creations are not restricted to the British skyline. Construction crews have been active in Egypt, the West Indies, Thailand and throughout Europe. Higgs and Hill is now working on projects in Poland and Czechoslovakia.

The company divides its business into four key segments:

- Traditional contracting. The company designs and builds a wide range of structures, including shopping centers, sports facilities, hospitals and office buildings. It has also handled the refurbishing of a number of established landmarks such as the Courage Brewery in Bristol and the National Gallery in London.
- Management contracting. The company handles the planning, coordinating and construction of many of its projects, including the renovation

254

of the Alhambra Theatre in Bradford and the construction of new stands at Lord's Cricket Ground in London.

- Developments. Incorporated in 1962, Higgs and Hill Developments plans, finances, builds and manages its own commercial and retail projects in England and Europe.
- Homes. The company's homes division builds a variety of homes— apartment buildings and complexes and single-family homes— throughout the United Kingdom.
- Higgs and Hill also owns Diespeker Concrete Company, which designs and erects concrete structures.

EARNINGS GROWTH

The company has had solid earnings growth the past five years. Its earnings per share increased 147 percent over the period, 20 percent per year.

Higgs & Hill reported total revenue of 419 million pounds (750 million in U.S. dollars) in 1989.

STOCK GROWTH

The company's stock price increased steadily the past five years, climbing 215 percent for the period—26 percent per year.

Including reinvested dividends, a $10,000 investment in Higgs stock at the end of 1984 would have grown to about $37,000 five years later. Average annual compounded rate of return (including stock growth and reinvested dividends): about 30 percent.

DIVIDEND YIELD

The company generally pays an excellent yield, which has averaged about 3.5 percent over the past five years. During the most recent two-year rating period (1988 and 1989), the stock paid an average annual current return (dividend yield) of 4.1 percent.

DIVIDEND GROWTH

Higgs traditionally raises its dividend each year. The dividend increased 233 percent (27 percent per year) over the five-year period from 1984 to 1989.

CONSISTENCY

The company has had very consistent growth in its earnings per share, revenues, operating income and book value per share. Its price-earnings ratio of about 6.5 is excellent for a fast-growing company.

MOMENTUM

Higgs has had strong growth the past two years, although its 1989 earnings per share increase of 15 percent was somewhat below its five-year average. In 1988 earnings per share grew 41 percent. The company's revenues also have continued to grow well over the past couple of years.

SUMMARY

Fiscal year ended: Dec. 31
(British pounds; revenue and operating income in millions)

	1990*	1989	1988	1987	1986	1985	1984	5-year growth, %† (annual/total)
Revenue	—	419	343	267	239	206	190	17/120
Operating income	—	26	25	18	12	11	7	30/271
Earnings/share	—	0.52	0.45	0.32	0.24	0.21	0.21	20/147
Dividend/share	—	0.20	0.12	0.09	0.08	0.07	0.06	27/233
Dividend yield, %	7.8	4.3	3.8	3.1	2.8	3.1	4.3	—/—
Stock price	3.40	4.55	3.13	2.91	2.70	2.18	1.44	26/215
P/E ratio	6.5	8.7	7.0	9.1	11.4	9.6	6.7	—/—
Book value/share	—	—	2.62	2.17	1.91	1.79	1.64	12/78

* 6–1–90
† 1984–89
Source: Company sources and Worldscope.

Note: No ADR; stock price quoted in the *European Wall Street Journal* and the *Financial Times;* 5-year average annual return in U.S. currency: 39%.

16

Glaxo

GLAXO HOLDINGS PLC

Clarges House, 6-12 Clarges Street
London W1Y 8DH
United Kingdom
Tel: 01-493 4060
Chairman: Sir Paul Girolami
Chief Executive: Dr. Ernest Mario

EARNINGS GROWTH	★ ★ ★ ★
STOCK GROWTH	★ ★ ★ ★
DIVIDEND YIELD	★ ★ ★
DIVIDEND GROWTH	★ ★ ★ ★
CONSISTENCY	★ ★ ★ ★
MOMENTUM	★ ★ ★
LON, NYSE, TSE, LSE, TYO	**22 points**

Spicy diets and churning stomachs have helped make Glaxo Holdings the world's fastest-growing major pharmaceutical company for seven consecutive years. The company's ulcer remedy, ranitidine (sold under the brand name Zantac), is the world's largest-selling prescription drug.

But if the bottom ever were to fall out of the ranitidine market—not that there's any real threat of that—Glaxo's management might be nursing a serious ulcer of its own. With annual sales of about $2 billion (1.3 billion pounds), ranitidine accounts for about half of the company's total revenue.

In addition to its anti-ulcer medication, Glaxo has developed drugs for a wide range of other ailments. About 23 percent of its revenue comes from the sale of its respiratory drugs. Its leading anti-asthma medication, Ventolin, is the top-selling drug in its segment, according to the company. Glaxo also produces several other anti-asthma drugs, including the second best seller, Becotide (sold as Beclovent in the United States), plus Volmax and Beconase.

Antibiotics account for about 15 percent of the company's revenue. Its leading injectable antibiotic—used for the treatment of bacterial infections—is Fortum (sold as Fortaz in the United States). The company reports that Fortum is the world's third-largest-selling "injectable cephalosporin."

Glaxo also produces a line of cardiovascular drugs (2 percent of revenues) and a line of dermatologicals (4 percent of sales). Glaxo reports that it is the world's second largest producer of topical steroids.

Worldwide, Glaxo has operating companies in about 50 countries and sells its products in nearly 150 countries.

Glaxo's largest market is North America, which accounts for about 45 percent of the company's revenue. Its sales volume in the United States is more than three times as high as at home in the United Kingdom. Glaxo has an office and a factory in North Carolina, where it employs about 4,000 American workers.

Glaxo's other major source of sales is Europe, which accounts for about 30 percent of the company's revenue.

EARNINGS GROWTH

The company has had outstanding growth the past few years. Its earnings per share increased 300 percent over the past five years, 32 percent per year.

Glaxo reported total revenue of 2.6 billion pounds (4 billion in U.S. dollars) in 1989. The company has 38,000 employees.

STOCK GROWTH

The company's stock price has increased 214 percent over the past five years, 26 percent per year.

Including reinvested dividends, a $10,000 investment in Glaxo's stock in 1984 would have grown to about $34,000 five years later. Average annual compounded rate of return (including stock growth and reinvested dividends): about 28 percent.

DIVIDEND YIELD

The company generally pays a modest yield, which has averaged under 2 percent over the past five years. During the most recent two-year rating period (1988 and 1989), the stock paid an average annual current return (dividend yield) of 2.6 percent.

DIVIDEND GROWTH

Glaxo traditionally raises its dividend every year. The dividend increased 400 percent (39 percent per year) over the five-year period from 1984 to 1989.

CONSISTENCY

Glaxo has compiled a flawless record of growth in every key financial category the past five years. Its recent price-earnings ratio of about 15 is a normal level for a growing company.

MOMENTUM

Glaxo's earnings-per-share growth has been very good the past two years but not quite up to its five-year average. On the other hand, its revenue and book value growth in 1989 exceeded its five-year average. So, overall, the company's growth still appears to be on an upward surge.

SUMMARY

Fiscal year ended: June 30
(British pounds; revenue and operating income in millions)

	1990*	1989	1988	1987	1986	1985	1984	5-year growth, %† (annual/total)
Revenue	—	2,570	2,059	1,741	1,429	1,412	1,200	16/114
Operating income	—	876	764	695	517	3,760	249	31/286
Earnings/share	—	0.46	0.39	0.34	0.27	0.19	0.12	32/300
Dividend/share	—	0.18	0.13	0.10	0.07	0.05	0.04	39/400
Dividend yield, %	3.0	2.6	2.5	1.1	1.4	1.6	1.5	—/—
Stock price	7.85	6.81	4.91	8.30	5.07	3.08	2.47	26/214
P/E ratio	15.1	15.0	12.9	24.8	18.7	16.3	18.9	—/—
Book value/share	—	1.54	1.21	0.98	0.74	0.56	0.46	27/234

* 6–1–90
† 1984–89
Source: Company sources and Worldscope.

Note: ADR; stock price quoted in *Barron's*, the *Wall Street Journal*, the *European Wall Street Journal* and the *Financial Times*; 5-year average annual return in U.S. currency: 37%.

22

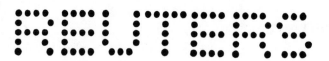

REUTERS HOLDINGS PLC

85 Fleet Street
London EC4P 4AJ
United Kingdom
Tel: 01 250 1122
Chairman: Sir Christopher Hogg

EARNINGS GROWTH	★ ★ ★ ★
STOCK GROWTH	★ ★ ★ ★
DIVIDEND YIELD	★ ★
DIVIDEND GROWTH	★ ★ ★ ★
CONSISTENCY	★ ★ ★ ★
MOMENTUM	★ ★ ★
LON, OTC (ADR)	**21 points**

What do you get when you cross the "Paperless Society" with the "Information Age"? The answer is Reuters, the world's leading electronic financial news and information service.

Reuters has assembled a worldwide news gathering network, with bureaus in 77 countries. The information goes out 24 hours a day, providing businesses, financial institutions and newspapers with instant access to breaking news, stock quotes and a wide range of financial information.

While Reuters hasn't always had the advantage of satellite transmissions and on-line computer monitors, from its very beginning, the company has built its business on fast delivery.

Shortly after Paul Julius Reuter started the business in 1849, he began using carrier pigeons to bridge a gap in the European telegraphic system. When the first telegraph link was established between Europe and North America in 1866, Reuters was one of its first users. And when international communications circuits became available in the early 1960s, Reuters again was one of the first users, transmitting up-to-the-minute financial data around the world.

Today, Reuters uses satellites and cable links to transmit data to its global customer base.

The company offers a wide range of information services:

- Real-time information on financial markets and breaking news transmitted to client terminals;
- Automated stock and bond trading systems that allow brokers to complete international trades;
- Trading room services to allow brokers and analysts to review and analyze market data and information from around the world;
- Historical information services that provide stock prices and company news dating back several years;
- Media services that provide news stories and photographs from around the world for newspapers and other publications.

EARNINGS GROWTH

Reuters has had outstanding growth the past five years, with an excellent earnings per share gain of 290 percent for the period—31 percent per year. The company has total annual sales of 1.2 billion pounds, about 1.9 billion in U.S. dollars.

STOCK GROWTH

The company's stock price has climbed rapidly the past five years—nearly doubling in 1989. Over the past five years, the stock price has increased 247 percent (28 percent per year).

Including reinvested dividends, a $10,000 investment in Reuters stock at the closing 1984 stock price would have grown to about $36,000 five years later. Average annual compounded rate of return (including stock growth and reinvested dividends): about 29 percent.

DIVIDEND YIELD

The company tends to pay a low yield, which has averaged just over 1 percent over the past five years. During the most recent two-year rating period (1988 and 1989), the stock paid an average annual current return (dividend yield) of 1.5 percent.

DIVIDEND GROWTH

Reuters traditionally raises its dividend every year. Over the past five years, the dividend has increased 300 percent—32 percent per year.

CONSISTENCY

The company has had consistent annual growth in earnings, revenue, operating income and total assets for many years. Its ratio of long-term-debt-to-capital has traditionally been moderate, but its price-earnings ratio of around 26 is a bit on the high side—especially for a British company.

MOMENTUM

The company continues to maintain its strong record of growth in every key category. Even in early 1990, as other British stocks faltered, Reuters moved gently upward.

SUMMARY

Fiscal year ended: Dec. 31
(British pounds; revenue and operating income in millions)

	1990*	1989	1988	1987	1986	1985	1984	5-year growth, %† (annual/total)
Revenue	—	1,185	1,003	866	620	434	330	29/259
Operating income	—	—	207	168	123	85	68	31/290
Earnings/share	—	0.43	0.32	0.26	0.19	0.13	0.11	31/290
Dividend/share	—	0.12	0.09	0.07	0.06	0.03	0.03	32/300
Dividend yield, %	1.4	1.3	1.7	1.5	1.0	0.9	0.9	—/—
Stock price	11.97	10.14	5.15	4.93	5.50	3.68	2.92	28/247
P/E ratio	26.0	23.0	16.0	19.0	28.4	27.9	27.8	—/—
Book value/share	—	0.79	0.65	0.52	0.43	0.44	0.36	17/119

* 6–1–90
† 1984–89, except operating income, 1983–88
Source: Company sources and Worldscope.

Note: ADR; stock price quoted in *Barron's,* the *Wall Street Journal,* the *European Wall Street Journal* and the *Financial Times;* 5-year average annual return in U.S. currency: 38%.

24

⌗ Tarmac

TARMAC PLC

Hilton Hall
Essington, Wolverhampton WV11 2BQ
United Kingdom
Tel: (0902) 307407
Chairman: Sir Eric Pountain

EARNINGS GROWTH	★ ★ ★
STOCK GROWTH	★ ★
DIVIDEND YIELD	★ ★ ★ ★
DIVIDEND GROWTH	★ ★ ★ ★
CONSISTENCY	★ ★ ★ ★
MOMENTUM	★ ★ ★ ★
LON	21 points

Tarmac may well be the biggest name in the British building industry. Through its broad network of subsidiaries, Tarmac claims to be Britain's leading home builder, its largest building and civil engineering contractor and one of its largest construction materials suppliers.

The firm has fortified its position in the building industry by acquiring well over 100 smaller construction-related companies. Tarmac employs a loose management style, encouraging its subsidiaries to operate autonomously.

The company divides its operations into several key segments, including:

- Housing (28 percent of revenue). Tarmac builds roughly 15,000 new homes a year through its 20 locally-based house-building subsidiaries. It is the largest house-building business in the United Kingdom.
- Construction (24 percent of revenue). Tarmac is Britain's biggest building and civil engineering contractor. The company is involved in road, bridge and tunnel projects and construction of large office and residential developments.

263

- Quarry products (17 percent of revenue). The company is the British market leader in the production of aggregates, blacktop and ready-mix concrete. It also operates a waste disposal landfill and a road-surfacing company.
- Industrial products (13 percent of revenue). The company produces roofing products, insulation, doors, partitions, screens and a variety of other related products.
- Tarmac America (11 percent of revenue). Tarmac has operations in Virginia, North and South Carolina, Florida, Texas and California that produce aggregates, cement and construction products.
- Building materials (5 percent of revenue). Tarmac is a major supplier of clay, concrete, stone and tile building products.

EARNINGS GROWTH

The company has had excellent earnings per share growth the past five years, increasing 183 percent for the period, 23 percent per year.

Tarmac has annual revenue of 2.8 billion pounds (5 billion in U.S. dollars).

STOCK GROWTH

The company's stock price has climbed steadily the past five years, rising 97 percent for the period, 15 percent per year.

Including reinvested dividends, a $10,000 investment in Tarmac stock in 1984 would have grown to about $23,000 five years later. Average annual compounded rate of return (including stock growth and reinvested dividends): about 18 percent.

DIVIDEND YIELD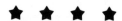

The company generally pays a good yield, which has averaged nearly 4 percent over the past five years. During the most recent two-year rating period (1988 and 1989), the stock paid an average annual current return (dividend yield) of 5.0 percent.

DIVIDEND GROWTH

Tarmac traditionally raises its dividend each year. The dividend increased 250 percent (28 percent per year) over the five-year period from 1984 to 1989.

CONSISTENCY

The company has had a flawless record of growth in its earnings per share, revenues, operating income and book value per share for several years. Its price-earnings ratio of about 8 is a very favorable level for a growing company.

MOMENTUM

Tarmac continues to grow at a fast pace. Its earnings per share were up 46 percent in 1988. In 1990, even in a down British market, Tarmac stock continued to creep up.

SUMMARY

Fiscal year ended: Dec. 31
(British pounds; revenue and operating income in millions)

	1990*	1989	1988	1987	1986	1985	1984	5-year growth, %† (annual/total)
Revenue	—	—	2,754	2,163	1,718	1,536	1,277	20/145
Operating income	—	—	404	285	178	140	115	38/392
Earnings/share	—	—	0.34	0.24	0.18	0.14	0.13	23/183
Dividend/share	—	0.14	0.10	0.07	0.05	0.05	0.04	28/250
Dividend yield, %	5.8	5.6	4.3	3.3	2.6	2.5	3.1	—/—
Stock price	2.59	2.52	2.30	2.22	2.09	1.86	1.28	15/97
P/E ratio	8.0	—	6.7	9.4	11.9	13.4	10.0	—/—
Book value/share	—	—	1.11	1.00	0.78	0.68	0.53	19/141

* 6–1–90
† 1983–88, except stock price and dividend/share, 1984–89
Source: Worldscope.

Note: No ADR; stock price quoted in *Barron's,* the *Wall Street Journal,* the *European Wall Street Journal* and the *Financial Times;* 5-year average annual return in U.S. currency: 26%.

28

RANKS HOVIS MCDOUGALL PLC

RHM Centre
Alma Road
Windsor, Berkshire SL4 3ST
United Kingdom
Tel: 0753 857123
Chairman: Stanley G. Metcalfe

EARNINGS GROWTH	★ ★ ★
STOCK GROWTH	★ ★ ★ ★
DIVIDEND YIELD	★ ★ ★
DIVIDEND GROWTH	★ ★ ★ ★
CONSISTENCY	★ ★ ★ ★
MOMENTUM	★ ★
LON	**20 points**

For years, the kitchens of Ranks Hovis McDougall have turned out a palatable array of British favorites: Mr. Kipling cakes, Robertson's marmalades, Capri-Sun pouch drinks and Hovis breads, among others. But now the Berkshire-based foods company has its own "All-American" label and is gradually nibbling its way deeper into the U.S. food market.

RHM has added several regional U.S. food companies, as well as a number of Pacific basin firms, to its growing list of subsidiaries.

In the United States, RHM owns All American Nut peanut butter, Carriage House Foods, National Preserve, Pilgrim Farms and the Red Wing Company. RHM also has divisions in Australia (Cerebos Pacific Ltd.), New Zealand (Cerebos Gregg's), Singapore, Malaysia, Taiwan and Thailand.

About 11 percent of the company's total sales are generated by its U.S. divisions, and 6 percent come from its Pacific basin companies.

The company's largest division is its milling and bread baking division (35 percent of sales). RHM produces several brands of breads, flours and cereals, including McDougalls, Bisto, Paxo, Be-Ro and Granary flours. Its Hovis breads are among the most popular in Britain.

Other divisions include:

- Grocery products (20 percent of sales). Among the major brand names produced by RHM's grocery division are Just Juice, Capri-Sun, Sharwood's (Indian and Chinese foods) and Shredded Wheat cereal (not to be confused with Nabisco Shredded Wheat).
- Cakes and confectionery (11 percent of sales). RHM's Manor Foods division produces Mr. Kipling and Cadbury's desserts and O.P. Chocolate candies and wafers.
- Food services (15 percent of sales). The company operates a chain of self-service restaurants and bakeries, as well as a catering service and specialty foods production operation.

EARNINGS GROWTH

The company has had solid growth the past few years, with an increase in earnings per share of 183 percent over the past five years, 23 percent per year.

RHM reported total revenue of 1.8 billion pounds (2.8 billion in U.S. dollars) in 1989.

STOCK GROWTH

The company's stock price has moved up very quickly the past five years, increasing 414 percent for the period—39 percent per year.

Including reinvested dividends, a $10,000 investment in RHM stock in 1984 would have grown to about $57,000 five years later. Average annual compounded rate of return (including stock growth and reinvested dividends): about 42 percent.

DIVIDEND YIELD

The company generally pays a good yield, which has averaged about 3 percent over the past five years. During the most recent two-year rating period (1988 and 1989), the stock paid an average annual current return (dividend yield) of 2.8 percent.

DIVIDEND GROWTH

RHM traditionally raises its dividend nearly every year. The dividend increased 225 percent (27 percent per year) over the five-year period from 1984 to 1989.

CONSISTENCY

The company has had very consistent growth in its earnings per share, revenues and operating income over the past five years. Its growth in book value per share, however, has been somewhat volatile during the period. The company's 1989 price-earnings ratio of about 13 is consistent with other growing British companies.

MOMENTUM

RHM had fairly good growth in most of its key categories in 1989, but results were not quite up to par with its average increases over the past five years.

SUMMARY

Fiscal year ended: Sept. 2
(British pounds; revenue and operating income in millions)

	1990*	1989	1988	1987	1986	1985	1984	5-year growth, %† (annual/total)
Revenue	—	1,786	1,669	1,544	1,414	1,314	1,213	8/47
Operating income	—	203	174	129	98	78	56	33/320
Earnings/share	—	0.34	0.31	0.24	0.21	0.15	0.12	23/183
Dividend/share	—	0.13	0.11	0.08	0.07	0.05	0.04	27/225
Dividend yield, %	4.6	2.9	2.7	2.6	2.6	3.2	4.5	—/—
Stock price	3.49	4.53	4.07	3.27	2.68	1.54	0.88	39/414
P/E ratio	10.1	13.3	13.1	13.6	12.8	10.3	7.3	—/—
Book value/share	—	2.60	2.61	0.74	1.06	1.15	1.11	19/136

* 6–1–90
† 1984–89
Source: Company sources and Worldscope.

Note: No ADR; stock price quoted in *Barron's,* the *European Wall Street Journal* and the *Financial Times;* 5-year average annual return in U.S. currency: 52%.

33 ◧ POLLY PECK
INTERNATIONAL PLC

POLLY PECK INTERNATIONAL PLC

42 Berkeley Square
London W1X 5DB
England
Tel: 01-499 0890
Fax: 01-491 1718
Chairman and Chief Executive: Asil Nadir

EARNINGS GROWTH	★
STOCK GROWTH	★ ★ ★ ★
DIVIDEND YIELD	★ ★ ★
DIVIDEND GROWTH	★ ★ ★ ★
CONSISTENCY	★ ★ ★ ★
MOMENTUM	★ ★ ★ ★
LON, NYSE, ADR	**20 points**

For 10 years, Polly Peck has been Britain's fastest-growing business. Now the foods, textiles and electronics conglomerate has set its sights on the rest of the world. In 1989 it acquired controlling interest in Sansui, the Japanese electronics firm, and Del Monte, the U.S. foods company.

In 1980 Polly Peck was an obscure London foods importer, with annual sales of just 6 million pounds (about $10 million). By 1990, the company's sales were expected to eclipse 2 billion pounds—an incredible 10-year growth rate of about 33,000 percent (75 percent per year).

By acquiring Del Monte and Sansui, Polly Peck has established itself as an international force in both foods and electronics. Del Monte, which is a leading producer and marketer of bananas, pineapples and other exotic fruits, has had annual sales of about $750 million.

Sansui, with annual sales of about $120 million, has been a leader in the hi-fi stereo market since 1954, when it began to manufacture stereo amplifiers. Its primary business the past few years has been the manufacture of car and home stereo equipment.

Both acquisitions would seem to fit well into Polly Peck's corporate structure. The company's leading business segment has been the production, packaging and marketing of fruits, vegetables, juices, concentrates and nuts (44 percent of sales and 76 percent of earnings). The company has operations in Great Britain and throughout Europe as well as in North and South America.

Polly Peck has also developed a strong electronics division (44 percent of sales; 20 percent of profits). The company has several electronics subsidiaries scattered around the globe, including Capetronic of Hong Kong, which makes home entertainment systems and computer peripherals, Vestel of Turkey, a stereo equipment manufacturer, and British-based Russell Hobbs Tower, a manufacturer of home appliances and cookware.

Polly Peck also has three smaller divisions: textiles (3 percent of earnings), leisure (the company owns a Sheraton hotel and some Pizza Hut restaurants in Turkey) and pharmaceuticals (the firm owns two small pharmaceutical companies in Turkey).

EARNINGS GROWTH

The company's earnings per share has moved up only modestly the past five years (70 percent total, 11 percent per year), but that is not a true indicator of the company's overall growth. Its revenue, assets and book value per share have grown very rapidly and would tend, in this case, to be a more accurate reflection of the company's overall growth in value.

The company reported revenue of 1.2 billion pounds (1.9 billion in U.S. dollars) in 1989.

STOCK GROWTH

The company's stock price has climbed quickly the past five years, increasing 232 percent for the period—27 percent per year.

Including reinvested dividends, a $10,000 investment in Polly Peck stock in 1984 would have grown to about $37,000 five years later. Average annual compounded rate of return (including stock growth and reinvested dividends): about 30 percent.

DIVIDEND YIELD

The company generally pays a good yield, which has averaged about 3 percent over the past five years. During the most recent two-year rating period (1988 and 1989), the stock paid an average annual current return (dividend yield) of 3 percent.

DIVIDEND GROWTH

Polly Peck has given its shareholders several large dividend hikes the past few years. The dividend has increased 500 percent (43 percent per year) over the five-year period from 1984 to 1989.

CONSISTENCY

The company has had very consistent growth in its earnings per share, revenues and operating income. Its price-earnings ratio of about 10 is very favorable for a fast-growing company.

MOMENTUM

Polly Peck continues to grow at an exceptional clip. Its revenue was up 60 percent in 1989 and was expected to be up as much as 80 percent in 1990 (thanks to its new acquisitions). Even earnings per share made a nice move in 1989, climbing 24 percent.

SUMMARY

Fiscal year ended: Dec. 31
(British pounds; revenue and operating income in millions)

	1990*	1989	1988¹	1987	1986	1985	1984	5-year growth, %† (annual/total)
Revenue	—	1,162	725	381	274	206	137	54/748
Operating income	—	139	110	93	76	64	50	22/178
Earnings/share	—	0.41	0.33	0.30	0.28	0.26	0.24	11/70
Dividend/share	—	0.12	0.05	0.05	0.03	0.03	0.02	43/500
Dividend yield, %	3.5	3.3	2.6	2.2	3.7	2.9	1.6	—/—
Stock price	4.25	3.59	2.03	2.08	0.90	0.90	1.08	27/232
P/E ratio	10.7	8.9	6.1	6.8	3.2	3.4	4.5	—/—
Book value/share	—	2.02	1.17	1.20	0.50	0.45	0.45	35/348

* Stock price as of 6–1–90
† 1984–89
1. Prior to 1988, fiscal year ended Aug. 30
Source: Worldscope.

Note: ADR; stock price quoted in *Barron's,* the *Wall Street Journal,* the *European Wall Street Journal* and the *Financial Times;* 5-year average annual return in U.S. currency: 39%.

36

LADBROKE GROUP PLC

Chancel House
Neasden Lane
London NW10 2XE
United Kingdom
Tel: 01-459 8031
Chairman and Managing Director: Cyril Stein

EARNINGS GROWTH	★ ★ ★ ★
STOCK GROWTH	★ ★ ★
DIVIDEND YIELD	★ ★ ★ ★
DIVIDEND GROWTH	★ ★
CONSISTENCY	★ ★ ★ ★
MOMENTUM	★ ★ ★
LON	**20 points**

As anyone who's ever laid a wager would tell you, the odds always favor the house—which is why your safest bet may be on Ladbroke. Ladbroke, after all, *is* the house. It is the world's largest commercial off-track betting organization.

The London-based holding company also owns Hilton International hotels, several property development subsidiaries and a chain of British housewares stores called Texas Homecare.

Most of Ladbroke's off-track revenue comes from England, where it operates about 2,000 betting shops, and Belgium, where it operates about 1,000 shops. The company also has begun to establish a presence in the United States, where it has opened off-track betting businesses in five states, including California.

The company recently purchased Canterbury Downs horse race track in Minneapolis, one of a number of U.S. tracks Ladbroke has purchased in recent years. Other recent acquisitions include The Meadows track in Pittsburgh and Golden Gate Fields in San Francisco. The company has gained a reputation for turning losing track operations into money-makers.

Ladbroke's racing revenues account for about 56 percent of its total revenue and 30 percent of its profit.

Other divisions include:

- Hotels (24 percent of revenues; 45 percent of profits). Ladbroke recently acquired Hilton International, which operates about 150 hotels in 47 countries (not to be confused with Hilton Hotels, a publicly traded U.S. company that operates 250 hotels in the United States).
- Properties (4 percent of revenues; 12 percent of profits). Ladbroke operates five major property development subsidiaries, including New York-based London & Leeds. The company specializes in developing office buildings and retail centers.
- Retail (15 percent of revenues; 13 percent of profits). The company operates more than 200 Texas Homecare stores throughout the United Kingdom. The stores specialize in kitchen and bathroom appliances, furniture and other products for the home.

EARNINGS GROWTH

The company has had excellent growth the past few years. Its earnings per share increased 380 percent over the past five years, 37 percent per year.

Ladbroke reported total revenue of 3.7 billion pounds (5.9 billion in U.S. dollars) in 1989.

STOCK GROWTH

The company's stock price has moved up steadily the past five years, increasing 180 percent for the period—23 percent per year.

Including reinvested dividends, a $10,000 investment in Ladbroke stock in 1984 would have grown to about $33,000 five years later. Average annual compounded rate of return (including stock growth and reinvested dividends): about 27 percent.

DIVIDEND YIELD

The company generally pays a good yield, which has averaged just under 4 percent over the past five years. During the most recent two-year rating period (1989 and 1990), the stock paid an average annual current return (dividend yield) of 3.9 percent.

DIVIDEND GROWTH

Ladbroke traditionally raises its dividend nearly every year. The dividend increased 100 percent (15 percent per year) over the five-year period from 1984 to 1989.

CONSISTENCY

The company has had very consistent growth in its earnings per share, revenues, operating income and book value per share. Its price-earnings ratio of around 11 is a very attractive level for a growing company.

MOMENTUM

Ladbroke has continued a strong pace of growth the past two years, although its 1989 earnings per share growth (20 percent) was not quite up to its five-year average. On the other hand, revenues were up 28 percent and operating income was up 56 percent. The company's stock price was driven down by the 1990 slump in the British market, making the stock, potentially, a very solid value.

SUMMARY

Fiscal year ended: Dec. 31
(British pounds; revenue and operating income in millions)

	1990*	1989	1988	1987	1986	1985	1984	5-year growth, %† (annual/total)
Revenue	—	3,659	2,848	2,135	1,766	1,343	1,116	27/227
Operating income	—	431	277	179	127	87	55	51/683
Earnings/share	—	0.24	0.20	0.15	0.12	0.10	0.05	37/380
Dividend/share	—	0.10	0.08	0.07	0.06	0.05	0.05	15/100
Dividend yield, %	5.0	2.9	3.8	4.3	3.3	3.5	3.8	—/—
Stock price	2.62	3.42	2.17	1.60	1.77	1.48	1.22	23/180
P/E ratio	10.5	14.1	10.9	10.9	15.2	15.0	14.6	—/—
Book value/share	—	2.84	2.35	1.46	1.20	1.23	0.87	27/226

* 5–1–90
† 1984–89
Source: Worldscope.

Note: ADR; stock price quoted in *Barron's,* the *Wall Street Journal,* the *European Wall Street Journal* and the *Financial Times;* 5-year average annual return in U.S. currency: 36%.

38

IBSTOCK JOHNSEN PLC

Lutterworth House
Lutterworth, Leicestershire LE17 4PS
United Kingdom
Tel: (0455) 553071
Fax: (0455) 553182
Chairman: Paul C. Hyde-Thomson

EARNINGS GROWTH	★ ★ ★ ★
STOCK GROWTH	★ ★
DIVIDEND YIELD	★ ★ ★ ★
DIVIDEND GROWTH	★ ★ ★ ★
CONSISTENCY	★ ★ ★ ★
MOMENTUM	★ ★
LON	**20 points**

Ibstock Johnsen has built its business brick by brick. First it established it-self as one of Britain's leading brick producers by slowly acquiring new sub-sidiaries and factories throughout the United Kingdom. Then it jumped into the U.S. brick market with the acquisition of Glen-Gery Brick. It has since added New Jersey Shale Brick and Midland Brick to its list of U.S. subsidi-aries.

The company produces a wide range of bricks, blocks and other ceramic building materials for the housing and commercial construction industry.

The company's sustained focus on the brick industry and its measured, persistent series of acquisitions has helped Ibstock Johnsen forge a balance sheet as solid as the proverbial brick outhouse. It has managed to keep its debt ratio at a modest level while consistently increasing sales, earnings, book value and shareholder dividends year after year.

Brick sales account for about 70 percent of the company's total profits (54 percent comes from its British operations, 16 percent from the United States).

The other 30 percent of the firm's profits (and 56 percent of its total rev-enues) comes from its forest products division. Its Price & Pierce subsidiary has divisions in both England and the United States. It also recently acquired a large forest products company in Portugal. In all, the company owns about 62,000 acres of woodlands.

EARNINGS GROWTH

The company has had outstanding growth the past few years. Its earnings per share increased 375 percent over the past five years, 37 percent per year.

Ibstock had annual revenue of 367 million pounds (665 million in U.S. dollars) in 1988.

STOCK GROWTH

The company's stock price has increased 110 percent over the past five years, 18 percent per year.

Including reinvested dividends, a $10,000 investment in Ibstock stock in 1984 would have grown to about $26,000 five years later. Average annual compounded rate of return (including stock growth and reinvested dividends): about 21 percent.

DIVIDEND YIELD

The company generally pays a good yield, which has averaged about 3.5 percent over the past five years. During the most recent two-year rating period (1988 and 1989), the stock paid an average annual current return (dividend yield) of 4.0 percent.

DIVIDEND GROWTH

Ibstock traditionally raises its dividend nearly every year. The dividend increased 500 percent (43 percent per year) over the recent five-year period.

CONSISTENCY

The company has had very consistent growth in its earnings per share, revenues and operating income. Its price-earnings ratio of under 8 is very attractive for a growing company.

MOMENTUM

Ibstock Johnsen had a good year in 1988, but its stock price declined about 10 percent in 1989—after years of sustained growth.

SUMMARY

Fiscal year ended: Dec. 31
(British pounds; revenue and operating income in millions)

	1990*	1989	1988	1987	1986	1985	1984	5-year growth, %† (annual/total)
Revenue	—	—	367	145	130	116	110	33/321
Operating income	—	—	52	31	19	14	14	43/491
Earnings/share	—	—	0.19	0.15	0.10	0.07	0.06	37/375
Dividend/share	—	—	0.06	0.04	0.03	0.02	0.02	43/500
Dividend yield, %	5.3	5.2	3.7	2.8	3.2	3.4	3.0	—/—
Stock price	1.39	1.37	1.48	1.41	0.94	0.68	0.65	18/110
P/E ratio	7.2	7.0	7.9	9.2	9.7	10.2	10.2	—/—
Book value/share	—	—	0.98	0.79	0.57	0.45	0.51	18/133

* 6–1–90
† 1983–88, except stock price, 1984–89
Source: Worldscope.

Note: No ADR; stock price quoted in the *European Wall Street Journal* and the *Financial Times;* 5-year average annual return in U.S. currency: 29%.

40 CARLTON
Communications Plc

CARLTON COMMUNICATIONS PLC

15 St. George Street
Hanover Square
London W1R 9DE
England
Tel: 01-499 8050
Chairman and Chief Executive: Michael Green

EARNINGS GROWTH	★ ★ ★ ★
STOCK GROWTH	★ ★ ★ ★
DIVIDEND YIELD	★ ★
DIVIDEND GROWTH	★ ★ ★ ★
CONSISTENCY	★ ★ ★
MOMENTUM	★ ★
LON, NASDAQ	**19 points**

The video production market has been one of the most explosive growth areas of the 1980s, and Carlton Communications—with a growth curve to match—has been leading the way. It is the world's leading producer of prerecorded video cassettes.

The London-based company has its hands in a wide variety of video-related businesses, including production of television programs and the design and manufacture of digital and analogue video production equipment.

The bulk of Carlton's video production work is done in the United States. In 1988 it acquired Technicolor, the fabled North Hollywood-based production facility, where color film processing was originally developed. The company now processes more films and video cassettes than any other facility in the world.

With Technicolor, Carlton has a total production capacity of over 100 million video cassettes per year, giving it the dominant position in one of the great growth areas of this era. Total sales of prerecorded video cassettes grew from just 5 million in 1982 to more than 150 million in 1989, and all indications are that that growth should continue at a strong pace both in the United States and abroad.

Television and video products comprise about 35 percent of Carlton's annual sales. The other 65 percent of sales come from video-related services. The company operates a number of video and film production facilities such as the Moving Picture Company in Britain (where European Coca-Cola ads are produced), Complete Post in Los Angeles and Post Perfect in New York. The facilities are used to produce television shows, advertisements and videos for major advertisers and television stations.

Carlton also has a fleet of mobile camera units for location production. It recently signed a five-year agreement with ABC Television to cover various European sporting events, including the British Open Golf Championship.

The company has several subsidiaries that design and manufacture sophisticated video-related equipment. Carlton recently introduced its Abekas A84 digital vision mixer, which is able to manipulate up to eight layers of video simultaneously.

EARNINGS GROWTH

The company has had tremendous growth the past few years. Its earnings per share increased 562 percent over the past five years, 47 percent per year.

Carlton reported total revenue of 518 million pounds (839 million in U.S. dollars) in 1989.

STOCK GROWTH

The company's stock price jumped from 1.66 pounds in 1984 to 9.10 pounds in 1987 but has been bouncing up and down since then. Over the five-year rating period from 1984 to 1989, the stock grew 437 percent, 40 percent per year.

Including reinvested dividends, a $10,000 investment in Carlton stock at the end of 1984 would have grown to about $55,000 five years later. Average annual compounded rate of return (including stock growth and reinvested dividends): about 41 percent.

DIVIDEND YIELD

The company generally pays a modest yield, which has averaged about 1 percent over the past five years. During the most recent two-year rating period (1989 and 1990), the stock paid an average annual current return (dividend yield) of 2 percent.

DIVIDEND GROWTH

Carlton traditionally raises its dividend each year. The dividend increased 350 percent (35 percent per year) over the five-year period from 1984 to 1989.

CONSISTENCY

The company has had very consistent growth in its earnings per share, revenues, operating income and book value per share, with just a couple of glitches over the past five years. Its price-earnings ratio of about 11 is very attractive for a growing company.

MOMENTUM

Carlton's stock price has fallen the past year over speculation that the company's growth may be slowing down—although earnings per share grew 29 percent in 1989. Its book value per share, however, declined 17 percent.

SUMMARY

Fiscal year ended: Sept. 30
(British pounds; revenue and operating income in millions)

	1990*	1989	1988	1987	1986	1985	1984	5-year growth, %† (annual/total)
Revenue	—	518	174	89	58	38	21	90/2,360
Operating income	—	112	49	33	19	12	5	86/2,140
Earnings/share	—	0.53	0.41	0.31	0.21	0.15	0.08	47/562
Dividend/share	—	0.09	0.07	0.05	0.04	0.03	0.02	35/350
Dividend yield, %	3.0	1.0	1.2	0.6	0.9	0.8	1.3	—/—
Stock price	5.65	8.93	6.23	9.10	4.30	4.00	1.66	40/437
P/E ratio	10.5	16.8	14.3	27.7	19.3	26.6	22.4	—/—
Book value/share	—	1.23	1.61	1.30	1.65	0.84	0.76	10/61

* 6–1–90
† 1984–89
Source: Company sources, CompuStat, Worldscope.

Note: ADR; stock price quoted in *Barron's,* the *European Wall Street Journal* and the *Financial Times;* 5-year average annual return in U.S. currency: 51%.

43

STEETLEY

STEETLEY PLC

P.O. Box 53
Brownsover Road, Rugby
Warwickshire CV21 2UT
United Kingdom
Tel: 0788 535621
Chairman: David L. Donne

EARNINGS GROWTH	★ ★ ★
STOCK GROWTH	★ ★ ★
DIVIDEND YIELD	★ ★ ★ ★
DIVIDEND GROWTH	★ ★
CONSISTENCY	★ ★ ★ ★
MOMENTUM	★ ★ ★
LON	**19 points**

Where others see dirt, Steetley sees money. More than half of its approximately $1 billion a year in revenue comes straight out of the ground—and we're not talking about gold and diamonds here, or even coal. Steetley's business is sand and gravel.

Quarry operations account for about 51 percent of Steetley's revenue. The company operates about 80 quarries in the United Kingdom, France and Spain, extracting stone, sand and gravel for road and rail construction and the building of homes, factories and offices. It also operates quarries in the United States and Canada.

Bricks, tiles and concrete products account for about 24 percent of the company's revenues. Steetley turns out about 100 varieties of brick for the housing and commercial construction market. In all, it produces about 400 million bricks per year. It is the second largest brickmaker in the United Kingdom, with 11 brickworks. The company also has brickmaking operations in the United States.

The company's Steetley Concrete Products subsidiary makes blocks, paving products and reconstructed stone. Steetley has several other related divisions, which account for about 25 percent of the company's revenue.

281

Steetley Minerals is involved in trading industrial minerals, quarrying and exporting bentonite and china clay and processing and packaging a variety of absorbent materials.

Steetley Refractories makes refractory products for high-temperature application, including steel, glass, cement, ceramic and petrochemicals.

EARNINGS GROWTH

The company has had very good growth the past five years, with its earnings per share rising 187 percent for the period, 23 percent per year.

Steetley reported total revenue of 655 million pounds (1.05 billion in U.S. dollars) in 1989. The company has 7,000 employees.

STOCK GROWTH

The company's stock price has moved up steadily the past five years, increasing 177 percent for the period—23 percent per year.

Including reinvested dividends, a $10,000 investment in Steetley stock in 1984 would have grown to about $32,000 five years later. Average annual compounded rate of return (including stock growth and reinvested dividends): about 26 percent.

DIVIDEND YIELD

The company generally pays a very good yield, which has averaged about 3.5 percent over the past five years. During the most recent two-year rating period (1988 and 1989), the stock paid an average annual current return (dividend yield) of 3.8 percent.

DIVIDEND GROWTH

Steetley raises its dividend most years. The dividend increased 133 percent (19 percent per year) over the five-year period from 1984 to 1989.

CONSISTENCY

The company has had a flawless record of growth in its earnings per share, revenues, operating income and book value per share over the past five years. Its price-earnings ratio of under 10 is very favorable for a growing company.

MOMENTUM

During the past two years, Steetley has continued its solid growth, very much in line with its performance of past years.

SUMMARY

Fiscal year ended: Dec. 31
(British pounds; revenue and operating income in millions)

	1990*	1989	1988	1987	1986	1985	1984	5-year growth, %† (annual/total)
Revenue	—	655	525	487	419	409	421	9/55
Operating income	—	106	86	61	43	35	33	26/221
Earnings/share	—	0.46	0.40	0.30	0.23	0.18	0.16	23/187
Dividend/share	—	0.14	0.12	0.09	0.08	0.06	0.06	19/133
Dividend yield, %	4.3	4.1	3.5	2.9	3.4	3.4	4.1	—/—
Stock price	4.29	3.94	3.33	3.10	2.23	1.87	1.42	23/177
P/E ratio	9.4	8.6	8.3	10.3	9.5	10.5	8.8	—/—
Book value/share	—	2.40	2.18	1.76	1.63	1.50	1.48	10/62

* 6–1–90
† 1984–89
Source: Worldscope.

Note: No ADR; stock price quoted in the *European Wall Street Journal* and the *Financial Times;* 5-year average annual return in U.S. currency: 35%.

44

‖‖‖‖‖‖
TESCO

TESCO PLC

Tesco House
Delamare Road
Cheshunt, Hertfordshire EN8 9SL
United Kingdom
Tel: 0992-32222
Chairman: Sir Ian MacLaurin

EARNINGS GROWTH	★ ★
STOCK GROWTH	★ ★ ★
DIVIDEND YIELD	★ ★
DIVIDEND GROWTH	★ ★ ★ ★
CONSISTENCY	★ ★ ★ ★
MOMENTUM	★ ★ ★ ★
LON, OTC	**19 points**

Tesco sells groceries by the acre. Its new line of Tesco superstores offers customers, on average, some 35,000 square feet of meats, produce and other grocery products.

The company has grown steadily over the years (its operating earnings have increased seven-fold since 1980), and it now boasts 375 stores throughout the United Kingdom. It has about 15 stores in Scotland, 25 in Wales and the balance in England. Tesco opens about 20 new stores a year (although, at the same time, it might close 5 to 10 of its less profitable stores).

The firm has its own computer-linked network of regional warehouses, each over 250,000 square feet. The warehouse network helps keep costs down and profit margins up. By maintaining its own warehouses, the company not only can buy in volume but it can more closely monitor delivery schedules and inventory.

The company adds about 1,000 new products a year to its list of store offerings. In addition to the major name-brand products, Tesco stores offer hundreds of its own branded products.

In conjunction with its grocery stores, Tesco also operates 92 gas (petrol) stations.

In addition to its low overhead and broad volume of groceries, the company attributes part of its popularity to its new shop-within-a-shop concept. Stores are subdivided into smaller specialty areas that give even the huge superstores more of a boutique-like atmosphere.

EARNINGS GROWTH

The company has had excellent growth the past few years. Its earnings per share increased 140 percent over the past five years, 19 percent per year.

Tesco reported total revenue of 4.7 billion pounds (8.2 billion in U.S. dollars) in 1989.

STOCK GROWTH

The company's stock price has increased rapidly the past five years, climbing 177 percent for the period—23 percent per year.

Including reinvested dividends, a $10,000 investment in Tesco stock in 1985 would have grown to about $30,000 five years later. Average annual compounded rate of return (including stock growth and reinvested dividends): about 25 percent.

DIVIDEND YIELD

The company generally pays a moderate yield, which has averaged about 2 percent over the past five years. During the most recent two-year rating period (1989 and 1990), the stock paid an average annual current return (dividend yield) of 2.3 percent.

DIVIDEND GROWTH

Tesco has raised its dividend 300 percent over the past five years, 32 percent per year.

CONSISTENCY

The company has had a flawless record of growth the past several years in its earnings per share, revenues, operating income and book value per share. Its price-earnings ratio of about 14 is consistent with other growing British companies.

MOMENTUM

Tesco has had excellent earnings and revenue growth the past couple of years. Even in a sluggish British stock market, its share price jumped 30 percent in its fiscal 1990.

SUMMARY

Fiscal year ended: Feb. 27
(British pounds; revenue and operating income in millions)

	1990	1989	1988	1987	1986	1985	1984	5-year growth, %† (annual/total)
Revenue	—	4,718	4,119	3,593	3,355	3,000	2,595	13/81
Operating income	—	277	214	175	124	82	69	32/301
Earnings/share	—	0.12	0.11	0.10	0.07	0.06	0.05	19/140
Dividend/share	—	0.04	0.03	0.02	0.02	0.02	0.01	32/300
Dividend yield, %	2.3	2.3	1.8	1.6	1.6	2.2	2.3	—/—
Stock price	1.99	1.53	1.55	1.56	1.19	0.73	0.58	23/177
P/E ratio	14.0	13.1	14.2	16.4	17.0	12.7	12.5	—/—
Book value/share	—	0.67	0.59	0.55	0.48	0.37	0.33	14/103

† 1984–89, except stock price, 1985–90
Source: Worldscope.

Note: ADR; stock price quoted in the *Barron's,* the *Wall Street Journal,* the *European Wall Street Journal* and the *Financial Times;* 5-year average annual return in U.S. currency: 34%.

63 Glynwed International plc

GLYNWED INTERNATIONAL PLC

Headland House, New Coventry Road
Sheldon
Birmingham B26 3AZ
United Kingdom
Tel: 021-742 2366
Chairman and Chief Executive: Gareth Davies

EARNINGS GROWTH	★ ★ ★	
STOCK GROWTH	★ ★ ★	
DIVIDEND YIELD	★ ★ ★ ★	
DIVIDEND GROWTH	★ ★	
CONSISTENCY	★ ★ ★	
MOMENTUM	★ ★	
LON	**17 points**	

Glynwed International can trace its roots to the Industrial Revolution. Its Coalbrookdale Iron subsidiary was founded in 1709 by Abraham Darby, who was credited with being the first to use coke for the commercial smelting of iron.

Today, Glynwed is still in the iron and steel business, but it has expanded into several other areas as well. It's a diversified manufacturer of building, consumer and engineering materials.

The company breaks its operations into five key segments including:

- Consumer and building products (16 percent of revenues; 21 percent of earnings). Glynwed makes Aga-Rayburn multi-fuel cooking and heating appliances (now sold primarily in the United Kingdom but coming to America), Falcon Catering Equipment, Flavel-Leisure gas and electric cookers and gas fires, Leisure sinks, basins and showers, and Glynwed Foundries cast iron building products.
- Metal services (30 percent of revenues; 17 percent of earnings). Through its Aalco and Amari subsidiaries, the company produces aluminum and stainless steel sheets, plates, strips, bars, tubes and pipes. It also produces

287

nickel and copper. The company has operations in the United Kingdom, Europe, the United States and Canada.

- Plastics (17 percent of revenues; 20 percent of earnings). Glynwed Plastics International is a world leader in thermoplastic pressure pipework systems, including pipe fittings and valves.
- Steel and engineering (22 percent of revenues; 27 percent of earnings). The company is a world leader in the production of hardened and tempered steel. Its engineering subsidiaries make nails, rivets, plastic cable fixing clips, lifting equipment, fabrications for aircraft engines and stairways, flooring and security fencing systems.
- Tubes and fittings (15 percent of revenues; 8 percent of earnings). The company's Wednesbury Tube subsidiary exports copper tubing to 47 countries. Glynwed also produces steel tubing through its other subsidiaries.

EARNINGS GROWTH

Glynwed has enjoyed solid growth the past few years. Its earnings per share increased 158 percent over the past five years, 21 percent per year.

Glynwed reported total revenue of 1.1 billion pounds (2 billion in U.S. dollars) in 1989.

STOCK GROWTH

The company's stock price the past five years has increased 192 percent—24 percent per year.

Including reinvested dividends, a $10,000 investment in Glynwed stock at the end of 1984 would have grown to about $35,000 five years later. Average annual compounded rate of return (including stock growth and reinvested dividends): about 28 percent.

DIVIDEND YIELD

The company generally pays a good yield, which has averaged about 4 percent over the past five years. During the most recent two-year rating period (1988 and 1989), the stock paid an average annual current return (dividend yield) of 4.7 percent.

DIVIDEND GROWTH

Glynwed traditionally raises its dividend each year. The dividend increased 140 percent (19 percent per year) over the five-year period from 1984 to 1989.

CONSISTENCY

The company has had steady growth through much of the past five years, with just a couple of glitches: operating income dropped slightly in 1987, revenue dropped slightly in 1985 but earnings per share and book value have gone up each year. Its price-earnings ratio of about 8 is very attractive for a growing company.

MOMENTUM

Glynwed's steady earnings growth appeared to be leveling off in 1989. Earnings per share grew only 7 percent, but revenues were up 34 percent, a healthy sign in a sluggish British economy.

SUMMARY

Fiscal year ended: Dec. 31
(British pounds; revenues and operating income in millions)

	1990*	1989	1988	1987	1986	1985	1984	5-year growth, %† (annual/total)
Revenue	—	1,125	839	556	478	464	514	17/118
Operating income	—	—	94	63	68	63	58	14/88
Earnings/share	—	0.31	0.29	0.23	0.18	0.15	0.12	21/158
Dividend/share	—	0.12	0.10	0.08	0.07	0.06	0.05	19/140
Dividend yield, %	6.4	5.8	3.6	2.7	3.3	4.3	5.6	—/—
Stock price	2.52	2.60	2.68	2.95	2.07	1.32	0.89	24/192
P/E ratio	8.0	8.3	9.3	12.7	8.9	7.4	7.1	—/—
Book value/share	—	—	0.90	0.83	0.79	0.75	0.74	4/23

*5–1–90
† 1984–89, except operating income and book value, 1983–88
Source: Company sources and Worldscope.

Note: No ADR; stock price quoted in the *European Wall Street Journal* and the *Financial Times;* 5-year average annual return in U.S. currency: 37%.

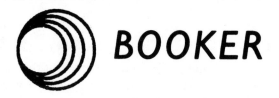

BOOKER

BOOKER PLC

Portland House
Stag Place
London SW1E 5AY
United Kingdom
Tel: 01-828 9850
Fax: 01-630 8029
Chairman: Sir Michael Caine
Chief Executive: Jonathan F. Taylor

EARNINGS GROWTH	★ ★ ★ ★
STOCK GROWTH	★
DIVIDEND YIELD	★ ★ ★ ★
DIVIDEND GROWTH	★ ★
CONSISTENCY	★ ★ ★ ★
MOMENTUM	★ ★
LON	**17 points**

Make no mistake about it: Booker is *not* the creator of all life.

But it does do its share.

Booker owns the world's largest chicken-breeding business (Connecticut-based Arbor Acres Farms), is the world's leading producer of breeding stock for large white turkeys (California-based Nicholas Turkey), is one of the United Kingdom's largest seed producers (Booker Seeds), conducts the second largest fish hatchery business in the United Kingdom (McConnell Salmon) and is the largest mushroom producer in the United Kingdom (Middlebrook Mushrooms).

Booker's Arbor Acres subsidiary has chicken-breeding operations in 26 countries and distribution operations in 70 countries.

About 10 percent of the company's revenue and roughly half of its profit comes from its agribusiness operations.

Booker's other leading business segments include:

- Food distribution (about 85 percent of revenue and 25 percent of profit).
  Booker is the leading food wholesaler in the United Kingdom. It oper-

ates 170 cash-and-carry food warehouse depots to serve about 400,000 commercial clients, including caterers, independent grocers, and confectionery, tobacco and news shop owners.

The company's wholesale food division is the leading distributor to British convenience stores and the largest wholesaler of frozen foods in the United Kingdom. Booker also owns a catering supply operation and a major health food wholesaler.

- Health products (6 percent of revenue; 10 percent of profit). Booker operates the United Kingdom's largest health products retail chain, Holland & Barrett, which has 180 stores. The company is also the United Kingdom's leading supplier of branded nutritional and dietary supplements, and it owns P Leiner, a California-based company that is the largest supplier of vitamins and dietary supplements in the United States.
- Booker's other divisions include Loseley Dairy Products and "Plenty," an engineering company that concentrates on the oil and gas industry. The company holds controlling interest in Agatha Christie Limited and Glidrose Publications, which manage the copyrights of Agatha Christie and Ian Fleming and other James Bond books.

EARNINGS GROWTH

The company has had excellent growth the past few years. Its earnings per share increased 208 percent over the past five years, 25 percent per year.

Booker reported total revenue of 1.8 billion pounds (3.3 billion in U.S. dollars) in 1988.

STOCK GROWTH

The company's stock price has moved up steadily the past five years, increasing 91 percent for the period—14 percent per year.

Including reinvested dividends, a $10,000 investment in Booker stock in 1984 would have grown to about $23,000 five years later. Average annual compounded rate of return (including stock growth and reinvested dividends): about 18 percent.

DIVIDEND YIELD

The company generally pays a good yield, which has averaged about 4.5 percent over the past five years. During the most recent two-year rating period (1988 and 1989), the stock paid an average annual current return (dividend yield) of 4.6 percent.

DIVIDEND GROWTH

Booker traditionally raises its dividend each year. The dividend increased 111 percent (16 percent per year) over the five-year period from 1984 to 1989.

CONSISTENCY

The company has had consistent growth in its earnings per share, revenues and operating income. Its price-earnings ratio of about 12 is favorable for a growing company.

MOMENTUM

Booker has continued its steady earnings and revenue growth during the past couple of years, although its stock price moved very little between 1987 and 1990.

SUMMARY

Fiscal year ended: Dec. 31
(British pounds; revenue and operating income in millions)

	1990*	1989	1988	1987	1986	1985	1984	5-year growth, %† (annual/total)
Revenue	—	—	1,839	1,263	1,263	1,188	1,097	12/78
Operating income	—	—	66	54	48	42	29	21/153
Earnings/share	—	—	0.37	0.32	0.27	0.23	0.19	25/208
Dividend/share	—	10.19	0.18	0.15	0.13	0.12	0.09	16/111
Dividend yield, %	6.3	4.5	4.7	4.2	4.1	4.4	3.9	—/—
Stock price	3.99	4.30	3.79	3.70	3.27	2.64	2.24	14/91
P/E ratio	11.7	10.9	10.4	11.7	12.2	11.4	12.1	—/—
Book value/share	—	—	1.05	1.15	1.10	0.93	0.95	4/15

*5-1-90
† 1983–88, except dividend per share and stock price, 1984–89
Source: Company sources and Worldscope.

Note: ADR; stock price quoted in the *European Wall Street Journal* and the *Financial Times;* 5-year average annual return in U.S. currency: 26%.

68

J SAINSBURY PLC

J. SAINSBURY PLC

Stamford House
Stamford Street
London SE1 9LL
United Kingdom
Tel: 01 921 6000
Chairman and Chief Executive: Sir John Sainsbury

EARNINGS GROWTH	★ ★ ★
STOCK GROWTH	★
DIVIDEND YIELD	★ ★ ★
DIVIDEND GROWTH	★ ★ ★
CONSISTENCY	★ ★ ★ ★
MOMENTUM	★ ★ ★
LON, OTC	**17 points**

J. Sainsbury has been selling groceries in Britain for more than 120 years, but its balance sheet hardly looks the part of a mature company. The London retailer has had 10 consecutive years of profit growth of 20 percent or more, a record unmatched by any other major British corporation.

Sainsbury is Britain's leading food retailer, locking up an 11-percent share of the food and drink market. Its 1989 sales of 5.7 billion pounds (9.6 billion in U.S. dollars) is the highest of any U.K. retail company.

The company operates about 300 supermarkets throughout Great Britain. It also owns about 10 massive Savacentre supermarkets and about 60 Homebase home improvement and garden stores. In the United States, the company recently opened several Shaw's supermarkets in Rhode Island and New Hampshire.

In recent years Sainsbury has followed the industry trend of offering more products and services and expanding the floor space of its stores. Its new stores (the company adds about 20 new stores a year) average over 30,000 square feet—about twice the size of its older stores.

Among the features added to some of the new stores are coffee shops, floral shops and gas (petrol) stations.

Over the years, the company has engendered a strong sense of brand loyalty among its customers. Sainsbury brand foods account for about 55 percent of the company's sales. Such customer loyalty may well be justified: the *Green Consumer Guide,* a British periodical that rates products and companies, recently ranked Sainsbury as the country's number-one retailer in terms of environmental policies.

Another British magazine, *Marketing Week,* ranked Sainsbury as Britain's top company in terms of "quality of service," "overall financial performance in its sector" and "profitable pricing of products and services."

The company was originally founded in 1869 by John James Sainsbury, and it has been managed by Sainsburys ever since. Its present chairman and CEO, John Sainsbury, represents the fourth generation of Sainsburys to manage the firm.

EARNINGS GROWTH

Sainsbury has had 10 consecutive years of increased earnings per share—and 10 straight years of increased profits of 20 percent or more. Over the past five years, earnings per share have climbed 183 percent—23 percent per year.

Sainsbury, with total annual revenues of 5.7 billion pounds (9.6 billion in U.S. dollars), has about 35,000 full-time and 55,000 part-time employees. It has 70,000 shareholders of record.

STOCK GROWTH

While earnings growth has been strong, the company's stock price has not grown as quickly as one might have expected, but it still has offered a fair return the past five years. The stock has increased 71 percent (12 percent per year) during the five-year period through fiscal 1989.

Including reinvested dividends, a $10,000 investment in Sainsbury stock at its median price in 1985 would have grown to about $19,000 five years later. Average annual compounded rate of return (including stock growth and reinvested dividends): about 14 percent.

DIVIDEND YIELD

The company generally pays a modest yield, which has averaged just under 2 percent over the past five years. During the most recent two-year rating period (1989 and 1990), the stock paid an average annual current return (dividend yield) of 2.6 percent.

DIVIDEND GROWTH

Sainsbury traditionally raises its dividend every year. The dividend increased 150 percent (20 percent per year) over the five-year period from 1984 to 1989.

CONSISTENCY

The company has had very consistent growth in its earnings per share, revenues, operating income and book value per share, with increases in all areas every year of the five-year rating period.

MOMENTUM

Sainsbury's growth has continued at a strong sustained pace the past couple of years—well in line with its excellent historic growth record.

SUMMARY

Fiscal year ended: Mar. 19
(British pounds; revenue and operating income in millions)

	1990	1989	1988	1987	1986	1985	1984	5-year growth, %† (annual/total)
Revenue	—	5,659	4,791	3,857	3,414	2,999	2,575	17/119
Operating income	—	373	306	281	190	161	129	24/189
Earnings/share	—	0.17	0.14	0.11	0.09	0.08	0.06	23/183
Dividend/share	—	0.05	0.04	0.04	0.03	0.02	0.02	20/150
Dividend yield, %	2.9	2.3	1.8	1.4	1.4	1.5	1.4	—/—
Stock price	2.65	2.23	2.31	2.48	1.98	1.55	1.33	12/71
P/E ratio	14.0	13.4	17.0	21.9	21.8	19.9	20.6	—/—
Book value/share	—	0.78	0.69	0.55	0.47	0.40	0.35	17/122

† 1984–89, except stock price, 1985–90
Source: Company sources and Worldscope.

Note: ADR; stock price quoted in *Barron's,* the *Wall Street Journal,* the *European Wall Street Journal* and the *Financial Times;* 5-year average annual return in U.S. currency: 22%.

IMI

IMI PLC

P.O. Box 216
Witton, Birmingham B6 7BA
United Kingdom
Tel: 021-356 4848
Chairman: Sir Eric Pountain

EARNINGS GROWTH	★ ★
STOCK GROWTH	★ ★
DIVIDEND YIELD	★ ★ ★ ★
DIVIDEND GROWTH	★
CONSISTENCY	★ ★ ★ ★
MOMENTUM	★ ★ ★
LON	**16 points**

IMI has used its engineering expertise to establish itself as an emerging world force in a wide range of high-tech markets—from drink dispensers to titanium jet engine parts.

The company divides its business into five primary segments:

- Building products (25 percent of revenues; 20 percent of earnings). IMI makes copper tubes and fittings, hot water cylinders, radiator valves and other components for home plumbing and heating systems.
- Refined and wrought metals (31 percent of revenues; 19 percent of earnings). IMI is the United Kingdom's leading copper refinery and its only manufacturer of titanium. IMI recently developed a titanium alloy capable of withstanding temperatures of up to 650°C—the highest temperature ever achieved for titanium. The alloy is used primarily for jet engine parts and other aerospace applications.
- Drinks dispensers (17 percent of revenues; 18 percent of earnings). IMI's Cornelius drinks dispenser business is the world's leading manufacturer of soft drink and beer dispenser equipment for restaurants and bars. It has manufacturing operations in the United Kingdom, the United States (Cornelius was originally a Minnesota-based company), Germany, Can-

ada, Brazil and Spain and has distribution operations in all of the major markets throughout the world.

- Fluid control (20 percent of revenues; 29 percent of earnings). The company manufactures air service equipment, pneumatic control components and systems, compressors and dryers. It also manufactures industrial automation systems through a German subsidiary.
- Special engineering (14 percent of revenues and earnings). IMI manufactures automobile radiators for cars and trucks, air conditioners, heat exchangers and sporting ammunition.

EARNINGS GROWTH

The company has had solid growth the past few years. Its earnings per share increased 127 percent over the past five years, 18 percent per year.

IMI reported total revenue of 1.1 billion pounds (1.95 billion in U.S. dollars) in 1989.

STOCK GROWTH

The company's stock price has moved up steadily the past five years, increasing 121 percent for the period—17 percent per year.

Including reinvested dividends, a $10,000 investment in IMI stock in 1984 would have grown to about $26,000 five years later. Average annual compounded rate of return (including stock growth and reinvested dividends): about 21 percent.

DIVIDEND YIELD

The company generally pays a very good yield, which has averaged about 4.5 percent over the past five years. During the most recent two-year rating period (1988 and 1989), the stock paid an average annual current return (dividend yield) of 4.4 percent.

DIVIDEND GROWTH

IMI traditionally raises its dividend nearly every year. The dividend increased 80 percent (13 percent per year) over the five-year period from 1984 to 1989.

CONSISTENCY

The company has had very consistent growth in its earnings per share, revenues, operating income and book value per share. Its price-earnings ratio of about 8 to 10 is a very attractive level for a growing company.

MOMENTUM

IMI has continued to increase its earnings per share each year, although growth has leveled off the past two or three years.

SUMMARY

Fiscal year ended: Dec. 31
(British pounds; revenue and operating income in millions)

	1990*	1989	1988	1987	1986	1985	1984	5-year growth, %† (annual/total)
Revenue	—	1,079	902	860	780	766	737	8/46
Operating income	—	121	102	88	71	61	50	19/142
Earnings/share	—	0.25	0.22	0.19	0.17	0.15	0.11	18/127
Dividend/share	—	0.09	0.08	0.07	0.06	0.05	0.05	13/80
Dividend yield, %	5.0	4.3	4.5	3.8	3.4	4.4	4.5	—/—
Stock price	2.44	2.22	1.83	1.84	1.76	1.19	1.00	17/121
P/E ratio	10.0	8.8	8.2	9.6	10.3	8.0	9.3	—/—
Book value/share	—	1.15	1.02	1.00	0.90	0.89	0.86	6/33

*6–1–90
† 1984–89
Source: Company sources and Worldscope.

Note: ADR; stock price quoted in the *European Wall Street Journal* and the *Financial Times;* 5-year average annual return in U.S. currency: 29%.

75
Reckitt & Colman

RECKITT & COLMAN PLC

One Burlington Lane
London W4 2RW
United Kingdom
Tel: 01-994 6464
Chairman: Sir Michael Colman
Chief Executive: John St. Lawrence

EARNINGS GROWTH	★ ★	
STOCK GROWTH	★ ★	
DIVIDEND YIELD	★ ★ ★	
DIVIDEND GROWTH	★ ★	
CONSISTENCY	★ ★ ★ ★	
MOMENTUM	★ ★ ★	
LON	**16 points**	

Through much of the 1800s and into the early 1900s, London-based Reckitt & Sons and cross-town rival J&J Colman were fierce competitors. They battled for market share of the English flour and starch trade in the late 1800s, then extended their rivalry abroad in the early 1900s, engaging in a cutthroat competition for the South American market.

The two companies finally agreed to bury the hatchet in 1913, establishing a joint business to handle their trading operations in South America. But not until 40 years later did the two firms finally decide to tie the knot officially. The merger forming Reckitt & Colman Holdings Ltd. was finalized in 1954. Later that year, the combined company brought another old rival into the fold when it merged with Chiswick Products.

Reckitt & Colman breaks its operations into five primary segments, including:

- Household and toiletry (51 percent of revenues). The company makes a wide range of cleaning products, including Cleen O Pine, Dettox, Gumption Cream, Harpic bathroom cleaner, Haze and Stick Up air fresheners, Robin Frend laundry products, Mr. Sheen and Mansion polishes, Brasso

299

metal polishes, Windolene window cleaners, Cherry Blossom shoe polishes, Once, Supersoft and Cossack hair products and Veet and Nulon skin lotions.

- Foods (33 percent of revenues). Reckitt & Colman make Colman's mustards and condiments, Robinsons baby foods and juices and Jif lemon juice.
- Pharmaceutical (11 percent of revenues). The company makes Dettol soaps and antiseptics, Lemsip cold treatments and a variety of other over-the-counter and prescription medications.
- Fine art and graphics (2 percent of revenues). The firm produces Winsor & Newton paints, brushes and pads, Reeves children's art supplies and Dryad crafts and publications.
- Colors (3 percent of revenues). The company produces a line of industrial dyes and pigments.

EARNINGS GROWTH

The company has had solid growth the past five years, with an increase in its earnings per share of 118 percent for the period, 17 percent per year.

R&C had revenues of 1.4 billion pounds (2.5 billion in U.S. dollars) in 1988.

STOCK GROWTH

The company's stock price has increased steadily the past five years, climbing 120 percent for the period—17 percent per year.

Including reinvested dividends, a $10,000 investment in R&C stock in 1984 would have grown to about $25,000 five years later. Average annual compounded rate of return (including stock growth and reinvested dividends): about 20 percent.

DIVIDEND YIELD

The company generally pays a good yield, which has averaged about 2.5 percent over the past five years. During the most recent two-year rating period (1988 and 1989), the stock paid an average annual current return (dividend yield) of 2.8 percent.

DIVIDEND GROWTH

R&C traditionally raises its dividend each year. The dividend increased 116 percent (17 percent per year) over the most recent five-year period.

CONSISTENCY

The company has had very consistent growth in its earnings per share, revenue, and operating income. Its price-earnings ratio of about 13 is consistent with other growing British companies.

MOMENTUM

R&C has continued to sustain solid growth through 1988 and 1989, with earnings-per-share increases in line with its average over the past five years.

SUMMARY

Fiscal year ended: Dec. 31
(British pounds; revenue and operating income in millions)

	1990*	1989	1988	1987	1986	1985	1984	5-year growth, %† (annual/total)
Revenue	—	—	1,394	1,493	1,329	1,267	1,124	7/42
Operating income	—	—	190	180	149	121	100	17/121
Earnings/share	—	—	0.81	0.68	0.58	0.48	0.42	17/118
Dividend/share	—	—	0.26	0.22	0.19	0.16	0.14	17/116
Dividend yield, %	3.0	2.8	2.8	2.8	2.1	2.5	2.5	—/—
Stock price	12.66	12.49	9.20	7.85	8.62	6.51	5.68	17/120
P/E ratio	13.0	13.0	11.4	11.5	14.9	13.5	13.6	—/—
Book value/share	—	—	3.47	3.15	2.86	2.57	2.78	10/60

*6–1–90
† 1983–88, except stock price, 1984–89
Source: Worldscope.

Note: No ADR; stock price quoted in *Barron's,* the *Wall Street Journal,* the *European Wall Street Journal* and the *Financial Times;* 5-year average annual return in U.S. currency: 28%.

77

Redland

REDLAND PLC

Redland House
Reigate, Surrey RH2 0SJ
United Kingdom
Tel: 0737 242488
Chairman: Sir Colin Corness

EARNINGS GROWTH	★ ★
STOCK GROWTH	★
DIVIDEND YIELD	★ ★ ★ ★
DIVIDEND GROWTH	★ ★
CONSISTENCY	★ ★ ★ ★
MOMENTUM	★ ★ ★
LON	**16 points**

Business is always looking up at Redland—it's the world's largest producer of pitched roofing tiles.

The Surrey-based manufacturer produces roofing products at 138 manufacturing plants in 22 countries. In the United States its Monier Roof Tile subsidiary is the country's largest producer of roofing tiles. Redland is also the leading roofing tile manufacturer in nearly every country in Western Europe and a major force in the roofing industry in Australia, the Far East and South Africa.

Roofing products account for about 35 percent of the company's revenues.

About 50 percent of Redland's revenue comes from its U.K. operations. The rest comes primarily from Europe (26 percent), the United States (16 percent) and Australia and the Far East (7 percent).

In addition to its roofing products, the company is involved in manufacturing a variety of other construction-related materials, including:

- Aggregates (27 percent of revenue). Redland is the fourth-largest producer of aggregates (stone, cement, blacktop, concrete, etc.) in the United Kingdom and the United States. It also has operations in France and the Middle East. The company is involved not only in mining stone from quarries and producing cement and concrete mix, but it also has its own paving operations.

- Bricks (5 percent of revenue). With operations in the United Kingdom, Australia and the Netherlands, Redland is one of the world's largest brickmakers. In all, it has 36 brickmaking plants, with total production capacity of about a billion bricks a year.
- Other activities (32 percent of revenue). The company is involved in a number of other construction-related ventures, including the production of plasterboard and ceramic wall and floor tile.

EARNINGS GROWTH

The company has enjoyed steady growth the past five years, with earnings per share climbing 125 percent for the period, 18 percent per year.

Redland reported total revenue of 1.5 billion pounds (2.8 billion in U.S. dollars) in 1989.

STOCK GROWTH

The company's stock price has had solid growth the past five years, increasing 96 percent for the period—14 percent per year.

Including reinvested dividends, a $10,000 investment in Redland stock in 1984 would have grown to about $22,000 five years later. Average annual compounded rate of return (including stock growth and reinvested dividends): about 17 percent.

DIVIDEND YIELD

The company generally pays a good yield, which has averaged about 3.5 percent over the past five years. During the most recent two-year rating period (1988 and 1989), the stock paid an average annual current return (dividend yield) of 4.0 percent.

DIVIDEND GROWTH

Redland traditionally raises its dividend each year. The dividend increased 130 percent (18 percent per year) over the five-year period from 1984 to 1989.

CONSISTENCY

The company has had very consistent growth in its earnings per share, operating income and book value per share. Its price-earnings ratio of about 10 is very favorable for a growing company.

MOMENTUM

Redland has maintained solid growth in its operating income and earnings per share the past couple of years.

SUMMARY

Fiscal year ended: Dec. 31[1]
(British pounds; revenue and operating income in millions)

	1990*	1989	1988	1987	1986	1985	1984	5-year growth, %† (annual/total)
Revenue	—	1,548	1,899	1,800	1,300	1,292	1,247	5/24
Operating income	—	260	231	196	144	125	119	17/118
Earnings/share	—	0.61	0.52	0.43	0.36	0.31	0.27	18/125
Dividend/share	—	0.23	0.20	0.16	0.13	0.11	0.10	18/130
Dividend yield, %	5.3	4.2	3.7	3.8	2.7	2.4	3.6	—/—
Stock price	5.88	5.53	5.40	4.12	4.82	4.61	2.82	14/96
P/E ratio	9.9	9.1	10.4	9.5	13.4	14.8	10.3	—/—
Book value/share	—	—	—	1.88	1.85	1.39	1.31	—/—

*6–1–90
† 1984–89, except book value per share, 1983–88
1. Redland changed its year-end from March to December in 1988. But all figures represent 12-month growth. Year-ends were: 3-30-85, 3-29-86, 3-28-87, 3-26-88, 12-31-88 and 12-31-89.
Source: Company sources.

Note: ADR; stock price quoted in *Barron's,* the *Wall Street Journal,* the *European Wall Street Journal* and the *Financial Times;* 5-year average annual return in U.S. currency: 25%.

84

AAH HOLDINGS PLC

76 South Park
Lincoln LN5 8ES
United Kingdom
Tel: (0522) 546577
Chairman: William M. Pybus

EARNINGS GROWTH	★ ★
STOCK GROWTH	★ ★
DIVIDEND YIELD	★ ★ ★ ★
DIVIDEND GROWTH	★ ★
CONSISTENCY	★ ★ ★
MOMENTUM	★
LON	**14 points**

You're the administrator of a London hospital and you find that the facility has become perilously low on some key medical supplies.

Or you're a Liverpool pharmacist and you've just portioned out the last of your supply of a popular antibiotic for a customer—and the day is still early.

You need drugs and medical supplies, and you need them *now!*

Who you gonna call?

In the United Kingdom the answer, most often, is AAH.

As the kingdom's leading wholesale distributor of drugs and medical supplies, AAH stocks more than 20,000 different items in medical warehouses all over Britain. Company drivers often make as many as two delivery stops a day at many of the busier medical facilities.

AAH also operates a chain of Vantage pharmacies, develops and markets computer information systems for medical research and manufactures a line of beauty products. The company's pharmaceutical division accounts for 75 percent of its total revenue and 59 percent of its profit.

AAH's other business segments include:

- Builders supplies (8 percent of revenue; 16 percent of profit). AAH operates a network of building-supply yards geared to building professionals. The centers carry about 15,000 product lines.
- AAH also owns a building materials manufacturing operation (Supamix), a plumbing supplies distributor and a brick manufacturing plant.
- Electrical supplies (5 percent of revenues; 10 percent of profit). Through its Hamilton Electric Supplies subsidiary, the company is a wholesaler of home appliances.
- AAH's transport services division and its environmental services division each account for about 2 percent of revenues and 4 percent of profits.

At one time, AAH derived the bulk of its revenue from the sale of fuels. In fact, the company began as a coal producer in South Wales in 1923. But because of declining profits in the industry, the company has phased out its fuel division, selling off the last of its holdings in 1988.

EARNINGS GROWTH

AAH has had five good, though somewhat erratic, years of earnings growth. Its earnings per share has increased, on average, 16 percent per year over the past five years.

With total annual revenues of 1 billion pounds (1.7 billion in U.S. dollars), AAH has 6,200 employees.

STOCK GROWTH

The company's stock has had fairly good growth the past five years, although, like most of the British market, it dropped off significantly early in 1990. Over the past five years, the stock price has increased 126 percent (18 percent per year).

Including reinvested dividends, a $10,000 investment in AAH stock at the end of 1984 would have grown to about $27,000 five years later. Average annual compounded rate of return (including stock growth and reinvested dividends): about 22 percent.

DIVIDEND YIELD

The company generally pays a fairly good yield, which has averaged about 4 percent over the past five years. During the most recent two-year rating period (1989 and 1990), the stock paid an average annual current return (dividend yield) of 4.0 percent.

DIVIDEND GROWTH

AAH traditionally raises its dividend every year. The dividend increased 100 percent (15 percent per year) over the five-year period from 1984 to 1989.

CONSISTENCY

The company has been pretty consistent, with increased revenues and earnings per share four of the past five years. Its book value has gone up each year. Its price-earnings ratio of around 11 is at an attractive level.

MOMENTUM

AAH has lost momentum the past couple of years. Its earnings per share went up only 6 percent in 1989, and its revenues have not increased since 1987. Half-way through its fiscal 1990, however, the company appeared to be headed toward a record high in earnings, although the increase was not expected to be dramatic.

SUMMARY

Fiscal year ended: Mar. 31
(British pounds; revenue and operating income in millions)

	1990	1989	1988	1987	1986	1985	1984	5-year growth, %† (annual/total)
Revenue	—	1,024	1,008	1,024	976	521	501	15/104
Operating income	—	31	27	26	22	13	12	21/158
Earnings/share	—	0.30	0.28	0.24	0.18	0.13	0.14	16/114
Dividend/share	—	0.12	0.10	0.09	0.08	0.07	0.06	15/100
Dividend yield, %	4.9	3.1	4.0	3.0	3.8	4.6	5.3	—/—
Stock price	3.35	3.84	2.56	2.98	2.06	1.48	1.13	18/126
P/E ratio	11.0	12.8	9.1	12.4	11.4	11.4	8.1	—/—
Book value/share	—	1.83	1.71	1.42	1.30	1.27	0.99	13/84

† 1984–89, except stock price, 1985–90
Source: Company sources and Worldscope.

Note: No ADR; stock price quoted in the *European Wall Street Journal* and the *Financial Times;* 5-year average annual return in U.S. currency: 38%.

United States

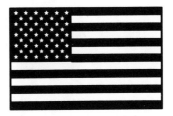

The U.S. dominance of the world stock market may indeed be a thing of the past, but the United States is still *the* major player in the global market.

In 1970 U.S. companies accounted for 66 percent of the total world market capitalization (market capitalization refers to the total value of all stocks based on the price of those stocks). Twenty years later, the United States accounted for only about 34 percent of the world market capitalization. Only about 20 percent of the world's major blue-chip stocks are U.S. companies.

The United States had actually fallen behind Japan in total market capitalization until the Japanese market was beset with troubles. The yen dropped 24 percent relative to the dollar from the beginning of 1989 through mid-1990, and the Japanese stock market dropped 33 percent the first nine months of 1990. The crash in the Japanese market helped reestablish the United States as the world leader in total market capitalization.

Although the U.S. market is not growing as quickly as some of the other emerging markets around the world, it remains a relatively stable and successful market. Aside from the crash of 1987, the U.S. market has had an impressive run of success throughout most of the past 10 years.

The country's GNP was $5.44 trillion in the first quarter of 1990. Its inflation rate the past three years (through 1989) has averaged 4.2 percent. Real economic growth the past three years has averaged 3.4 percent per year. The market value of all domestic stocks traded on U.S. exchanges was $3 trillion as of September, 1989.

In 1989 the U.S. market was up 26.9 percent. Through the first six months of 1990, the U.S. market was up about 2 percent.

Future prospects for U.S. growth hinge in part on the ability of its corporations to remain competitive in the European market. While U.S. companies may be at a disadvantage to their European competitors in the East European market, many U.S. companies already have strong international operations, with ties to the East and, in some cases, signed alliances with East European firms.

5

PHILIP MORRIS COMPANIES INC.

120 Park Avenue
New York, NY 10017
Tel: (212) 880-5000
Chairman and CEO: Hamish Maxwell
President: John A. Murphy

EARNINGS GROWTH	★ ★ ★ ★
STOCK GROWTH	★ ★ ★ ★
DIVIDEND YIELD	★ ★ ★ ★
DIVIDEND GROWTH	★ ★ ★
CONSISTENCY	★ ★ ★ ★
MOMENTUM	★ ★ ★ ★
NYSE	**23 points**

Hand it to Philip Morris. The New York-based consumer products giant has tried its best to diversify, to take the heat, so to speak, off its tobacco sales and spread out its profit base. The firm has been on a corporate buying binge the past few years that could fill a shopping cart:

It owns Tang and Jello, Miracle Whip, Cool Whip and Kool-Aid. It owns Maxwell House and Sanka coffees, Frusen Glädje and Breyers ice creams, Stove Top stuffing, Velveeta cheese food and Parkay margarine. It owns Kraft Foods, Oscar Mayer meats, Post cereals and Miller beer.

But Philip Morris is not only big in the U.S. market; it's also the third-largest consumer-products company in Europe, thanks in large part to its June, 1990, acquisition of Switzerland-based chocolates and coffee giant Jacobs Suchard.

In all, Philip Morris puts more than 3,000 products on the consumer market.

But stack them all into one grocery sack and the company's line-up of consumer staples still doesn't measure up to the incredible profit power of its tobaccos. Led by Marlboro and Marlboro Lights, the $5.1 billion a year in profit the company pockets from cigarette sales is nearly three times its earnings from all of its other consumer products combined.

This, of course, is all great news for Philip Morris shareholders, whose worries over the potential ill effects of an anti-tobacco backlash have long since dissipated into a cloud of money. In 1989 alone, Philip Morris stock soared 68 percent (plus a 3 percent dividend yield). The company has enjoyed 35 consecutive years of record earnings.

Marlboro alone earns about $3 billion a year—roughly twice the profits of the company's entire foods division. Marlboro is the country's and the world's largest-selling cigarette. It accounts for 26 percent of the 523 billion cigarettes sold in the United States each year. Marlboro Lights, the leading low-tar brand, accounts for another 10 percent of all U.S. sales. Philip Morris, which also makes Merit, Virginia Slims, Benson & Hedges, Parliament and Cambridge, is the world's leading cigarette manufacturer, holding about a 7 percent share of the 5 trillion-unit world market.

By sheer revenue—total dollars taken in—Philip Morris's gang of non-tobacco consumer products actually eclipses its tobacco sales. Food sales accounted for $23 billion—51 percent of the company's total revenue of $45 billion in 1989. Beer sales equaled 8 percent of the total, and smokes accounted for 40 percent of sales.

So with well under half of the company's revenue coming from its tobacco segment, how could tobacco still pull a full 72 percent of the firm's operating profit?

Call it "profit margin."

While Philip Morris, on average, earns 7 cents on every dollar of goods it sells from its non-tobacco segment, cigarette sales bring in a hefty 28 cents on the dollar—four times the average profit margin from its other products. *That* is how Philip Morris keeps its earnings growing even as tobacco sales simmer.

EARNINGS GROWTH

The company has had excellent growth the past five years, with an increase in earnings per share of 249 percent for the period, 28 percent per year.

Philip Morris reported total revenue of $44.7 billion in 1989.

STOCK GROWTH

The company's stock price has climbed rapidly the past five years, increasing 311 percent for the period—33 percent per year.

Including reinvested dividends, a $10,000 investment in Philip Morris stock in 1984 would have grown to about $48,000 five years later. Average annual compounded rate of return (including stock growth and reinvested dividends): about 37 percent.

DIVIDEND YIELD

The company generally pays a very good yield, which has averaged just over 4 percent over the past five years. During the most recent two-year rating period (1988 and 1989), the stock paid an average annual current return (dividend yield) of 4 percent.

DIVIDEND GROWTH

Philip Morris has raised its dividend 25 times in the last 22 years. The dividend rose 190 percent (24 percent per year) over the five-year period from 1984 to 1989.

CONSISTENCY

With 35 consecutive years of record earnings, Philip Morris has been one of the most consistent companies in America. The firm's price-earnings ratio of 10 to 12 is consistent with other U.S. tobacco companies.

MOMENTUM

How long can Philip Morris continue to increase its profits in the face of ever-mounting opposition to cigarettes? Since 1971 when cigarette ads were banned from TV, the company has continued to rack up year after year of record earnings. With increased pressure on restricting cigarettes in offices and public places, and with new measures pending that could put cigarette vending machines out of business, the tobacco industry could face further erosion in cigarette sales. But tobacco companies have been down this road before, and they've always survived by keeping cigarette prices rising. Expect more of the same in the future. For the near term, at least, Philip Morris shows no signs of burning out.

SUMMARY

Fiscal year ended: Dec. 31
(U.S. dollars; revenue and operating income in millions)

	1990*	1989	1988	1987	1986	1985	1984	5-year growth, %† (annual/total)
Revenue	—	44,759	31,742	28,183	25,883	16,267	14,102	26/217
Operating income	—	6,789	4,397	3,990	3,537	2,664	1,908	29/255
Earnings/share	—	3.18	2.51	1.94	1.55	1.31	0.91	28/249
Dividend/share	1.37	1.25	1.01	0.79	0.62	0.50	0.43	24/190
Dividend yield, %	3.3	3.5	4.5	3.4	3.8	4.8	4.7	—/—
Stock price	42.00	41.62	25.50	21.37	18.00	11.00	10.12	33/311
P/E ratio	12.0	11.7	10.3	11.8	10.6	8.2	8.5	—/—
Book value/share	—	10.35	8.30	7.20	5.95	4.95	4.20	20/144

*5-1-90
† 1984-89
Source: Company sources.

Note: Stock price quoted in *Barron's,* the *Wall Street Journal* and the *European Wall Street Journal.*

10

MIRRO·FOLEY
WEAREVER·REMA
AMEROCK·COUNSELOR
ANCHOR HOCKING GLASS
EZ PAINTR·BERNZOMATIC
BULLDOG·DORFILE
ANCHOR HOCKING PLASTICS
NEWELL WINDOW FURNISHINGS

The newell group ™

NEWELL CO.

29 East Stephenson Street
Freeport, IL 61032
Tel: (815) 235-4171
Chairman: William R. Cuthbert
Vice-Chairman and CEO: Daniel C. Ferguson
President and COO: William P. Sovey

EARNINGS GROWTH	★ ★ ★ ★
STOCK GROWTH	★ ★ ★ ★
DIVIDEND YIELD	★ ★
DIVIDEND GROWTH	★ ★ ★ ★
CONSISTENCY	★ ★ ★ ★
MOMENTUM	★ ★ ★ ★
NYSE	**22 points**

For most of its history, Newell has envisioned a future of maturing baby boomers, buying homes and pouring their dollars into housewares and do-it-yourself hardware. Now, for Newell, the future—and the do-it-yourself generation—has arrived. And so has Newell.

Over the past five years, the Freeport, Illinois, manufacturer has been one of the fastest-growing companies in the world. Its operating earnings have increased, on average, 34 percent per year during the five-year period. Over the past 20 years, the company has increased its annual sales from $30 million to $1.1 billion.

Newell operates in two market segments, hardware and houseware products (72 percent of sales) and industrial products (28 percent of sales), which includes packaging, plastic and glass products. Anchor-Hocking, the glassware, cookware and plastics manufacturer that Newell acquired in 1987, accounts for most of the sales in the company's industrial products segment.

Newell owns a wide range of consumer houseware brands sold in major retail stores such as Wal-Mart, K Mart, Target and Sears. Among its product lines, in addition to Newell and Anchor-Hocking, are Foley and Mirro cookware, Amerock cabinet hardware, window and bath hardware, BernzOmatic

315

and Surefire hand torches, WearEver pots and pans, Bulldog hardware and EZ Paintr.

Within its hardware and houseware division, cabinet and window hardware accounts for about 24 percent of sales, and cookware and bakeware account for 21 percent. The other 55 percent is divided among glassware, window furnishings, paints and other hardware and houseware products.

Newell's industrial products division produces packaging materials primarily for the foods and consumer goods industry, glass containers, a line of disposable and reusable food service items and metal, plastic and composite packaging closures.

EARNINGS GROWTH

The company has had exceptional growth the past few years. Its earnings per share increased 244 percent over the past five years, 28 percent per year.

Newell reported total revenue of $1.1 billion in 1989.

STOCK GROWTH

The company has also had exceptional stock price appreciation the past five years. The stock soared 375 percent during the period, 37 percent per year.

Including reinvested dividends, a $10,000 investment in Newell stock at its median price in 1984 would have grown to about $53,000 five years later. Average annual compounded rate of return (including stock growth and reinvested dividends): about 40 percent.

DIVIDEND YIELD

The company generally pays a fairly good yield, which has averaged just under 3 percent over the past five years. During the most recent two-year rating period (1988 and 1989), the stock paid an average annual current return (dividend yield) of 2.4 percent.

DIVIDEND GROWTH

Newell traditionally raises its dividend each year. The dividend rose 230 percent (27 percent per year) over the five-year period from 1984 to 1989.

CONSISTENCY

The company has had a flawless run of growth the past few years in all of its financial categories, earnings per share, revenues, operating income and book value per share. Its 1989 price-earnings ratio of about 14 is very favorable for a fast-growing company.

MOMENTUM

Newell has picked up the pace of its growth the past two years. Its earnings per share increased 46 percent in 1988 and 40 percent in 1989. Its book value per share jumped 73 percent in 1989.

SUMMARY

Fiscal year ended: Dec. 31
(U.S. dollars; revenue and operating income in millions)

	1990*	1989	1988	1987	1986	1985	1984	5-year growth, %† (annual/total)
Revenue	—	1,123	988	719	401	350	308	30/268
Operating income	—	170	160	103	57	44	39	34/330
Earnings/share	—	1.41	1.01	0.69	0.55	0.52	0.41	28/244
Dividend/share	0.50	0.43	0.28	0.21	0.19	0.13	0.13	27/230
Dividend yield, %	1.9	2.2	2.5	2.5	2.6	3.0	3.3	—/—
Stock price[1]	26.00	19.00	12.00	8.00	7.00	7.00	4.00	37/375
P/E ratio	18.0	14.0	10.0	12.0	13.0	8.0	9.0	—/—
Book value/share	—	9.20	5.30	4.70	4.00	3.05	2.65	28/244

*5–1–90
† 1984–89
1. Average stock price
Source: Company sources.

Note: Stock price quoted in *Barron's*, the *Wall Street Journal* and the *European Wall Street Journal*.

12

MERCK & CO., INC.

126 East Lincoln Ave.
P.O. Box 2000
Rahway, NJ 07065-0909
Tel: (201) 594-4000
Chairman, President and CEO: P. Roy Vagelos

EARNINGS GROWTH	★ ★ ★ ★
STOCK GROWTH	★ ★ ★ ★
DIVIDEND YIELD	★ ★
DIVIDEND GROWTH	★ ★ ★ ★
CONSISTENCY	★ ★ ★ ★
MOMENTUM	★ ★ ★ ★
NYSE	**22 points**

Over the years, Merck & Co. has developed medications for everything from swollen prostates to dry-eye syndrome. In all, it produces about 150 different medications and vaccines. But the heart of Merck's operation, its principal focus both financially and scientifically, has been finding new ways to keep the human heart beating.

Merck is America's largest pharmaceutical producer and unequivocally its most celebrated. It has been *Fortune's* "Most Admired Company" four years running and *Forbes's* "most innovative pharmaceutical company." It has made lists for being among the "best managed" *(Business Week* and *Business Month)*, "best for working women" *(New Woman),* "best for black employees" *(Black Enterprise)* and "best in public service" *(Business Week).*

Merck has operations in about 20 countries and sells its products in over 100 countries. Roughly half of its $6.6 billion in annual revenue comes from foreign sales.

Among the company's pharmaceutical sales, heart-related medications constitute its largest profit center, accounting for 34 percent of total revenue. Its leading drug is Vasotec, a blood pressure medication that has been one of the world's hottest sellers, with revenues of about $1 billion a year. The company reports that Vasotec is the only drug in its class proven to reduce the death rate of patients with severe heart failure.

Mevacor, a cholesterol-lowering medication, has also been a leading seller for Merck, setting a U.S. sales record for new drugs the year it was released in 1987. A single daily dose of Mevacor reportedly helps normalize cholesterol levels even among patients with extremely high levels. The company says the development of Mevacor came after 35 years of study and testing. The drug was named one of *Fortune* magazine's "products of the year" in 1987.

In addition to its list of successful cardiovascular-related medications, Merck has also developed some leading prescription drugs in several other fields. Antibiotics account for 15 percent of the company's revenues, antiinflammatories account for 14 percent, ophthalmologicals (eye treatments) account for 7 percent and ulcer medications and vaccines account for about 5 percent each.

Merck has also been on the leading edge of AIDS research.

In addition to its human health focus, the company has a strong interest in animal medications (9 percent of revenues) and specialty chemicals for water treatment, oil field drilling, food processing, cleaning, disinfecting and skin care (8 percent of revenue).

One of the keys to Merck's success has been its outstanding research program. The company employs about 5,000 people in research activities and spends about $750 million a year in research and development.

EARNINGS GROWTH

The company has had excellent growth the past few years. Its earnings per share increased 237 percent over the past five years, 27 percent per year.

Merck reported total revenue of $6.55 billion in 1989. The company has 32,000 employees.

STOCK GROWTH

The company's stock price has moved up very quickly the past five years, increasing 293 percent for the period—32 percent per year.

Including reinvested dividends, a $10,000 investment in Merck stock at its median price in 1984 would have grown to about $43,000 five years later. Average annual compounded rate of return (including stock growth and reinvested dividends): about 34 percent.

DIVIDEND YIELD

The company generally pays a fairly good yield, which has averaged about 2.5 percent over the past five years. During the most recent two-year rating

period (1988 and 1989), the stock paid an average annual current return (dividend yield) of 2.3 percent.

DIVIDEND GROWTH

Merck traditionally raises its dividend every year. The dividend increased 228 percent (27 percent per year) over the five-year period from 1984 to 1989.

CONSISTENCY

The company has had very consistent growth in its earnings per share, revenues, operating income and book value per share. Its price-earnings ratio of about 19 is consistent with other quickly growing U.S. companies.

MOMENTUM

Merck has continued to maintain a strong pace of growth the past couple of years. Its earnings per share rose 37 percent in 1988 and 24 percent in 1989.

SUMMARY

Fiscal year ended: Dec. 31
(U.S. dollars; revenue and operating income in millions)

	1990*	1989	1988	1987	1986	1985	1984	5-year growth, %† (annual/total)
Revenue	—	6,550	5,939	5,061	4,128	3,547	3,559	13/84
Operating income	—	—	2,072	1,579	1,235	1,022	964	—/—
Earnings/share	—	3.78	3.05	2.23	1.62	1.26	1.12	27/237
Dividend/share	1.80	1.64	1.28	0.82	0.63	0.53	0.50	27/228
Dividend yield, %	2.5	2.3	2.3	1.5	2.0	2.9	3.4	—/—
Stock price¹	73.25	59.00	54.00	58.00	33.00	19.00	15.00	32/293
P/E ratio	19.0	18.5	18.0	25.2	19.8	14.5	13.2	—/—
Book value/share	—	9.50	7.25	5.40	6.30	6.25	5.90	10/59

*5–1–90
† 1984–89
1. Average stock price
Source: Company sources.

Note: Stock price quoted in *Barron's,* the *Wall Street Journal* and the *European Wall Street Journal.*

18

WM. WRIGLEY JR. COMPANY

410 North Michigan Avenue
Chicago, IL 60611
Tel: (312) 644-2121
President and CEO: William Wrigley

EARNINGS GROWTH	★ ★ ★
STOCK GROWTH	★ ★ ★ ★
DIVIDEND YIELD	★ ★ ★
DIVIDEND GROWTH	★ ★ ★
CONSISTENCY	★ ★ ★ ★
MOMENTUM	★ ★ ★ ★
NYSE	**21 points**

Here's a thought to chew over: the William Wrigley Jr. Company sells but a single product, gum, and that lone product is in a very mature market. So how does Wrigley manage to keep wringing out rising revenues and profits year after year?

Over the past five years, the Chicago gum maker has increased its earnings per share an average of 24 percent per year and has provided a return to its shareholders (including dividend and stock price increases) of about 35 percent per year.

Wrigley is the world's largest gum manufacturer. It sells its gum in more than 100 countries. European sales make up about 20 percent of total revenue, other foreign sales account for about 15 percent and U.S. sales comprise about 65 percent. An estimated 47 percent of all gum chewed in the United States is produced by Wrigley.

Part of Wrigley's success has come through product-line expansion. Over the past several years, the company has added about 15 new brands and flavors to its longstanding favorites. For most of the company's 98-year history, Wrigley was known for its Juicy Fruit, Spearmint, Doublemint and Big Red gums.

Now the company offers Freedent (spearmint, peppermint, icemint and cinnamon), Extra (bubble, spearmint, peppermint, cinnamon and wintergreen), Hubba Bubba (original, cola, strawberry, raspberry, blueberry, grape) and Sugarfree Hubba Bubba (original and grape). The company's Extra gum is the top-selling sugarless gum in the U.S. market.

Wrigley also owns Amurol Products, which manufactures children's novelty bubble gum and other confectionery products, including Big League Chew and baseball trading cards. One of the company's newest offerings, Bubble Tape, has been a growing favorite in the bubblegum market.

EARNINGS GROWTH

The company has had excellent growth the past few years. Its earnings per share increased 190 percent over the past five years, 24 percent per year.

Wrigley reported total revenue of $992 million in 1989. The company has about 5,000 employees.

STOCK GROWTH

The company's stock price has moved up very quickly the past five years, increasing 400 percent for the period—32 percent per year.

Including reinvested dividends, a $10,000 investment in Wrigley stock at its median price in 1984 would have grown to about $45,000 five years later. Average annual compounded rate of return (including stock growth and reinvested dividends): about 35 percent.

DIVIDEND YIELD

The company generally pays a good yield, which has averaged about 3.5 percent over the past five years. During the most recent two-year rating period (1988 and 1989), the stock paid an average annual current return (dividend yield) of 3.1 percent.

DIVIDEND GROWTH

Wrigley traditionally raises its dividend every year. The dividend increased 189 percent (23 percent per year) over the five-year period from 1984 to 1989.

CONSISTENCY

The company has had very consistent growth in its earnings per share, revenues, operating income and book value per share. Its 1989 price-earnings ratio of about 16 is consistent with other quickly growing U.S. companies.

MOMENTUM

Wrigley has had excellent growth the past two years. Its earnings per share increased 29 percent in 1988 and 24 percent in 1989.

SUMMARY

Fiscal year ended: Dec. 31
(U.S. dollars; revenue and operating income in millions)

	1990*	1989	1988	1987	1986	1985	1984	5-year growth, %† (annual/total)
Revenue	—	992	891	781	699	620	590	11/68
Operating income	—	178	153	136	115	91	81	17/119
Earnings/share	—	2.70	2.18	1.69	1.28	1.03	0.93	24/190
Dividend/share	—	1.36	1.09	0.85	0.64	0.52	0.47	23/189
Dividend yield, %	3.5	3.1	3.0	3.1	3.1	4.3	5.3	—/—
Stock price	52.25	45.00	37.00	28.00	20.00	13.00	9.00	32/400
P/E ratio	19.0	16.0	16.0	16.0	16.0	11.0	9.0	—/—
Book value/share	—	9.25	7.77	7.18	6.93	6.13	5.43	11/70

*5–1–90
† 1984–89
Source: Company sources.

Note: Stock price quoted in *Barron's,* the *Wall Street Journal* and the *European Wall Street Journal.*

21
WAL-MART

WAL-MART STORES, INC.

702 S.W. 8th St.
Bentonville, AR 72716-0112
Tel: (501) 273-4000
Chairman: Sam M. Walton
President and CEO: David D. Glass

EARNINGS GROWTH	★ ★ ★ ★
STOCK GROWTH	★ ★ ★ ★
DIVIDEND YIELD	★
DIVIDEND GROWTH	★ ★ ★ ★
CONSISTENCY	★ ★ ★ ★
MOMENTUM	★ ★ ★ ★
NYSE	**21 points**

Attention shoppers: Wal-Mart is coming to town.

For most of its incredibly successful 26-year history, Wal-Mart stores have avoided the major markets, settling instead on smaller, less competitive rural markets. Most of the company's 1,300 stores are located in towns such as Rogers, Arkansas; Grapevine, Texas; and Blue Earth, Minnesota.

But now that Wal-Mart has begun to saturate America's heartland, it is beginning to take aim at the major markets. That's good news for urban area shoppers, bad news for Sears, K Mart, Target and Wal-Mart's other discount competitors.

Wal-Mart has been America's fastest-growing, most profitable department store almost since its inception in 1962. The company has never had a year in which it didn't set new records for sales and earnings.

Wal-Mart opens a new store, on average, about every three days. In 1980 there were 330 Wal-Mart stores in 11 states. Now the 1,300-store chain stretches through 25 states. And the company has begun breaking with tradition by adding stores in some major metropolitan areas.

Aside from their rural locations, Wal-Mart stores are much the same as any other discount department store. The corporate formula calls for each store to be divided into 36 departments, including apparel, housewares, hardware, appliances, automotive accessories, cameras, toys, sporting goods, health and beauty aids, jewelry and a variety of other merchandise.

The company achieved its early success largely by opening stores in locations where there was little competition from other discounters. It buys its merchandise in large volume, and, through discount pricing, turns it over quickly, incurring a minimum of overhead in the process. It adheres to a concept of "everyday low prices." While its competitors typically run 50 to 100 advertising circulars a year, Wal-Mart publishes only 12 per year.

The first Wal-Mart store (called Wal-Mart Discount City) was opened in Rogers, Arkansas, in 1962 by Samuel M. Walton. By the time he opened his first Wal-Mart, Mr. Walton was already well-schooled in the art of operating discount department stores. His original foray into retailing came in 1945, when he opened a Ben Franklin variety store franchise in Newport, Arkansas. He's been in the discount retailing business ever since and still serves as Wal-Mart's chairman of the board. Mr. Walton is reported to be one of the richest men in America.

In addition to its namesake stores, Wal-Mart also operates 105 Sam's Wholesale Club stores, which tend to be located in larger metropolitan markets; 14 dot Discount Drug stores, 3 Hypermart * USA stores, which are essentially expanded versions of Wal-Mart that include both groceries and general merchandise; and 2 Wal-Mart Supercenters, which also include general merchandise and groceries.

EARNINGS GROWTH

The company has had outstanding growth the past few years. Its earnings per share was up 322 percent over the past five years, 33 percent per year.

Wal-Mart reported total revenue of $21 billion in 1989.

STOCK GROWTH

The company's stock price has jumped 270 percent the past five years, 30 percent per year.

Including reinvested dividends, a $10,000 investment in Wal-Mart stock at its median price in 1984 would have grown to about $38,000 five years later. Average annual compounded rate of return (including stock growth and reinvested dividends): about 30.5 percent.

DIVIDEND YIELD

The company generally pays a very modest yield, which has averaged about 0.5 percent over the past five years. During the most recent two-year rating period (1989 and 1990), the stock paid an average annual current return (dividend yield) of 0.55 percent.

DIVIDEND GROWTH

Wal-Mart traditionally raises its dividend every year. The dividend increased 300 percent (32 percent per year) over the five-year period from 1984 to 1989.

CONSISTENCY

The company has had a flawless record of growth in its earnings per share, revenues, operating income and book value per share for many years. Its price-earnings ratio of about 28 is high for a U.S. company but should be no problem if Wal-Mart continues its impressive growth.

MOMENTUM

Hard as it may be to believe, Wal-Mart still hasn't lost a step. The company's earnings per share jumped 39 percent in 1988 and 33 percent in 1989.

SUMMARY

Fiscal year ended: Jan. 31
(U.S. dollars; revenue and operating income in millions)

	1990*	1989	1988	1987	1986	1985	1984	5-year growth, %† (annual/total)
Revenue	—	20,649	15,959	11,909	8,451	6,400	4,666	35/342
Operating income	—	1,540[1]	1,240	972	695	563	405	30/280
Earnings/share	—	1.48	1.11	0.80	0.58	0.48	0.35	33/322
Dividend/share	0.28	0.16	0.12	0.09	0.07	0.05	0.04	32/300
Dividend yield, %	0.6	0.5	0.4	0.4	0.5	0.5	0.4	—/—
Stock price	49.62	37.00[2]	30.00	31.00	21.00	13.00	10.00	30/270
P/E ratio	27.0	28.0	27.0	28.0	22.0	20.0	26.0	—/—
Book value/share	—	5.30	4.00	3.00	2.25	1.75	1.30	32/303

*5-1-90
† 1984-89
1. Estimated
2. Calendar year
Source: Company sources.

Note: Stock price quoted in *Barron's,* the *Wall Street Journal* and the *European Wall Street Journal.*

26
✸ Shaw Industries, Inc.

SHAW INDUSTRIES, INC.

P.O. Drawer 2128
Dalton, GA 30722-2128
Tel: (404) 278-3812
Chairman: J.C. Shaw
President and CEO: Robert E. Shaw

EARNINGS GROWTH	★ ★
STOCK GROWTH	★ ★ ★ ★
DIVIDEND YIELD	★ ★ ★
DIVIDEND GROWTH	★ ★ ★ ★
CONSISTENCY	★ ★ ★
MOMENTUM	★ ★ ★ ★
NYSE	**20 points**

In an era of rampant diversification, carpet-maker Shaw Industries is one company that has stuck to its knitting. Carpet is not only Shaw's principal business, it's its only business. It is also big business. With annual sales of over $1 billion, the Dalton, Georgia-based operation is the nation's leading carpet manufacturer.

Shaw Industries is a relatively young company, formed in 1967 by brothers J.C. and Robert E. Shaw. The brothers, now in their late 50s, still serve as chairman and president, respectively, and control about 16 percent of the company's stock.

Over its 23-year history, Shaw has enjoyed spectacular success. During the past 10 years, the company's earnings per share have increased about 700 percent.

Shaw's carpeting is marketed under the Magee, Philadelphia, Cabin Crafts and Stratton labels, as well as some private labels for distributors and retailers. The company sells carpeting through about 25,000 retail stores and 150 wholesale distributors in the United States. It also claims some foreign sales, although its foreign business accounts for less than 1 percent of the company's total revenue.

Like 95 percent of the U.S. carpeting industry, Shaw makes "tufted" carpet from nylon yarn. Shaw is vertically integrated, handling every step of the carpet-making process: spinning the fiber, dyeing it, weaving the rug and cutting it to size. In all, Shaw makes about 500 styles of tufted carpet for residential and commercial customers.

A couple of other factors have helped Shaw rise to the top of the carpet industry over its roughly 250 U.S. competitors. Through its rather aggressive acquisitions program, the company has been able to bring some of the best-known carpet brands into its fold. By integrating those operations and marketing them through one sales force, it has been able to reduce overhead and sales costs. It also attempts to provide more efficient and timely distribution through its 11 regional distribution centers.

EARNINGS GROWTH

The company has had strong growth the past few years. Its earnings per share increased 130 percent over the past five years, 18 percent per year.

Shaw reported total revenue of $1.2 billion in 1989. The company has 5,000 employees.

STOCK GROWTH

The company's stock price has jumped 450 percent over the past five years, 41 percent per year.

Including reinvested dividends, a $10,000 investment in Shaw stock at its median price in 1984 would have grown to about $61,000 five years later. Average annual compounded rate of return (including stock growth and reinvested dividends): about 44 percent.

DIVIDEND YIELD

The company generally pays a good yield, which has averaged under 3 percent over the past five years. During the most recent two-year rating period (1988 and 1989), the stock paid an average annual current return (dividend yield) of 2.9 percent.

DIVIDEND GROWTH

Shaw traditionally raises its dividend every year. The dividend rose 208 percent (25 percent per year) over the five-year period from 1984 to 1989.

CONSISTENCY

The company has had fairly consistent growth in all of its key financial areas, although it did have a dip in earnings per share and operating earnings in 1986. Its price-earnings ratio of about 16 is favorable for a growing U.S. company.

MOMENTUM

Shaw has had excellent growth the past two years. Its earnings per share increased 26 percent in 1988 and 47 percent in 1989.

SUMMARY

Fiscal year ended: June 30
(U.S. dollars; revenue and operating income in millions)

	1990*	1989	1988	1987	1986	1985	1984	5-year growth, %†(annual/total)
Revenue	—	1,176	958	694	550	519	454	21/159
Operating income	—	138	106	86	66	68	57	19/142
Earnings/share	—	1.57	1.07	0.85	0.71	0.76	0.68	18/130
Dividend/share	0.50	0.37	0.32	0.25	0.17	0.14	0.12	25/208
Dividend yield, %	1.6	2.6	3.2	2.3	2.3	2.8	2.7	—/—
Stock price[1]	31.75	22.00	10.00	11.00	9.00	6.00	4.00	41/450
P/E ratio	16.0	16.0	9.0	12.0	10.0	6.0	6.0	—/—
Book value/share	—	6.15	5.10	4.60	4.15	3.50	2.90	16/110

*5–1–90
† 1984–89
1. Average stock price for calendar year
Source: Company sources.

Note: Stock price quoted in *Barron's,* the *Wall Street Journal* and the *European Wall Street Journal.*

³² Torchmark Corporation

TORCHMARK CORPORATION

2001 Third Avenue South
Birmingham, AL 35233
Tel: (205) 325-4200
Chairman and CEO: R. K. Richey
President: Jon W. Rotenstreich

EARNINGS GROWTH	★ ★ ★
STOCK GROWTH	★ ★ ★ ★
DIVIDEND YIELD	★ ★ ★
DIVIDEND GROWTH	★ ★ ★
CONSISTENCY	★ ★ ★ ★
MOMENTUM	★ ★ ★
NYSE	**20 points**

In a decade that was among the most turbulent ever in the financial services industry, Torchmark never missed a beat. The Birmingham-based parent company of Liberty National Life Insurance Co. and Waddell & Reed financial services has been the best performing company in the American financial services sector, compiling a remarkable string of 38 consecutive years of record earnings.

Liberty National is the largest of Torchmark's small battery of insurance companies, with $20 billion of life insurance in force and annual total premiums of more than $400 million. The company employs 2,500 agents in 101 sales offices throughout the Southeast and sells a complete line of life and health insurance and annuity policies.

Liberty's casualty insurance arm, Liberty National Fire, offers a range of fire, property and casualty insurance for individuals and businesses.

Waddell & Reed (which is a branch of United Investors Management Company, a Torchmark subsidiary) offers financial planning services for individual investors and investment management services for large institutional investors. The company manages 16 mutual funds, with assets of $7.5 billion, and offers a number of other investment products.

Waddell & Reed (W&R) has 3,500 financial services representatives in 190 offices across all 50 states. They serve 900,000 customers nationwide. In addition to mutual funds and financial planning assistance, W&R reps sell life and health insurance policies from another Torchmark subsidiary, United Investors Life, and oil and gas limited partnerships managed by another subsidiary, Torch Energy.

W&R's sales force attracts its client base, in large part, through public seminars on money management aimed at individual investors. The company's representatives conduct nearly 4,000 seminars a year, which draw, in total, about 100,000 prospective clients.

Torchmark's other two major subsidiaries are United American Insurance, which sells Medicare supplement insurance through some 61,000 independent agents nationwide, and Globe Life and Accident Insurance, which markets health insurance through 1,400 agents in 76 branch offices. Globe also sells life insurance through 300 agents.

EARNINGS GROWTH

The company has had steady, solid growth the past few years. Its earnings per share increased 145 percent over the past five years, 20 percent per year.

Torchmark reported total revenue of $1.6 billion in 1989.

STOCK GROWTH

The company's stock price has moved up quickly the past five years, increasing 238 percent for the period—28 percent per year.

Including reinvested dividends, a $10,000 investment in Torchmark stock at its median price in 1984 would have grown to about $39,000 five years later. Average annual compounded rate of return (including stock growth and reinvested dividends): about 31 percent.

DIVIDEND YIELD

The company generally pays a good yield, which has averaged just over 3 percent over the past five years. During the most recent two-year rating period (1988 and 1989), the stock paid an average annual current return (dividend yield) of 3.4 percent.

DIVIDEND GROWTH

Torchmark traditionally raises its dividend every year. The dividend grew 160 percent (21 percent per year) over the five-year period from 1984 to 1989.

CONSISTENCY

The company has had very consistent growth in its earnings per share and revenues, including 38 consecutive years of record earnings. Its price-earnings ratio of about 10 is a very attractive level for a growing company.

MOMENTUM

Torchmark still appears to be on the fast track. Its earnings per share increased 14 percent in 1988 and 21 percent in 1989.

SUMMARY

Fiscal year ended: Dec. 31
(U.S. dollars; revenue and net income in millions)

	1990*	1989	1988	1987	1986	1985	1984	5-year growth, %† (annual/total)
Revenue	—	1,633	1,611	1,532	1,458	1,296	1,097	8/48
Operating income[1]	—	211	182	201	205	165	168	5/25
Earnings/share	—	3.88	3.20	2.80	2.64	2.17	1.58	20/145
Dividend/share	1.40	1.25	1.15	1.00	0.90	0.55	0.48	21/160
Dividend yield, %	3.2	3.0	3.8	3.5	3.0	2.5	3.9	—/—
Stock price[2]	43.62	44.00	29.00	29.00	30.00	21.00	13.00	28/238
P/E ratio	10.0	10.0	9.5	10.0	11.0	10.0	8.0	—/—
Book value/share	—	15.10	13.25	13.50	12.50	12.30	10.40	8/45

*5-1-90
† 1984-89
1. Net income is given here.
2. Average stock price given.
Source: Company sources.

Note: Stock price quoted in *Barron's,* the *Wall Street Journal* and the *European Wall Street Journal.*

39

WASTE MANAGEMENT, INC.

3003 Butterfield Road
Oak Brook, IL 60521
Tel: (708) 572-8800
Chairman and CEO: Dean L. Buntrock
President: Phillip B. Rooney

EARNINGS GROWTH	★ ★ ★ ★
STOCK GROWTH	★ ★ ★ ★
DIVIDEND YIELD	★
DIVIDEND GROWTH	★ ★ ★
CONSISTENCY	★ ★ ★ ★
MOMENTUM	★ ★ ★
NYSE	**19 points**

The smell of money can at times take on a very earthy, even pungent air. But Waste Management, Inc., whose very name has become synonymous with the gritty yet gainful business of waste control, learned long ago that a dollar by any other smell is just as sweet.

The Chicago-based waste treatment company has carved out its niche amidst slime, sludge, toxic chemicals and low-grade nuclear wastes. In the process, it has become one of the most profitable corporations in American industry.

The company has increased its earnings and revenues every year since it went public in 1971. Over the past five years, shareholders have received an average annual return on investment of about 43 percent.

Waste Management is the largest provider of solid and hazardous waste management and recycling services in the world. It has over 450 subsidiaries and divisions in North America and a dozen more overseas. It manages 125 landfills in the United States, with more under development, and provides trash collection services for 8 million homes and apartments and 700,000 commercial and industrial customers.

The company's recently launched Recycle America program now serves over a million households in 130 North American cities.

Waste Management has also been making swift progress in its waste-to-energy program. The company has about a dozen facilities in operation that convert landfill gases to electrical energy, with several more facilities now under construction. In all, the company's operating facilities provide the energy equivalent of about 2 million barrels of oil a year.

Through its Chemical Waste Management subsidiary (of which Waste Management owns 78 percent), the company provides disposal and treatment of hazardous chemical wastes and low-level radioactive wastes. Its Chem-Nuclear Systems subsidiary is the largest provider of low-level radioactive waste management services in the United States.

Waste Management has also made major inroads into the medical waste business through its Medical Services subsidiary. The company operates nine medical waste incinerators.

The firm is also involved in several related ventures. It provides street-sweeping services for municipal and commercial customers, operates municipal water and waste water treatment plants, markets Port-O-Let portable lavatories and has built a thriving business in lawn care and pest control through the acquisition of several small regional firms.

Waste Management has expanded its solid waste services beyond North America with several key acquisitions in Europe in 1989. The firm also has operations in Argentina, Australia, New Zealand and Saudi Arabia.

EARNINGS GROWTH

The company has had excellent growth the past few years. Its earnings per share increased 229 percent over the past five years, 27 percent per year.

Waste Management reported total revenue of $4.5 billion in 1989.

STOCK GROWTH

The company's stock price has soared the past five years, increasing 460 percent for the period—42 percent per year.

Including reinvested dividends, a $10,000 investment in Waste Management stock at its median price in 1984 would have grown to about $60,000 five years later. Average annual compounded rate of return (including stock growth and reinvested dividends): about 43 percent.

DIVIDEND YIELD

The company generally pays a modest yield, which has averaged just over 1 percent over the past five years. During the most recent two-year rating period (1988 and 1989), the stock paid an average annual current return (dividend yield) of 1.1 percent.

DIVIDEND GROWTH

Waste Management traditionally raises its dividend every year. The dividend increased 170 percent (22 percent per year) over the five-year period from 1984 to 1989.

CONSISTENCY

The company has had very consistent growth in its earnings per share, revenues, operating income and book value per share. Its price-earnings ratio of about 28 is quite high for U.S. companies but should not be a factor if the company continues its strong growth.

MOMENTUM

Waste Management has had excellent growth the past two years. Its earnings per share increased 41 percent in 1988 and 18 percent in 1989, well in line with its five-year average.

SUMMARY

Fiscal year ended: Dec. 31
(U.S. dollars; revenue and operating income in millions)

	1990*	1989	1988	1987	1986	1985	1984	5-year growth, %† (annual/total)
Revenue	—	4,459	3,565	2,757	2,017	1,625	1,314	28/239
Operating income	—	1,365²	1,109	876	559	518	388	29/251²
Earnings/share	—	1.22	1.03	0.73	0.53	0.43	0.37	27/229
Dividend/share	0.32	0.27	0.23	0.18	0.14	0.11	0.10	22/170
Dividend yield, %	0.9	1.0	1.2	0.9	1.1	1.6	2.1	—/—
Stock price¹	36.10	28.00	19.00	19.00	12.00	7.00	5.00	42/460
P/E ratio	28.0	22.0	18.0	26.0	22.0	16.0	12.0	—/—
Book value/share	—	5.75	4.82	4.16	3.67	2.79	2.27	20/153

*5-1-90
† 1984-89
1. Average stock price.
2. Estimated.
Source: Company sources.

Note: Stock price quoted in *Barron's,* the *Wall Street Journal* and the *European Wall Street Journal.*

BROWNING-FERRIS INDUSTRIES, INC.

Browning-Ferris Building
757 N. Eldridge
P.O. Box 3151
Houston, TX 77079
Tel: (713) 870-8100
Chairman and CEO: William D. Ruckelshaus
President and COO: John E. Drury

EARNINGS GROWTH	★ ★ ★
STOCK GROWTH	★ ★ ★ ★
DIVIDEND YIELD	★ ★
DIVIDEND GROWTH	★ ★
CONSISTENCY	★ ★ ★ ★
MOMENTUM	★ ★ ★
NYSE	**18 points**

Somewhere in a world swimming in plastic wrappers, disposable diapers and industrial toxins a very lucrative profit opportunity exists—a fact underscored by Browning-Ferris's bulging balance sheet. The nation's second largest waste management operation has enjoyed many years of increased earnings and has provided its shareholders with an average return on investment of 33 percent per year over the past five years.

And it's still growing quickly. In 1989 alone, the Houston-based company acquired more than 80 smaller refuse collection companies in the United States and 18 waste management companies abroad.

Browning-Ferris (BFI) provides waste collection and disposal services for homes, businesses and factories in 600 communities in 43 states—plus operations in Canada and several other countries. It operates 105 solid waste landfills and manages hazardous waste disposal sites in several states. In all, it provides solid waste disposal service for 5.4 million U.S. households and 622,000 commercial and industrial customers.

The company's commercial and industrial solid waste business accounts for 58 percent of its revenue, its residential service accounts for 16 percent of revenue, solid waste processing and disposal brings in another 16 percent of revenue and special services account for 8 percent of the company's revenue.

BFI has made major inroads into the nation's growing recycling trade. The company operates 130 curbside collection programs, serving nearly a million households. It also serves a number of commercial and industrial customers and operates 34 recycling centers.

Among its other more successful specialized services is Medical Waste Systems, which operates 23 processing sites, including 18 incinerators. It serves medical clients in 42 states plus Canada.

BFI is also expanding its recently established garbage-to-energy "resource recovery" services. American Ref-Fuel Company, which BFI owns jointly with Air Products and Chemicals, Inc., has a new facility in Long Island, New York, that burns 2,300 tons of garbage a day to generate electricity.

The company has two other similar facilities under construction, two more under contract and two more in the planning stages. Construction costs range from $100 million to $350 million per plant, with plant capacities of 600 to 3,000 tons per day.

Browning-Ferris also has subsidiaries involved in street and parking lot sweeping, portable restroom rental and bus and van transportation services.

EARNINGS GROWTH

The company has had 14 consecutive years of record earnings. Its earnings per share increased 155 percent over the past five years, 21 percent per year.

BFI reported total revenue of $2.6 billion in 1989. It has 26,000 employees.

STOCK GROWTH

The company's stock price has increased quickly the past five years, advancing 288 percent for the period—31 percent per year.

Including reinvested dividends, a $10,000 investment in BFI stock at its median price in 1984 would have grown to about $42,000 five years later. Average annual compounded rate of return (including stock growth and reinvested dividends): about 33 percent.

DIVIDEND YIELD

The company generally pays a modest yield, which has averaged about 2 percent over the past five years. During the most recent two-year rating period (1988 and 1989), the stock paid an average annual current return (dividend yield) of 1.9 percent.

DIVIDEND GROWTH

BFI traditionally raises its dividend every year. The dividend increased 133 percent (18 percent per year) over the five-year period from 1984 to 1989.

CONSISTENCY

Over the past five years, the company has had a flawless record of growth in its earnings per share, revenues, operating income and book value per share. Its price-earnings ratio of about 18 is about average for a growing American company.

MOMENTUM

BFI is still climbing quickly in revenues and operating income, although its 15 percent increase in earnings per share in 1989 was somewhat below its five-year average.

SUMMARY

Fiscal year ended: Sept. 30
(U.S. dollars; revenue and operating income in millions)

	1990*	1989	1988	1987	1986	1985	1984	5-year growth, %† (annual/total)
Revenue	—	2,550	2,067	1,656	1,328	1,144	1,000	21/155
Operating income	—	730[2]	606	503	385	318	274	22/166
Earnings/share	—	1.74	1.51	1.15	0.95	0.80	0.68	21/155
Dividend/share	0.64	0.56	0.48	0.40	0.32	0.27	0.24	18/133
Dividend yield, %	1.8	1.8	1.9	1.5	1.8	2.5	2.7	—/—
Stock price[1]	35.37	35.00	25.00	27.00	19.00	13.00	9.00	31/288
P/E ratio	19.0	18.0	16.0	23.0	18.0	13.0	13.0	—/—
Book value/share	—	8.33	7.05	5.93	5.11	3.95	3.39	20/146

*5-1-90
† 1984-89
1. Calendar year, average stock price
2. Estimated
Source: Company sources.

Note: Stock price quoted in *Barron's,* the *Wall Street Journal* and the *European Wall Street Journal.*

51

SARA LEE CORPORATION

SARA LEE CORPORATION

Three First National Plaza
Chicago, IL 60602-4260
Tel: (312) 726-2600
Chairman and CEO: John H. Bryan, Jr.
President: Paul Fulton

EARNINGS GROWTH	★ ★
STOCK GROWTH	★ ★ ★ ★
DIVIDEND YIELD	★ ★ ★
DIVIDEND GROWTH	★ ★
CONSISTENCY	★ ★ ★ ★
MOMENTUM	★ ★ ★
NYSE	**18 points**

It should come as no surprise to any American who has ever dipped into a frozen cheesecake, poundcake, coffeecake or snack cake that Sara Lee is corporate America's queen of frozen desserts. A quarter of all frozen baked goods sold in the United States is prepared by Sara Lee.

But the Chicago-based bakery caters to more than just America's sweet tooth. It's also the nation's leader in women's hosiery (Hanes, L'eggs, Isotoner) and the second leading manufacturer of brassieres, men's and boys' underwear and printed T-shirts.

Sara Lee is also particularly strong in the frozen meats department. It ranks number one in hot dogs, smoked sausage and breakfast sausage (Hillshire and Jimmy Dean). Internationally, it is the leading coffee distributor in the Netherlands and Belgium.

The company has operations in more than 30 countries and markets its products in nearly 150 countries around the world. Of its $12 billion in total annual sales, 73 percent comes from within the United States and 27 percent comes from abroad.

Sara Lee's packaged foods division—its meats, desserts and other frozen baked goods—accounts for about 29 percent of the company's revenue.

In addition to its packaged foods division, Sara Lee divides its operations into four other key segments:

- Packaged consumer products (25 percent of sales). This is the company's fastest-growing segment, and it includes Hanes (underwear, T-shirts, Isotoner and Silk Reflections hosiery) and L'eggs (Sheer Energy and Sheer Elegance). The company also owns Fuller Brush, Coach Leatherware (a nationwide chain of leather goods stores) and Socks Galore & More, a retail and mail order socks business.
- Food service (22 percent of sales). Sara Lee's PYA/Monarch is one of the largest food service operations in the United States. It supplies food and non-food items to institutional dining facilities (hospitals, schools, factories, etc.). Sara Lee recently sold its chain of Lyon's Restaurants.
- Household and personal care products (10 percent of revenue). Based in Utrecht, the Netherlands, Sara Lee's household goods and personal care products division does most of its business outside the United States. About 69 percent of its revenue comes from Europe and the United Kingdom. The company makes shoe care products (Kiwi and Esquire shoe polish), toiletries, over-the-counter medications, specialty detergents and insecticides.
- Coffee and grocery products (15 percent of sales). Sara Lee owns Douwe Egberts, one of Europe's leading brands of coffee and tea, and several other European coffee and tea lines. It also owns Duyvis nuts, the leading marketer of nuts in both the Netherlands and France.

EARNINGS GROWTH

Sara Lee has had 15 consecutive years of increased earnings. Its earnings per share increased 109 percent over the past five years, 16 percent per year.

The company has annual revenues of $11.7 billion. It has 100,000 employees and 45,000 shareholders of record.

STOCK GROWTH

The company's stock price has climbed quickly the past five years, increasing 250 percent for the period—28 percent per year.

Including reinvested dividends, a $10,000 investment in Sara Lee stock at its median price in 1984 would have grown to about $40,000 five years later. Average annual compounded rate of return (including stock growth and reinvested dividends): about 32 percent.

DIVIDEND YIELD

The company generally pays a good yield, which has averaged about 3.5 percent over the past five years. During the most recent two-year rating

period (1988 and 1989), the stock paid an average annual current return (dividend yield) of 3.0 percent.

DIVIDEND GROWTH

Sara Lee traditionally raises its dividend every year. The dividend increased 115 percent (17 percent per year) over the five-year period from 1984 to 1989.

CONSISTENCY

The company has had very consistent growth in its earnings per share, operating income and book value per share. Its price-earnings ratio of about 15 is consistent with other growing U.S. companies.

MOMENTUM

Sara Lee has continued to maintain a solid growth pace in every key category the past two years—well in line with its five-year growth record.

SUMMARY

Fiscal year ended: July 1
(U.S. dollars; revenue and operating income in millions)

	1990*	1989	1988	1987	1986	1985	1984	5-year growth, %† (annual/total)
Revenue	—	11,718	10,424	9,155	7,938	8,117	7,000	11/67
Operating income	—	1,021	807	684	553	529	470	17/117
Earnings/share	—	1.70	1.42	1.18	1.01	0.90	0.81	16/109
Dividend/share	0.84	0.69	0.58	0.48	0.39	0.35	0.32	17/115
Dividend yield, %	3.1	3.0	2.9	2.5	3.0	4.1	5.0	—/—
Stock price[1]	27.00	28.00	21.00	19.00	15.00	10.00	8.00	28/250
P/E ratio	15.0	14.0	14.0	16.0	13.0	9.0	8.0	—/—
Book value/share	—	8.40	7.10	6.40	5.40	4.65	4.30	14/94

*5–1–90
† 1984–89
1. Average stock price
Source: Company sources.
Note: Stock price quoted in *Barron's,* the *Wall Street Journal* and the *European Wall Street Journal.*

52

ALBERTSON'S, INC.

250 Parkcenter Boulevard
P.O. Box 20
Boise, Idaho 83726
Tel: (208) 385-6200
Chairman and CEO: Warren E. McCain
President: John B. Carley

EARNINGS GROWTH	★ ★
STOCK GROWTH	★ ★ ★ ★
DIVIDEND YIELD	★ ★
DIVIDEND GROWTH	★ ★
CONSISTENCY	★ ★ ★ ★
MOMENTUM	★ ★ ★ ★
NYSE	**18 points**

In the new age of grocery superstores—where acres of groceries coexist with floral centers, pharmacies and full-scale bakeries—Albertson's is making small potatoes of most the competition. Its stores come in four main sizes: big, huge, colossal and gargantuan.

Albertson's conventional stores average 27,000 square feet—nearly three times the size of the original Albertson's grocery that founder Joe Albertson opened in Boise in 1939.

But the company's conventional groceries are mere pantries compared with the 42,000-square-foot superstores. Even the superstores, however, may seem a bit cramped once you've experienced the company's 58,000-square-foot "combination" stores. But for the real megalomaniacs—the serious shoppers who want acres of offerings and elbow room to boot—Albertson's offers its final option, a 73,000-square-foot, no-frills discount "warehouse" store.

Of the company's 530 stores, 157 are conventional groceries, 200 are superstores, 140 are combination stores and 33 are warehouse stores.

Most of Albertson's stores are located in 15 Western states, although it also has some stores in Florida and Louisiana. Albertson's is strongest on the West Coast. Nearly half its stores are located in California, Washington and Oregon.

The company, now the sixth-largest food and drug chain in the United States, has posted 20 consecutive years of record sales and earnings. Albertson's consistent, sustained growth may be due in part to its commitment to updating, remodeling and expanding its stable of stores.

In 1990 the company began a five-year, $1.9-billion expansion and remodeling program. Plans call for the opening of 230 new stores, with primary emphasis on California, Texas and Arizona. The company will also remodel and, in some cases, expand 175 existing stores.

Albertson's has pinned much of its growth not only to its expanding store base but also to its expanding product base. In addition to standard grocery offerings, many of its larger stores have five special-service departments:

- Pharmacy. Low cost pharmacies are available in more than 200 Albertson's stores.
- Lobby departments. Many of its stores provide services for customers such as money orders, bus passes, lottery tickets, stamps, camera supplies, film developing and video tape rental.
- Service deli. Delicatessens in 441 of its stores offer take-home foods, meats, cheeses, fresh salads and fried chicken. Salad bars have been added in about 200 Albertson's stores.
- Service fish and meat departments. Most of the larger Albertson's stores have specialty departments with a full array of fresh fish, shellfish, premium cuts of meat and semi-prepared items such as stuffed pork chops.
- Bakeries. The company is moving toward a partial self-service concept in which customers may pick out the freshly baked breads, pastries, cakes and cookies on their own (or request personal service).

EARNINGS GROWTH

The company has had very consistent growth, with 20 consecutive years of record earnings per share. Over the past five years, the EPS has increased 98 percent (15 percent per year).

With total annual revenues of $7.4 billion, Albertson's has 55,000 employees.

STOCK GROWTH

The company's stock has had strong gains the past five years, increasing 276 percent (30 percent per year) during the period.

Including reinvested dividends, a $10,000 investment in Albertson's stock at its median price in 1984 would have grown to about $40,000 five years later. Average annual compounded rate of return (including stock growth and reinvested dividends): about 32 percent.

DIVIDEND YIELD

The company generally pays a fairly low yield, which has averaged about 2.0 percent over the past five years. During the most recent two-year rating period (1989 and 1990), the stock paid an average annual current return (dividend yield) of 1.7 percent.

DIVIDEND GROWTH

Albertson's traditionally raises its dividend every year. The dividend increased 135 percent (19 percent per year) over the five-year period from 1984 to 1989.

CONSISTENCY

The company has had very consistent growth in all the key categories of revenue, earnings, operating income and book value. Its price-earnings ratio of 17 to 20 is about average for growing U.S. stocks.

MOMENTUM

Albertson's has been on the rise the past couple of years. Its earnings per share rose 20 percent in 1989 and 30 percent in 1988.

SUMMARY

Fiscal year ended: Feb. 1
(U.S. dollars; revenue and operating income in millions)

	1990*	1989	1988	1987	1986	1985	1984	5-year growth, %† (annual/total)
Revenue	—	7,422	6,773	5,869	5,380	5,060	4,736	9/56
Operating income	—	348	289	255	218	199	176	15/97
Earnings/share	—	2.93	2.44	1.88	1.50	1.29	1.21	15/98
Dividend/share	0.96	0.80	0.56	0.48	0.42	0.38	0.34	19/135
Dividend yield, %	1.7	1.6	1.6	1.8	2.0	2.5	2.6	—/—
Stock price[1]	57.25	49.00	31.00	27.00	20.00	15.00	13.00	30/276
P/E ratio	20.0	17.0	13.6	14.3	13.8	11.8	10.8	—/—
Book value/share	—	13.95	11.96	10.20	8.90	7.80	6.87	15/103

*5–1–90
† 1984–89
1. Average stock price for calendar years
Source: Company sources.

Note: Stock price quoted in *Barron's,* the *Wall Street Journal* and the *European Wall Street Journal.*

55

KELLY SERVICES, INC.

999 W. Big Beaver Road
Troy, MI 48084
Tel: (313) 362-4444
Chairman: William R. Kelly
President and CEO: Terence E. Adderley

EARNINGS GROWTH	★ ★ ★
STOCK GROWTH	★ ★ ★ ★
DIVIDEND YIELD	★ ★
DIVIDEND GROWTH	★ ★
CONSISTENCY	★ ★ ★ ★
MOMENTUM	★ ★ ★
OTC	**18 points**

There was a time not long ago when a Kelly worker needed to know little more than how to work a typewriter and answer a phone. But technology has changed—and Kelly has tried to change with it.

Nowadays, Kelly workers may be expected to walk into an office and type out their work on any of 20 or 30 different software programs—and handle a complex office telephone system. The increasingly sophisticated corporate office has created both a challenge and a growing niche for Kelly Services.

Kelly is responding by providing advanced training for many of its 580,000 temporary workers. About 6,000 workers a week go through the Kelly PC-Pro hands-on training program that provides tutoring in nearly 30 different computer software programs, including DisplayWrite, Lotus 1-2-3, Microsoft, PCWriter, Professional Write, WordPerfect and most other commonly used programs.

If workers find that they're still stumped after arriving at their temporary assignment, they can call the Kelly Office Automation Hotline, where a helpful voice will talk them through their troubles.

Kelly's ability to adapt to the changing work environment has helped it stay on top as the world's leading temporary help service. The company has expanded beyond secretarial work and now also offers temporary marketing, technical, light industrial and home care services.

Kelly has 950 offices worldwide and serves 180,000 corporate customers, primarily in the United States, Canada, the United Kingdom and France.

Kelly counts on the unpredictable—as well as the predictable—for its steady flow of assignments. Its workers often step in for ailing full-time employees and help out at businesses during peak times or during special projects or new promotions.

Kelly Services was founded in 1946 by William Kelly, the 85-year-old chairman of the Michigan temp help firm. When he opened his first "service bureau" in 1946, Kelly sold his customers on the concept of sending their work to his office. But the temporary concept didn't really blossom until he altered the original plan and began sending workers into his clients' offices to handle the work. That change in strategy has helped keep Kelly's coffers growing for more than 40 years.

EARNINGS GROWTH

The company has had excellent growth the past few years. Its earnings per share increased 168 percent over the past five years, 22 percent per year.

Kelly reported total revenue of $1.4 billion in 1989.

STOCK GROWTH

The company's stock price has moved up steadily the past five years, increasing 240 percent for the period—28 percent per year.

Including reinvested dividends, a $10,000 investment in Kelly stock at its median price in 1984 would have grown to about $37,000 five years later. Average annual compounded rate of return (including stock growth and reinvested dividends): about 30 percent.

DIVIDEND YIELD

The company generally pays a modest yield, which has averaged under 2 percent over the past five years. During the most recent two-year rating period (1988 and 1989), the stock paid an average annual current return (dividend yield) of 1.6 percent.

DIVIDEND GROWTH

Kelly traditionally raises its dividend each year. The dividend increased 141 percent (19 percent per year) over the five-year period from 1984 to 1989.

CONSISTENCY

The company has had very consistent growth in its earnings per share, revenues, operating income and book value per share. Its price-earnings ratio of about 15 is average for a growing U.S. company.

MOMENTUM

Over the past couple of years, Kelly's growth has been in line with its excellent rate of growth over the five-year period.

SUMMARY

Fiscal year ended: Dec. 31
(U.S. dollars; revenue and operating income in millions)

	1990*	1989	1988	1987	1986	1985	1984	5-year growth, %† (annual/total)
Revenue	—	1,377	1,269	1,161	1,033	876	741	13/86
Operating income	—	112¹	106	98	78	68	56	15¹/100
Earnings/share	—	2.36	2.01	1.68	1.21	1.07	0.88	22/168
Dividend/share	0.66	0.58	0.48	0.41	0.35	0.30	0.24	19/141
Dividend yield, %	1.8	1.6	1.5	1.3	1.2	1.7	2.5	—/—
Stock price²	36.10	34.00	32.00	31.00	28.00	18.00	10.00	28/240
P/E ratio	15.0	15.0	16.0	18.0	23.0	16.0	11.0	—/—
Book value/share	—	9.50	7.70	6.15	4.90	4.25	3.60	21/165

*5–1–90
† 1984–89
1. Estimate
2. Average stock price

Note: Stock price quoted in *Barron's,* the *Wall Street Journal* and the *European Wall Street Journal.*

57

ANHEUSER-BUSCH COMPANIES, INC.

One Busch Place
St. Louis, MO 63118
Tel: (314) 577-2000
Chairman of the Board and President: August A. Busch III

EARNINGS GROWTH	★ ★
STOCK GROWTH	★ ★ ★ ★
DIVIDEND YIELD	★ ★
DIVIDEND GROWTH	★ ★ ★
CONSISTENCY	★ ★ ★ ★
MOMENTUM	★ ★ ★
NYSE	**18 points**

Even in a beer market gone flat, the "King of Beer" has managed to keep the suds flowing and the profits growing.

Although U.S. beer sales peaked in 1986, Anheuser-Busch, the world's largest brewer, has continued to knock down record revenues and earnings, in part, by soaking up a larger share of the U.S. beer market. Some 42 percent of all beer consumed in the United States is produced by Anheuser-Busch. And if the shake-out in the beer market continues, Busch could emerge with an even larger stake.

Anheuser-Busch is the maker of Budweiser, Michelob, Bud Light, Busch and half a dozen other brews. It brews about 81 million barrels of beer a year. It also imports two European-brewed beers, Carlsberg and Elephant Malt Liquor. It recently discontinued its LA beer after the low-alcohol brew failed to attract a respectable following. Beer and beer-related products account for about 76 percent of the company's $9.5 billion a year in total revenue.

Internationally, the company's beer is sold in 40 countries.

Busch's brewing business is fully integrated. It operates a dozen breweries in the United States, owns a beverage can manufacturer, a barley processing plant, a label printing operation and a refrigerated rail car transportation subsidiary.

The company's other segments include:

- Food products (20 percent of revenues). Campbell Taggart, one of the country's largest bakery operations, has 43 bakeries and several other related production facilities. It markets its baked goods primarily under the Grant's Farm, Colonial, Rainbo or Kilpatrick's labels. The company also supplies sandwich buns to some of the major fast food chains.

  Eagle Snacks produces peanuts, pretzels, potato chips and other snack food products.
- Family entertainment (3 percent of revenues). Busch Entertainment operates a number of theme parks throughout the United States, including The Dark Continent (Busch Gardens) and Adventure Island in Tampa, Florida; The Old Country in Williamsburg, Virginia; and Sesame Place in Langhorne, Pennsylvania. In 1989 it acquired four Sea World parks and two other theme parks from Harcourt Brace Jovanovich.
- Anheuser-Busch also owns the St. Louis Cardinals National League baseball team, which has been one of the most successful franchises in sports history.

Anheuser-Busch traces its roots to a small St. Louis brewery started in 1852. After a few years of lackluster results, the original owner, George Schneider, sold out the struggling operation to an investment group headed by St. Louis soap tycoon Eberhard Anheuser. Anheuser ultimately turned the business over to his son-in-law, a portly, gregarious man by the name of Adolphus Busch.

Mr. Busch, who converted the small brewery into a national force, is generally recognized as the founder of Anheuser-Busch. Budweiser, which Mr. Busch helped develop in 1876, was one of the first beers to achieve widespread distribution. Michelob, the company's "premium" beer, was first brought to market in 1896. When Adolphus Busch died in 1913, his son August A. Busch assumed control of the business. The reins have since been passed through two more generations of the Busch family. August A. Busch III, 53, now directs the company as its chairman of the board, president and CEO.

EARNINGS GROWTH

Anheuser-Busch has had 13 consecutive years of record earnings. Over the past five years, its earnings per share increased 116 percent (17 percent per year).

The company has total annual revenues of $9.5 billion and has about 47,000 employees.

STOCK GROWTH

The company's stock has moved up very quickly the past five years, increasing 245 percent (28 percent per year) during the period.

Including reinvested dividends, a $10,000 investment in Busch stock at its median price in 1984 would have grown to about $37,000 five years later. Average annual compounded rate of return (including stock growth and reinvested dividends): about 30 percent.

DIVIDEND YIELD

The company pays a fair yield, which has averaged about 2 percent over the past five years. During the most recent two-year rating period (1988 and 1989), the stock paid an average annual current return (dividend yield) of 2.2 percent.

DIVIDEND GROWTH

Busch traditionally raises its dividend every year. The dividend increased 162 percent (21 percent per year) over the five-year period from 1984 to 1989.

CONSISTENCY

The company has had very consistent growth in all of the key categories of earnings per share, revenues, operating income and book value per share. Its 1989 price-earnings ratio of 14 is about average for growing U.S. companies.

MOMENTUM

Busch is facing an up-hill battle in the downward slide of beer consumption in the United States. But it has still managed to keep profits and sales moving up by capturing an ever-larger share of the U.S. market.

SUMMARY

Fiscal year ended: Dec. 31
(U.S. dollars; revenue and operating income in millions)

	1990*	1989	1988	1987	1986	1985	1984	5-year growth, %† (annual/total)
Revenue	—	9,481	8,924	8,258	7,677	7,000	6,501	8/45
Operating income	—	—	1,623	1,445	1,282	1,068	958	13/83
Earnings/share	—	2.68	2.45	2.01	1.69	1.42	1.24	17/116
Dividend/share	0.88	0.84	0.69	0.57	0.46	0.37	0.32	21/162
Dividend yield, %	2.3	2.2	2.2	1.7	1.8	2.4	3.0	—/—
Stock price[1]	43.00	38.00	32.00	33.00	25.00	17.00	11.00	28/245
P/E ratio	16.0	14.0	12.0	17.0	15.0	11.0	9.0	—/—
Book value/share	—	12.50	11.00	9.00	9.00	7.80	6.85	13/82

*6-1-90
† 1984–89, except operating income, 1983–88
1. Average stock price
Source: Company sources.

Note: Stock price quoted in *Barron's,* the *Wall Street Journal* and the *European Wall Street Journal.*

THE WALT DISNEY COMPANY

500 S. Buena Vista Street
Burbank, CA 91521
Tel: (818) 560-1000
Chairman and CEO: Michael D. Eisner
President and COO: Frank G. Wells

EARNINGS GROWTH	★ ★ ★ ★
STOCK GROWTH	★ ★ ★ ★
DIVIDEND YIELD	★
DIVIDEND GROWTH	(no points)
CONSISTENCY	★ ★ ★ ★
MOMENTUM	★ ★ ★ ★
NYSE	**17 points**

It was a corporate merger made in heaven. Miss Piggy and Mickey Mouse, Kermit the Frog and Donald Duck, the creative genius of Jim Henson wed to the resources and technology of The Walt Disney Company. In 1989, when Henson, creator of the Muppets, agreed to sell Henson Associates to Disney and join the Disney team himself, analysts bubbled over at the prospect of a Henson-Disney creative tandem.

But in a company that has become synonymous with happy endings, this tale ended suddenly and sadly in May, 1990, when the 53-year-old Henson died of pneumonia. The loss, said one company official, "is like Disney dying. This is a huge blow." Henson had been involved in every phase of Disney's operations.

Despite Henson's death, Disney officials say the merger stands—making Miss Piggy, Kermit and the other Muppets permanent fixtures in the Disney family—although final terms of the reported $100 to $150 million buyout agreement have not been finalized.

The Muppets should keep plenty busy at Disney. The Burbank, California-based entertainment enterprise has been bursting at the seams. Its profits—from its theme park and resort business, its motion picture division, its TV and cable programming—have soared, on average, 46 percent per year for the past five years. Its stock price jumped 70 percent in 1989 alone.

Theme parks and resorts comprise the largest portion of the Disney kingdom, accounting for 56 percent of the company's revenue and 64 percent of operating income. In addition to Disneyland in California and Walt Disney World and the Epcot Center in Orlando, Florida, Disney opened a new $500 million Disney-MGM Studios Theme Park in its Orlando complex in 1989. The company is also associated with a Disney park in Japan, and one is being built in France.

Disney plans to spend several billion dollars over the next decade expanding its existing theme parks in Florida and California and adding a new park somewhere in Southern California, a second theme park in Tokyo and a second one in Europe.

Disney's other major segment, "filmed entertainment" (35 percent of revenues and 21 percent of operating earnings), has also been thriving lately. Walt Disney Studios—with its Touchtone Pictures, Disney and Hollywood Pictures divisions—has jumped from last in box office success among the major studios in 1985 to first in 1988 and 1989. The company's top films have included "Honey, I Shrunk the Kids," "Dead Poets Society," "Turner and Hooch," "The Little Mermaid," "Pretty Woman" and "Dick Tracy."

Disney's other filmed entertainment divisions also did well in 1989. Its television programs, "Golden Girls" and "Empty Nest," were among the top 10 rated programs, and "DuckTales" and "Chip 'n Dale's Rescue Rangers" ranked one-two in the afternoon children's programming niche.

The Disney (cable) Channel increased its subscriber base to nearly 5 million in 1989.

Disney's Buena Vista Home Video division was the industry leader in video sales for the third consecutive year. Its biggest sellers, "Bambi" and "Who Framed Roger Rabbit," sold a combined 18 million copies, placing them second and third among the all-time best-selling video releases.

The smallest of Disney's divisions—but the fastest growing—is its consumer products group (9 percent of revenue; 15 percent of operating income). The division, which is responsible for the sale of Disney apparel, dolls, software games, books and assorted merchandise, has doubled its sales and earnings the past two years. Mickey Mouse, now a spry 60 years old, remains the market leader among Disney buffs.

EARNINGS GROWTH

After some slow years in the early 1980s, Disney has managed to string together several years of outstanding earnings gains. Its earnings per share have jumped, on average, 46 percent per year over the past five years.

Disney reports total annual revenues of $4.6 billion in 1989. It has 47,000 employees and 170,000 shareholders.

STOCK GROWTH

The company's stock has enjoyed immense success the past five years, increasing 621 percent (49 percent per year) during the period.

Including reinvested dividends, a $10,000 investment in Disney stock at its median price in 1984 would have grown to about $75,000 five years later. Average annual compounded rate of return (including stock growth and reinvested dividends): about 50 percent.

DIVIDEND YIELD

The company pays a low yield, which has averaged under 1 percent the past five years. During the most recent two-year rating period (1988 and 1989), the stock paid an average annual current return (dividend yield) of 0.5 percent.

DIVIDEND GROWTH   (no points)

Dividends have been of little concern to Disney in recent years; it prefers to pour its profits back into the company. The dividend increased only 53 percent (9 percent per year) over the five-year period from 1984 to 1989.

CONSISTENCY

Disney has had very consistent growth in its earnings per share, revenues, operating income and book value per share over the past five years. Its price-earnings ratio has bounced around between 15 and 20 over the past few years.

MOMENTUM

The company still seems to be picking up steam. Its earnings per share have gone up 79 percent the past two years, and its revenues have increased 60 percent during the two-year period.

SUMMARY

Fiscal year ended: Sept. 30
(U.S. dollars; revenue and operating income in millions)

	1990*	1989	1988	1987	1986	1985	1984	5-year growth, %† (annual/total)
Revenue	—	4,594	3,438	2,877	2,166	1,700	1,656	22/177
Operating income	—	1,229	884	776	527	474	331	30/271
Earnings/share	—	5.10	3.80	2.85	1.82	1.29	0.75	46/580
Dividend/share	—	0.46	0.38	0.32	0.32	0.30	0.30	9/53
Dividend yield, %	0.5	0.5	0.6	0.5	0.9	1.6	2.1	—/—
Stock price[1]	110.50	101.00	61.00	62.00	42.00	22.00	14.00	49/621
P/E ratio	20.0	16.0	15.0	21.0	20.0	14.0	18.0	—/—
Book value/share	—	23.00	18.00	14.00	11.00	9.00	8.50	21/170

*5–1–90
† 1984–89
1. Average stock price
Source: Company sources.

Note: Stock price quoted in *Barron's,* the *Wall Street Journal* and the *European Wall Street Journal.*

62

CONAGRA, INC.

ConAgra Center
One Central Park Plaza
Omaha, NE 68102
Tel: (402) 978-4000
Chairman and CEO: Charles M. Harper
President and COO: Philip B. Fletcher

EARNINGS GROWTH	★ ★
STOCK GROWTH	★ ★ ★ ★
DIVIDEND YIELD	★ ★
DIVIDEND GROWTH	★ ★
CONSISTENCY	★ ★ ★ ★
MOMENTUM	★ ★ ★
NYSE	**17 points**

ConAgra's agricultural operations cut across the entire food chain from feeds and fertilizers to fresh fish and frozen dinners. But the true bread and butter of the company's operations is its meats—ham, poultry and beef—fresh, frozen and packaged.

The Omaha, Nebraska-based conglomerate owns a number of meats subsidiaries, including Banquet, Armour, Morton, Monfort, E.A. Miller, Country Pride, Decker, Golden Star, Pfaelzer, Cook Family Foods, Con-Agra Fresh Meats and ConAgra Poultry.

It also acquired Beatrice Foods in June, 1990, adding its list of well-known staples—Hunt's tomato products, Wesson cooking oils, Orville Redenbacher's popcorns and Swiss Miss puddings and cocoa mixes—to ConAgra's corporate spread.

ConAgra divides its operations into three primary segments:

- Prepared foods (63 percent of revenue). In addition to its meats, the company has other prominent holdings in the prepared foods market, including Banquet (frozen dinners, pot pies, chicken, etc.), Morton dinners, Home Brand peanut butter and Chun King dinners. The company also operates some specialized subsidiaries such as its pet products group.

- Agri-products (20 percent of revenue). The company sells a wide range of fertilizers, insecticides and crop-protection chemicals. It also sells animal feeds, nutrient additives for feeds and livestock health-care products.

    ConAgra owns a chain of 91 Country General Stores that carries merchandise targeted to country living such as boots, clothing, housewares, lawn and garden supplies, farm and ranch supplies, hardware, animal-care products and sporting goods. It also owns a chain of 86 Northwest Fabrics & Crafts stores.

- Trading and processing (17 percent of revenue). The company trades agricultural commodities and foodstuffs worldwide, with offices in 26 nations. It has food processing facilities throughout the United States, Canada, Europe and Latin America. Among its leading subsidiaries in the food trading and processing business are Berger and Company, Camerican International and Woodward & Dickerson. It also owns Peavey Grain Co. and recently acquired Pillsbury's grain merchandising division.

In all, ConAgra operates more than 40 different companies, with locations throughout North and South America, Europe, Asia and Australia.

EARNINGS GROWTH

The company has had solid growth the past few years. Its earnings per share increased 139 percent over the past five years, 19 percent per year.

ConAgra has total annual revenue of about $15.5 billion. The company has 55,000 employees.

STOCK GROWTH

The company's stock price has increased rapidly the past five years, climbing 212 percent for the period—26 percent per year.

Including reinvested dividends, a $10,000 investment in ConAgra stock at its median price in 1984 would have grown to about $35,000 five years later. Average annual compounded rate of return (including stock growth and reinvested dividends): about 28 percent.

DIVIDEND YIELD

The company generally pays a fairly good yield, which has averaged about 2.2 percent over the past five years. During the most recent two-year rating period (1989 and 1990), the stock paid an average annual current return (dividend yield) of 2.3 percent.

DIVIDEND GROWTH

ConAgra traditionally raises its dividend each year. The dividend increased 100 percent (15 percent per year) over the five-year period from 1984 to 1989.

CONSISTENCY

The company has had very consistent growth in its earnings per share, revenues, operating income and book value per share. Its price-earnings ratio of 13 to 15 is consistent with other growing U.S. companies.

MOMENTUM

ConAgra has been maintaining strong growth the past couple of years. Its earnings per share increased 26 percent in fiscal 1989 and was expected to move up 16 percent in fiscal 1990. Its revenue has increased about 70 percent over the past two years.

SUMMARY

Fiscal year ended: May 31
(U.S. dollars; revenue and operating income in millions)

	1990*	1989	1988	1987	1986	1985	1984	5-year growth, %† (annual/total)
Revenue	15,500²	11,340	9,475	9,001	5,911	5,498	3,301	28/243
Operating income	—	546	386	398	273	239	136	32/301
Earnings/share	1.90²	1.63	1.29	1.23	1.02	0.88	0.68	19/139
Dividend/share	0.58	0.50	0.43	0.37	0.33	0.28	0.25	15/100
Dividend yield, %	2.2	2.4	2.3	1.9	2.4	3.1	3.5	—/—
Stock price¹	27.80	25.00	20.00	20.00	17.00	12.00	8.00	26/212
P/E ratio	15.0	13.0	14.0	16.0	13.0	10.0	10.0	—/—
Book value/share	9.00²	7.90	7.00	6.15	5.15	4.60	4.10	14/92

*5–1–90
† 1984–89
1. Average stock price for calendar years
2. Estimated
Source: Company sources.

Note: Stock price quoted in *Barron's,* the *Wall Street Journal* and the *European Wall Street Journal.*

64

RUBBERMAID, INCORPORATED

1147 Akron Road
Wooster, Ohio 44691
Tel: (216) 264-6464
Chairman and CEO: Stanley C. Gault
President and COO: Walter W. Williams

EARNINGS GROWTH	★ ★
STOCK GROWTH	★ ★ ★ ★
DIVIDEND YIELD	★ ★
DIVIDEND GROWTH	★ ★
CONSISTENCY	★ ★ ★ ★
MOMENTUM	★ ★ ★
NYSE	**17 points**

What began 70 years ago as a small-time balloon manufacturer has now itself ballooned into one of the world's largest and most successful producers of housewares, toys and plastic office products.

Rubbermaid has enjoyed 38 consecutive years of record sales and 12 years (including 36 consecutive quarters) of record earnings. It has increased its dividend to shareholders for 35 consecutive years. The Wooster, Ohio-based manufacturer has been listed among *Fortune* magazine's "10 Most Admired Companies" for five consecutive years.

Rubbermaid opened its doors in 1920 as The Wooster Rubber Company. In the 1930s it began producing its first houseware products—rubber dustpans, drainboard mats and soap dishes. Now the company manufactures more than 1,000 different plastic products.

Rubbermaid has grown rapidly the past few years, eclipsing the $1 billion mark in sales for the first time in 1987. Its rapid growth is due in part to a number of key acquisitions, including Little Tikes (toys) in 1984, Gott Corp. (leisure products) in 1985, SECO Industries (floor maintenance products) and MicroComputer Accessories in 1986 and Viking Brush (Canada's leading maker of brushes, brooms and other cleaning aids) in 1987.

The company's products are geared to both consumers (77 percent of sales) and institutional customers (23 percent of sales). In addition to its U.S. sales, Rubbermaid also does a good foreign business and recently agreed to a joint venture with Curver Housewares Group of the Netherlands that will give Rubbermaid a prominent role in the European housewares market. Foreign sales account for about 15 percent of the company's revenue.

Rubbermaid breaks its U.S. operations into five divisions:

- Housewares. The oldest and largest of Rubbermaid's divisions manufactures such products as sinkware, space organizers, household containers, trash cans, cookware, food storage containers, rubber gloves, casual dinnerware, shelf liners and vacuum cleaner bags.
- Specialty products. This division makes lawn furniture, planters, bird feeders, thermos jugs, insulated food chests, canteens and water coolers.
- Commercial products. Products geared to the commercial, industrial and institutional markets include brooms, mops, brushes, trash cans, trays, pitchers and cups, food storage containers, housekeeping carts and other maintenance, food-service and office products.
- Office products. The company makes modular desk systems, floor mats and accessories for personal computers, word processors and data terminals, including plastic molded stands for computers and printers, storage racks and disk files.
- Toys. Through its Little Tikes subsidiary, the company makes a wide range of toys, pedal cars, children's furniture and other children's recreational equipment.

EARNINGS GROWTH

The company has had solid growth the past few years. Its earnings per share increased 128 percent over the past five years, 18 percent per year.

Rubbermaid reported total revenue of $1.3 billion in 1989. The company has 8,000 employees.

STOCK GROWTH

The company's stock price has moved up quickly the past five years, increasing 210 percent for the period—26 percent per year.

Including reinvested dividends, a $10,000 investment in Rubbermaid stock at its median price in 1984 would have grown to about $33,000 five years later. Average annual compounded rate of return (including stock growth and reinvested dividends): about 27 percent.

DIVIDEND YIELD

The company generally pays a modest yield, which has averaged about 1.5 percent over the past five years. During the most recent two-year rating period (1988 and 1989), the stock paid an average annual current return (dividend yield) of 1.5 percent.

DIVIDEND GROWTH

Rubbermaid has raised its dividend 35 consecutive years. The dividend increased 130 percent (18 percent per year) over the five-year period from 1984 to 1989.

CONSISTENCY

The company has had very consistent growth in its earnings per share, revenues, operating income and book value per share. Its price-earnings ratio of about 20 is a little higher than average for U.S. companies.

MOMENTUM

The company's consistent growth has continued the past two years in every key financial category.

SUMMARY

Fiscal year ended: Dec. 31
(U.S. dollars; revenue and operating income in millions)

	1990*	1989	1988	1987	1986	1985	1984	5-year growth, %† (annual/total)
Revenue	—	1,344	1,194	1,015	795	671	566	19/137
Operating income	—	250¹	218	207	168	141	108	18/131
Earnings/share	—	1.58	1.35	1.15	0.96	0.79	0.69	18/128
Dividend/share	0.52	0.46	0.38	0.32	0.26	0.23	0.20	18/130
Dividend yield, %	1.5	1.5	1.6	1.1	1.2	1.0	2.0	—/—
Stock price²	34.37	31.00	24.00	27.00	23.00	14.00	10.00	26/210
P/E ratio	21.0	20.0	18.0	24.0	23.0	17.0	14.0	—/—
Book value/share	—	8.05	6.95	5.95	4.90	4.15	3.50	18/128

*5-1-90
† 1984-89
1. Estimated
2. Average stock price
Source: Company sources.

Note: Stock price quoted in *Barron's,* the *Wall Street Journal* and the *European Wall Street Journal.*

ABBOTT LABORATORIES

One Abbott Park Road
Abbott Park, IL 60064
Tel: (708) 937-6100
Chairman and CEO: Duane L. Burnham
President and COO: Thomas R. Hodgson

EARNINGS GROWTH	★ ★
STOCK GROWTH	★ ★ ★
DIVIDEND YIELD	★ ★
DIVIDEND GROWTH	★ ★
CONSISTENCY	★ ★ ★ ★
MOMENTUM	★ ★ ★
NYSE	**16 points**

For 102 years, Abbott Laboratories has been a growing force in the fiercely competitive U.S. medical products market—and for good reason. This is a place that goes for blood.

In fact, blood banks the world over use Abbott's diagnostic screening equipment. Abbott was the first company to introduce an AIDS antibody test and continues to be a world leader in AIDS testing, controlling about 10 percent of the worldwide market.

Abbott's diagnostic equipment is also used to test for cancer, hepatitis, strep throat, high cholesterol and a wide range of other conditions. Its "Vision" desk-top blood analyzer screens for 25 different conditions on-site—printing out the results in about 20 minutes. The Chicago-area company is the world's leading manufacturer of "alternative site" testing equipment.

The company is also a major manufacturer of urine drug sample testing systems for corporations and other organizations.

Abbott's hospital and laboratory products segment accounts for 48 percent of annual revenue.

Pharmaceutical and nutritional products account for about 52 percent of the company's $5.4 billion a year in total revenue. Abbott makes drugs for the treatment of anxiety, epilepsy and hypertension. It is a leading producer of antibiotics, and it manufacturers a broad line of cardiovascular products, cough and cold formulas and vitamins.

While most of Abbott's products are specialized for the medical profession, the company produces a handful of consumer products such as Murine eye drops, Selsun Blue dandruff shampoo, Tronolane hemorrhoid medication and Isomil and Similac nutritional formulas for infants.

The company also does a good business in agricultural-related products such as plant growth regulators and herbicides, and it is the world's leading supplier of biological pesticides.

Abbott boasts a strong international business, which accounts for about 35 percent of total revenue. It has operations in more than 130 countries.

The company was founded in 1888 when Dr. Wallace C. Abbott began a sideline venture in his small Chicago apartment, making pills from the alkaloid of plants. Abbott Labs has experienced remarkably consistent growth during its 102-year history—particularly in recent years. The company has posted record sales, earnings and dividends every year since 1971.

EARNINGS GROWTH

Abbott has had excellent long-term earnings growth. Its earnings per share has increased 130 percent (an average of 18 percent per year) over the past five years.

With total annual revenues of $5.4 billion, Abbott has about 40,000 employees.

STOCK GROWTH

The company's stock price has had strong gains the past five years, increasing 176 percent (22 percent per year) during the period.

Including reinvested dividends, a $10,000 investment in Abbott stock at its median price in 1984 would have grown to about $30,000 five years later. Average annual compounded rate of return (including stock growth and reinvested dividends): about 24.5 percent.

DIVIDEND YIELD

The company generally pays a fairly good yield, which has averaged about 2.5 percent over the past five years. During the most recent two-year rating period (1988 and 1989), the stock paid an average annual current return (dividend yield) of 2.5 percent.

DIVIDEND GROWTH

Abbott has raised its dividend 17 consecutive years. The dividend increased 133 percent (18 percent per year) over the five-year period from 1984 to 1989.

CONSISTENCY

The company has had very consistent growth in its earnings, revenues, operating income and book value per share. Its earnings per share has increased 19 consecutive years. Its price-earnings ratio of about 14 to 17 over the past three years is about average for growing U.S. companies.

MOMENTUM

Abbott has had sustained growth in the key areas of earnings, operating income, revenues and book value. Its most recent reported increase in earnings per share of about 16 percent (in 1989) was just about in line with its average over the past five years.

SUMMARY

Fiscal year ended: Dec. 31
(U.S. dollars; revenue and operating income in millions)

	1990*	1989	1988	1987	1986	1985	1984	5-year growth, %† (annual/total)
Revenue	—	5,379	4,937	4,387	3,807	3,360	3,104	12/73
Operating income	—	1,221	1,102	1,006	879	737	677	13/80
Earnings/share	—	3.85	3.33	2.78	2.32	1.94	1.67	18/130
Dividend/share	1.68	1.40	1.20	1.00	0.84	0.70	0.60	18/133
Dividend yield, %	2.5	2.4	2.6	1.7	1.9	2.6	2.8	—/—
Stock price¹	66.75	58.00	48.00	54.00	43.00	28.00	21.00	22/176
P/E ratio	17.0	15.0	14.0	21.0	19.0	14.0	13.0	—/—
Book value/share	—	12.30	11.00	9.25	7.75	7.80	6.70	13/84

*5–1–90
† 1984–89
1. Average stock price
Source: Company sources.

Note: Stock price quoted in *Barron's,* the *Wall Street Journal* and the *European Wall Street Journal.*

RPM, INC.

2628 Pearl Road
P.O. Box 777
Medina, Ohio 44258
Tel: (216) 225-3192
Chairman and CEO: Thomas C. Sullivan
President: James A. Karman

EARNINGS GROWTH	★
STOCK GROWTH	★ ★
DIVIDEND YIELD	★ ★ ★ ★
DIVIDEND GROWTH	★ ★
CONSISTENCY	★ ★ ★ ★
MOMENTUM	★ ★ ★
OTC	**16 points**

It all began with "Alumanation," a coating process for outdoor metal structures that RPM founder Frank C. Sullivan brought to market 43 years ago. Alumanation today remains the world's leading liquid aluminum coating solution, and RPM has yet to have a single year when it didn't set new records for sales and earnings.

The Ohio-based manufacturer, which has built its business through internal growth and a robust appetite for acquisitions, has become one of the world's leading paints and coatings manufacturers. Its coatings cover the Statue of Liberty, the Eiffel Tower and hundreds of bridges, ships, highways, factories, office towers, warehouses and other structures in some 75 countries worldwide.

Most of RPM's 29 subsidiaries are involved in the manufacture of corrosion protection, waterproofing and maintenance products. Among its key products are paints, sealants, roofing materials and touch-up products for autos and furniture. It also makes fabrics and wallcoverings.

RPM divides its business into five market segments:

- Corrosion control (about 27 percent of revenue). RPM produces coatings and chemicals for power plants, oil rigs, rail cars, tankers, smoke stacks and other structures that are subject to harsh environments.
- Specialty chemicals (about 23 percent of revenue). The company makes concrete additives that provide corrosion resistance and add strength to cement used in construction; it makes additives for coatings and dyes; it makes coatings and cleaners for the textile trade; and it produces furniture stains, fillers and polishes, auto refinishing products and auto corrosion-control additives.
- Waterproofing and general maintenance (about 15 percent of revenue). The company makes coatings for metal structures such as buildings, bridges and industrial facilities; it also produces sheet roofing, sealants and deck coatings.
- Consumer hobby and leisure (15 percent of revenue). RPM's Testor subsidiary is America's leading producer of models, paints and accessory items for the model and hobby market. RPM's Craft House subsidiary makes Sesame Street and Magic Rocks toys and Paint-by-Numbers art kits.
- Consumer do-it-yourself (20 percent of revenue). The company's Bondex subsidiary makes patch and repair products and waterproofing products. Its Zinsser subsidiary makes shellacs, sealants and primers.

EARNINGS GROWTH

The company has had steady growth the past five years, with an increase in earnings per share of 86 percent, 13 percent per year.

RPM reported total revenue of $376 million in 1989. The company has 2,000 employees.

STOCK GROWTH

The company's stock price has moved up well the past five years, increasing 125 percent for the period—18 percent per year.

Including reinvested dividends, a $10,000 investment in RPM stock at its median price in 1984 would have grown to about $26,000 five years later. Average annual compounded rate of return (including stock growth and reinvested dividends): about 21 percent.

DIVIDEND YIELD

The company generally pays a good yield, which has averaged about 3.5 percent over the past five years. During the most recent two-year rating period (1989 and 1990), the stock paid an average annual current return (dividend yield) of 3.6 percent.

DIVIDEND GROWTH

RPM raises its dividend every year. The dividend increased 106 percent (16 percent per year) during the five-year period from 1985 to 1990.

CONSISTENCY

The company has been among the most consistent companies in American industry, with a flawless record of continuing growth in its earnings per share, revenues, operating income and book value per share for more than four decades. Its price-earnings ratio of about 15 to 17 is consistent with other growing U.S. companies.

MOMENTUM

RPM has had solid growth the past two years, very much in line with its five-year growth history.

SUMMARY

Fiscal year ended: May 31
(U.S. dollars; revenue and operating income in millions)

	1990	1989	1988	1987	1986	1985	1984	5-year growth, %† (annual/total)
Revenue	—	376	342	291	251	203	154	19/144
Operating income	—	55.8	50.3	41.5	29.6	24.8	18.3	25/205
Earnings/share	—	1.08	0.95	0.77	0.70	0.69	0.58	13/86
Dividend/share	0.68	0.61	0.54	0.45	0.39	0.33	0.21	16/106
Dividend yield, %	3.4	3.8	3.6	3.1	3.3	3.6	2.8	—/—
Stock price[1]	20.00	18.00	16.00	14.00	14.00	11.00	8.00	18/125
P/E ratio	17.0	14.8	15.7	18.6	17.0	13.5	13.0	—/—
Book value/share	—	6.54	6.09	5.73	5.43	4.11	3.78	12/73

† 1984–89, except dividend/share, 1985–90
1. Average stock price, calendar years
Source: Company sources.

Note: Stock price quoted in *Barron's,* the *Wall Street Journal* and the *European Wall Street Journal.*

MCDONALD'S CORPORATION

McDonald's Plaza
Oak Brook, IL 60521
Tel: (708) 575-3000
Senior Chairman: Fred L. Turner
Chairman and CEO: Michael R. Quinlan

EARNINGS GROWTH	★ ★
STOCK GROWTH	★ ★ ★ ★
DIVIDEND YIELD	★
DIVIDEND GROWTH	★
CONSISTENCY	★ ★ ★ ★
MOMENTUM	★ ★ ★
NYSE	**15 points**

Despite rumors to the contrary, the Berlin Wall has not been replaced by a pair of Golden Arches. But when the Wall did fall, one of the first side trips many East Germans took was a quick jaunt in their Trabants to the nearest McDonald's.

Even in Russia, Muscovites got a chance to enjoy their first Big Mac attack when a McDonald's opened in January, 1990, in the shadow of the Kremlin. Several more Moscow McDonald's were expected to open soon.

McDonald's is the most advertised single brand name in the world. Even before *perestroika,* the Golden Arches were well established on foreign soil. About 3,000 of McDonald's 11,000 restaurants are located outside the United States. There are about 1,000 in Europe, 1,200 in Asia and Australia and more than 600 in Canada.

And every 16 hours, somewhere in the world, a new McDonald's opens. The company opens more than 600 new restaurants each year. Each day, 22 million people dine at McDonald's. Since the late Ray Kroc opened his first McDonald's in 1955, the company has served more than 70 billion hamburgers.

Oddly enough, hamburger sales at McDonald's have slipped in recent years, but the company has stocked its menu with other items—breakfast dishes, salads, cookies and other types of sandwiches—to help keep profits rolling. The company has had 24 consecutive years of record earnings and revenue, dating back to the year the company went public.

Most McDonald's restaurants are owned by independent businesspeople who operate them through a franchise agreement with the company. Typically, the company tries to recruit investors who will be active, on-premises owners rather than outside investors. The conventional franchise arrangement is generally for a term of 20 years and requires an investment of about half a million dollars, 60 percent of which may be financed. Each outlet is also subject to franchise fees based on a percentage of sales.

Quality assurance is a major point of emphasis at McDonald's. The company goes to great extremes to see that each of its restaurants complies with company standards. Edward Rensi, the president and chief operating officer of McDonald's U.S. division, personally visits 15 to 20 restaurants a week and about 400 a year to assure that things are functioning properly out in the field.

EARNINGS GROWTH

The company has had steady growth, with earnings per share rising 101 percent over the past years, 15 percent per year.

McDonald's had revenues of $6.1 billion in 1989.

STOCK GROWTH

The company's stock price has moved up quickly the past five years, increasing 200 percent for the period—25 percent per year.

Including reinvested dividends, a $10,000 investment in McDonald's stock in 1984 would have grown to about $32,000 five years later. Average annual compounded rate of return (including stock growth and reinvested dividends): about 26 percent.

DIVIDEND YIELD

The company generally pays a modest yield, which has averaged just over 1 percent over the past five years. During the most recent two-year rating period (1988 and 1989), the stock paid an average annual current return (dividend yield) of 1.0 percent.

DIVIDEND GROWTH

McDonald's traditionally raises its dividend every year—although the increases often amount to no more than a penny or two a share. The dividend increased 76 percent (12 percent per year) over the five-year period from 1984 to 1989.

CONSISTENCY

The company has had very consistent growth in its earnings per share, revenues, operating income and book value per share. It has had 24 consecutive years of record earnings. Its price-earnings ratio of about 15 is average for U.S. companies.

MOMENTUM

While McDonald's growth has been steady, its days of rapid expansion are long gone. But as it spreads its Golden Arches around the globe, annual earnings and revenue growth could remain in the 10 to 20 percent range.

SUMMARY

Fiscal year ended: Dec. 31
(U.S. dollars; revenue and operating income in millions)

	1990*	1989	1988	1987	1986	1985	1984	5-year growth, %†(annual/total)
Revenue	—	6,142	5,566	4,894	4,240	3,761	3,415	13/79
Operating income	—	1,246	1,177	1,051	852	813	701	13/77
Earnings/share	—	1.95	1.71	1.45	1.24	1.11	0.97	15/101
Dividend/share	0.31	0.30	0.27	0.24	0.21	0.20	0.17	12/76
Dividend yield, %	1.0	0.9	1.1	1.0	1.0	1.1	1.4	—/—
Stock price	30.25	34.50	24.12	22.00	20.25	18.00	11.50	25/200
P/E ratio	15.0	17.6	14.1	15.1	16.3	16.2	11.8	—/—
Book value/share	—	10.65	9.09	7.72	6.45	5.67	4.94	17/115

*5–1–90
† 1984–89
Source: Company sources.

Note: Stock price quoted in *Barron's,* the *Wall Street Journal* and the *European Wall Street Journal.*

HONORABLE MENTION

AUSTRALIA

Amcor Ltd., South Gate, South Melbourne, Victoria 3205, Australia. Tel: (03) 615-9000. Australia's largest forest products and packaging company. 1989 revenue: AU$3.5 billion (US$2.8 billion).

Arnotts Ltd., 168-170 Kent St., 16th Floor, Sydney, N.S.W. 2000, Australia. Tel: (02) 27 3772. Produces biscuits, snack products, dietary foods, cakes, pet foods and other foods and beverages. 1988 revenue: AU$698 million (US$556 million).

Australian National Industries, 5 Birnie Ave., P.O. Box 105, Lidcombe, N.S.W. 2141, Australia. Diversified manufacturing, distribution and contracting. 1988 revenue: AU$1.4 billion (US$1.1 billion).

CRA Group, 31st Floor, 55 Collins St., Melbourne, Victoria 3001, Australia. Tel: 03 658 3333. Mining and manufacturing. 1988 revenue: AU$5.3 billion.

Comalco, 38th Floor, 55 Collins St., Melbourne, Victoria 3000, Australia. Tel: (03) 658-8300. Australia's largest aluminum production company. 1988 revenue: AU$2.5 billion.

F.H. Faulding, 183 Melbourne St., North Adelaide, S.A. 5006, Australia. Tel: (08) 267-1033. Manufacturer and wholesaler of pharmaceuticals, household and allied products; distribution agent for medical and dental supplies. 1989 revenue: AU$535 million (US$404 million).

MIM Holdings Ltd., MIM Plaza, 410 Ann St., Brisbane, Queensland 4000, Australia. Producer of copper, lead, silver, zinc, coal and gold. 1989 revenue: AU$1.8 billion.

National Consolidated Ltd., 180 Queen St., 3rd Floor, Melbourne, Victoria 3000, Australia. Tel: (03) 670 9562. Metal products, building products, heat-transfer products and printing products. 1988 revenue: AU$450 million (US$359 million).

News Corp. Ltd., News House, 2 Holt St., Sydney, N.S.W. 2010, Australia. Tel: (02) 228-3000. Rupert Murdoch's media empire—newspapers, magazines, films, television and commercial printing. 1989 revenue: AU$7.9 billion (US$6 billion).

TNT Ltd., TNT Plaza, Tower One, Lawson Square, Redfern, N.S.W. 2016, Australia. Tel: (02) 699-9238. Freight, transportation and international trading. 1989 revenue: AU$3.9 billion.

AUSTRIA

The Austria Fund (OST), a closed-end mutual fund traded on the New York Stock Exchange. It invests in a wide range of Austrian stocks.

BELGIUM

Sofina S.A., 38 Rue De Naples, 1050 Brussels, Belgium. Energy, technology, finance, insurance and real estate.

BRAZIL

The Brazil Fund (BZF), a closed-end mutual fund traded on the New York Stock Exchange. It invests in a diverse selection of Brazilian stocks.

CANADA

Cara Operations Ltd., 230 Bloor St. W., Toronto, Ontario M5S 1T8, Canada. Tel: 416-962-4571. Operates in the restaurant, airline catering, hospitality and retail sectors. 1988 revenue: 287 million Canadian dollars (US$232 million).

Imasco, 4 Westmount Square, Montreal, Quebec H3Z 2S8, Canada. Tel: 514-937-9111. Tobacco, banking, restaurants, retail drugs. 1989 revenue: 5.7 billion Canadian dollars (US$4.8 billion).

McMillan Bloedel Ltd., 1075 W. Georgia St., Vancouver, British Columbia V6E 3R9, Canada. Tel: 604-683-6711. Forest products and production. 1988 revenue: 529 million Canadian dollars (US$430 million).

Seagram Company, 1430 Peel St., Montreal, Quebec H3A 1S9, Canada. Tel: 514-849-5271. Producers of wine, spirits and other beverages. 1989 revenue: US$5.1 billion.

George Weston, 22 St. Clair Ave. East, Toronto, Ontario M4T 2S7, Canada. Tel: 416-922-4395. Food production. 1988 revenue: 10.8 billion Canadian dollars (US$8.9 billion).

CHILE

The Chile Fund (CH), a closed-end mutual fund traded on the New York Stock Exchange. It invests in a diverse selection of Chilean stocks.

DENMARK

This northern European country of 5 million people supports several key industries: machinery, textiles, furniture, electronics and dairy. Gross domestic product is about US $120 billion. Industrial production has increased an average of just under 1 percent per year over the past three years. The market value of domestic shares on the Copenhagen Exchange as of January 1, 1989, was US $27 billion.

Denmark's stock market was up 36.4 percent (42.3 percent in U.S. currency) in 1989.

International Service Systems, Kollegievej 6, 2920 Charlottenlund, Denmark. Tel: (451) 63 08 11. Products and services in the building maintenance and building automation business. 1988 revenue: 6.6 billion kroner (US$964 million).

FINLAND

Like Denmark, Finland is a northern European country of about 5 million people. Its chief industries include machinery, shipbuilding, textiles and clothing. Gross domestic product is just over US $100 billion. Industrial production has increased an average of about 3.5 percent per year over the past three years. The market value of domestic shares on the Helsinki Exchange as of January 1, 1990, was US $30.5 billion.

The Finland market was down 13.8 percent (11.2 percent in U.S. currency) in 1989 and down about 12 percent through the first half of 1990.

Pohjola Group, Lapinmaentie 1, 00300 Helsinki, Finland. Tel: 358 0 5591. Diversified insurance company. Consolidated income: 8.2 billion finmarks.

FRANCE

Carrefour SA, 5 Avenue Du Long Rayage, 91005 Lisses, Essonne, France. Tel: 33 1 60869652. Large-scale retailer of groceries, clothing and soft goods. 1988 revenue: 6.5 million francs.

Compagnie Generale D'Electricite SA, 54 Rue La Boetie, 75008 Paris, France. Tel: (1) 40 76 10 10. Telecommunications equipment and services, energy and transportation, electrical contracting. 1988 revenue: 128 billion francs (US$21 billion).

Compagnie Generale Des Eaux, 52 Rue D'Anjou, 75384 Paris Cedex 08, France. Tel: (1) 42669150. Water distribution and related services, building and real estate. 1987 revenue: 53 billion francs (US$10 billion.)

EuroDisneyland, P.O. Box BP100, 94350 Villiers-Surmarn, France. Operates new Disneyland in France.

Pernod Ricard, 142 Boulevard Haussmann, 75008 Paris, France. Tel: (1) 43 59 28 28. Wines, spirits and other beverages and food products. 1988 revenue: 11.6 billion francs (US$1.9 billion).

Thomson SA, Cedex 67, 92045 Paris-La Defense, France. Tel: 33 (1) 49 07 80 00. Consumer electronics, professional electronics for civil and defense applications, semiconductors, financial services. 1988 revenue: 75 billion francs.

GERMANY

Bayerische Motoren Werke (BMW), Postfach 40 02 40, D-8000 Munchen 40, Germany. Manufactures automobiles and motorcycles. 1988 revenue: 24 billion deutsche marks.

Commerzbank, Postfach 10 05 05, 6000 Frankfurt/Main 1, Germany. Tel: (069) 285389. One of Germany's largest banks. 1989 net income: 564 million deutsche marks; deposits: 75 billion deutsche marks.

Daimler-Benz AG, Postfach 60 02 02, D-7000 Stuttgart 60, Germany. Tel: (0711) 1755195. Manufactures passenger cars (43 percent of revenue), commercial vehicles (31 percent), electronics and aerospace (25 percent). 1988 revenue: 73 billion deutsche marks (US$41 billion).

Man Aktiengesellschaft, Postfach 40 13 47, D-8000 Munchen 40, Germany. Commercial trucks and other vehicles and building technology. Fiscal 1989 revenue: 17 billion deutsche marks.

Mannesman AG, Postfach 5501, D-4000 Dusseldorf 1, Germany. Tel: (0211) 8200. Heavy and light engineering, electrical and mechanical components and systems. 1988 revenue: 20 billion deutsche marks (US$11 billion).

Siemens AG, Wittelsbacherplatz 2, D-8000 Munchen 2, Germany. Tel: (089) 2340. Energy installation systems, information systems, telecom and security and medical engineering. 1988 revenue: 59 billion deutsche marks (US$32 billion).

Varta AG, Seedammweg 55 VD Hohe, Hesse, D-6380 Bad Hamburg, Germany. Tel: (49) 511-79031. Starter batteries, portable batteries, industrial batteries and plastics. 1988 revenue: 2 billion deutsche marks (US$1.1 billion).

HONG KONG

Hong Kong Electric Holdings Ltd., Electric House, 44 Kennedy Road, Hong Kong. Tel: (5) 843311. Hong Kong utility; pays excellent dividend. 1988 revenue: HK$3.3 billion (US$423 million).

Hong Kong & Shanghai Hotels Ltd., St. George's Bldg., 11th Floor, Hong Kong. Tel: 5-249391. Operates hotels, apartments, restaurants; develops property. 1988 revenue: HK$1.1 billion (US$146 million).

Hutchison Whampoa Ltd., Hutchison House, 22nd Floor, Hong Kong. Tel: 5-230161. Involved in retailing, property development, finance and shipping. 1988 revenue: HK$13 billion (US$1.6 billion).

Kowloon Motor Bus Co. Ltd., No. 1 Polun St., Lai Chi Kok, Kowloon, Hong Kong. Tel: 786-8888. Transportation and franchised public buses. 1988 revenue: HK$1.8 billion (US$227 million).

New World Development, New World Tower, 30th Floor, 18 Queen's Road Central, Hong Kong. Tel: (852) 523-1056. Construction, property development, hotels, rental property. 1989 revenue: HK$6.1 billion (US$784 million).

Winson Industrial Corp. Ltd., Prince's Bldg., 22nd Floor, Hong Kong. Tel: (5) 228071. Manufactures textiles and apparel. Also involved in property development. 1988 revenue: HK$2.4 billion (US$313 million).

ITALY

Located on the Mediterranean in southern Europe, Italy has a population of 57 million. Its major industries include steel, machinery, autos, textiles, shoes, machine tools and chemicals.

The currency is the Italian lira (ITL 1,229 = US $1, June, 1990). Its GNP was ITL 983 trillion (US$752 billion) in 1988. Italy's inflation rate the past three years has been around 5 percent. Real economic growth the past several years has also averaged about 5 percent per year. The market value of all domestic stocks traded on the Italian Stock Exchange was US $135 billion as of January 1, 1989. The main Italian exchange is in Milan.

In 1989 the Italian stock market was up 13.5 percent in Italian currency (17.3 percent in U.S. currency). Through the first six months of 1990, the Italian market was up about 9 percent.

Investing in Italian stocks has been an extreme hassle, to say the least. In years past it could take as long as six months for transactions to be settled. And while advances have been made the past two or three years, most international investors have found it best to avoid investing in Italian stocks until the exchange system is further modernized.

Italy Fund, Inc., 31 W. 52nd St., New York, NY 10019. Tel: 212-767-3034. The Italy Fund is a closed-end mutual fund that trades on the New York Stock Exchange and invests in a diverse selection of Italian stocks.

JAPAN

Hitachi Ltd., 6 Kanda-Surugadai 4-chome, Chiyoda-ku, Tokyo 101, Japan. Tel: (03) 258-1111. Produces information systems (33 percent of sales), wire and cable products (18 percent), industrial machinery (17 percent), consumer products (17 percent) and power systems (15 percent). 1989 revenue: 6.4 trillion yen (US$48 billion).

Jusco Co. Ltd., 1 1-chome, Kandanishiki-cho, Chiyoda-ku, Tokyo 101, Japan. Tel: (03) 296-7868. One of Japan's leading retail chains. 1989 revenue: 1.2 trillion yen (US$9.6 billion).

Kanegafuchi Chemical Ind. Co. Ltd., 2-4 Nakanoshima 3-chome, Kita-ku, Osaka 530, Japan. Tel: (06) 226-5152. Produces PVC resins and sodas, special resins and resin products (60 percent of sales), synthetic fibers (9 percent). 1988 revenue: 216 billion yen (US$1.7 billion).

Mitsubishi Corp., 2-6-3 Marunouchi, Chiyoda-ku, Tokyo 100-86, Japan. Tel: (03) 210-2121. Metal sales (29 percent of revenue); machinery and information systems (26 percent), fuels (14 percent), foods (14 percent), chemicals (9 percent). Fiscal 1990 revenue: 18.5 trillion yen (US$130 billion).

NEC Corp., 33-1 Shiba 5-chome, Minato-ku, Tokyo 108, Japan. Tel: (03) 454-1111 (International: 81-3-454-1111). Global supplier of communications systems and equipment; computers and electronic systems; electron devices, including semiconductor devices; home electronics products; and information services. 1989 revenue: 3 trillion yen (US$23 billion).

NCR Japan Ltd., 2-2 Akasaka 1-chome, Minato-ku, Tokyo 107, Japan. Tel: (03) 582-6111. Makes computer systems (87 percent of sales) and free-standing business equipment (13 percent). 1988 revenue: 109 billion yen (US$901 million).

Nippon Oil Co. Ltd., 3-12 Nishi Shimbashi 1-chome, Manato-ku, Tokyo 105, Japan. Tel: 502-1111. 1989 revenue: 2.2 trillion yen (US$17 billion).

Orix Corp., World Trade Center Building, 4-1 Hamamatsu-cho, 2-chome, Minato-ku, Tokyo 105, Japan. Tel: (03) 435-6641. Japan's largest leasing group. 1989 revenue: 228 billion yen (US$1.7 billion).

Sony Corp., 7-35 Kitashinagawa 6-chome, Shinagawa-ku, Tokyo 141, Japan. Tel: (03) 448-2111. Manufactures video equipment (27 percent of revenue), audio equipment (26 percent), TVs (16 percent), records (16 percent) and related products (15 percent). 1989 revenue: 2.1 trillion yen (US$16 billion).

Taisho Pharmaceutical Co., 24-1 Takada, 3-chome, P.O. Box 111, Toshima-ku, Tokyo 171, Japan. Tel: (03) 985-1111. Produces over-the-counter drugs and tonics (57 percent), nervous system agents (20 percent), toiletry goods (7 percent). 1988 revenue: 124 billion yen (US$995 million).

Takashimaya Co., 1-5 Namba 5-chome, Chuo-ku, Osaka 542, Japan. Tel: (06) 631-1101. Japan's leading department store chain. 1989 revenue: 600 billion yen (US$4.7 billion).

Toyo Trust & Banking Co. Ltd., 1-4-3 Marunouchi, Chiyoda-ku, Tokyo 100, Japan. Tel: (03) 287-2211. 1989 revenue: 948 billion yen (US$7 billion).

Toyota Motor Corp., 1 Toyotacho, Toyota City, Aichi 471, Japan. Tel: 0565 (28) 2121. 1988 revenue: 7.2 trillion yen (US$54 billion).

Yasuda Fire & Marine Insurance Co., 26-1 Nishi-Shinjuku, 1-chome, Shinjuku-ku, P.O. Box 1280, Tokyo Center, Tokyo 160, Japan. Tel: 03 (349) 3111. 1988 revenue: 723 billion yen (US$5.8 billion).

KOREA

The Korea Fund, 345 Park Ave., New York, NY 10154. Tel: 212-326-6200. The Korea Fund is a closed-end mutual fund that trades on the New York Stock Exchange. It invests in a diverse selection of Korean stocks.

MALAYSIA

Located on the southeast tip of Asia and the north coast of the island of Borneo, Malaysia is a country of 17 million people. Its major industries include rubber goods, steel and electronics.

The currency is the Malaysian ringgit (MYR 2.71 = US $1, June, 1990). Its GNP was MYR 85 billion (US $31 billion) in 1988. Malaysia's inflation rate the past three years has been about 1.5 percent. Real economic growth the past several years has averaged about 5 percent per year. The market value of all domestic stocks traded on the Kuala Lumpur Stock Exchange was US $23 billion as of September 1, 1989.

The Malaysian market is tied closely to the Singapore market, with many stocks cross-listed on both exchanges, although Malaysia has taken steps to pull away from the Singapore market. In 1989 the Malaysian and Singapore markets combined rose 40 percent (in U.S. currency).

Malaysia Fund (MF) is a closed-end mutual fund traded on the New York Stock Exchange. It invests in a diverse selection of Malaysian stocks.

Malaysian International Shipping Corp., 2nd Floor, Wisma Misc. No2, Jalan Conlay, P.O. Box 10371, 50712 Kuala Lumpur, Malaysia. International shipping company. 1988 revenue: 1.5 billion ringgit.

MEXICO

Cifra, Jose Ma. Castorena 470, Delegacion Cuajimalpa 05200, Mexico. Food, clothing and general merchandise retailing. 1989 revenue: 3.1 billion pesos (US$1.2 billion).

The Mexico Fund, One Liberty Plaza, 165 Broadway, New York, New York 10080. Tel: 212-637-9396. A closed-end mutual fund that trades on the New York Stock Exchange. It invests in a diverse selection of Mexican stocks.

THE NETHERLANDS

Akzo NV, Postbus 186, 6800 Ls Arnhem, the Netherlands. Tel: (085) 66 44 33. Produces chemicals, fibers, coatings and health-care products. 1988 revenue: 16.6 billion guilders (US$8.3 billion).

KLM Royal Dutch Airlines, Postbus 7700, 1117 ZL Schiphol Airport, the Netherlands. Tel: (020) 649 9123. Worldwide airline, with destinations in 141 cities in 77 countries. Fiscal 1989 revenue: 6 billion guilders (US$3 billion).

Royal Dutch Petroleum/Shell (KNPM), FNH/1 Division, 30 Carel van Bylandtlaan, 2596 HR The Hague, the Netherlands. Tel: (70) 3774540. (New York address: GSDF Division, Shell Oil Co., 30 Rockefeller Plaza, New York, NY 10112.) Major world producer of petroleum. 1989 revenue: 52 million pounds.

NEW ZEALAND

Carter Holt Harvey Ltd., 640 Great South Road, Manukau City, Auckland, New Zealand. Tel: (09) 278-0999. Produces wood and paper, building products and foods. 1989 revenue: NZ$14 billion (US$874 million).

NORWAY

Located in the western section of the Scandinavian Peninsula, Norway is a country of 4.2 million people. Its major industries include engineering, metals, chemicals, food processing, fishing, paper, shipbuilding and oil and gas.

The currency is the Norwegian krone (NOK 6.45 = US $1, June, 1990). Norway's GNP was NOK 576 billion (US $81 billion) in 1988. Its inflation rate the past three years has been around 7 percent. Real economic growth the past several years has averaged about 2 percent per year. The market value of all domestic stocks traded on the Oslo Exchange was US $15.8 billion as of January 1, 1989.

In 1989 the Norwegian stock market was among the fastest growing in the world, up 44 percent. It was still moving up well in 1990, up 22 percent through the first five months.

Hafslund Nycomed AS, P.O. Box 5010 Majorstua, Slemdalsveien 37, Oslo 3, N-0301, Norway. Tel: 472 463830. Produces imaging diagnostic equipment, pharmaceuticals, specialty metal products and a diversified range of other products. 1988 revenue: 2.6 billion kroner (US$400 million).

PHILIPPINES

First Philippine Fund (FPF), a closed-end mutual fund that invests in a diverse selection of Philippine stocks. It's traded on the New York Stock Exchange.

Philippine Long Distance Telephone Co., P.O. Box 952, Makati, Metro Manila, Philippines. The largest telephone service in the Philippines. 1989 revenue: 9.5 billion pesos.

San Miguel Corp., 40 San Miguel Ave., Mandaluyong, Metro Manila, Philippines. Tel: 722-3000. Generates 2.5 percent of the country's gross national product. Produces beer, beverages, foods, packaging and other agricultural-related products. 1988 revenue: 21 billion pesos.

SINGAPORE

Asia Pacific Breweries Ltd., 475 River Valley Road, Singapore 1024. Tel: 4730222. Produces beer and other alcoholic beverages, soft drinks and dairy products. 1989 revenue: 663 million Singapore dollars (US$338 million).

DBSLand, 68 Orchard Road, Plaza Singapura, Singapore 0923. Tel: 3363300. Land and property development. 1989 revenue: 157 million Singapore dollars (US$80 million).

Singapore Press Holdings, News Centre, 82 Genting Lane, Singapore 1334. Involved in advertising and publishing. 1989 revenue: 459 million Singapore dollars (US$250 million).

SPAIN

Banco Central, S.A., Alcala 49, Apartado 339, Madrid 14, Spain. Large Spanish bank. 1987 revenue: 416 billion pesetas (US$3.9 billion).

Telephonica de Espana, Gran Via 28, Madrid 28013, Spain. Tel: 231-76-34. Spanish telephone company. 1989 revenue: 710 billion pesetas (US$6.5 billion).

SWEDEN

Ericsson, (L.M.) Telefon AB, Telefonplan S-126 25 Stockholm, Sweden. Tel: 46 8-7-19 00 00. Telephone, radio and business communications (70 percent of revenue); engineering (9 percent); cables (9 percent). 1988 revenue: 31 billion kronor (US$5.1 billion).

Saab-Scania AB, S-581 88 Linkoping, Sweden. Tel: 4613 180000. Manufacturer of trucks and buses (49 percent of revenue), autos (38 percent), aircraft (9 percent) and industrial equipment and defense systems (4 percent). 1988 revenue: 42 billion kronor (US$7 billion).

SWITZERLAND

Located in the Alps of Europe, Switzerland, population 6.5 million, has long been a major center of international trade. The Zurich Stock Exchange is one of the largest in the world in terms of volume.

Switzerland's major industries include machinery, machine tools, steel, instruments, watches, textiles, foodstuffs, chemicals, drugs, banking and tourism.

The currency is the Swiss franc (CHF 1.41 = US $1, June, 1990). Its gross domestic product was CHF 270 billion (US $160 billion) in 1988. Its inflation rate the past three years has been about 1.5 percent. Real economic growth the past several years has averaged about 3 percent per year. The market value of all domestic stocks traded on the Zurich Exchange was US $140 billion as of January 1, 1989.

In 1989 the Swiss market was up 27.6 percent in local currency, 24.5 percent in U.S. currency. Through the first six months of 1990, it was up about 1 percent.

Foreign investors face many restrictions in attempting to buy Swiss stocks, although some stocks are open to foreign investors.

Brown, Boveri & Co., P.O. Box 58, Ch-5401 Baden, Switzerland. Tel: (056) 751111. Involved in electrical power supply and installation. 1988 revenue: 25 billion Swiss francs (US$17 billion).

Nestle SA, Avenue Nestle, Ch-1800 Cham & Vevey, Switzerland. Tel: 021 510112. Worldwide food and beverage production. 1988 revenue: 41 billion Swiss francs (US$27 billion).

Societe Generale De Surveillance, 8 Rue Des Alpes, Case Postal 898, Ch-1211 Geneve 1, Switzerland. Tel: (022) 39 94 989. Testing and valuation services for consumer and industrial products. 1988 revenue: 1.7 billion Swiss francs (US$1.1 billion).

TAIWAN

Taiwan Fund, Inc., 82 Devonshire St., Boston, MA 02109. Tel: 800-334-9393. The Taiwan Fund is a closed-end mutual fund traded on the New York Stock Exchange. It invests in a diverse selection of Taiwanese stocks.

UNITED KINGDOM

Allied-Lyons PLC, Allied House, 156 St. John St., London EC1P 1AR, U.K. Tel: 01 253-9911. Beer and retailing, wines, spirits and foods. 1989 revenue: 4.5 billion pounds (US$7.9 billion).

BAT PLC, Windsor House, 50 Victoria St., London SW1H ONL, U.K. Insurance, tobacco, retailing. 1988 revenue: 17.7 billion pounds.

BET PLC, Stratton House, Piccadilly, London W1X 6AS, U.K. Tel: 01 629 8886. International supplier of support services to the industrial, commercial and public sectors. 1989 revenue: 2.15 billion pounds (US$3.6 billion).

BPB Industries PLC, Langley Park House, Uxbridge Road, Sough SL3 6DU, U.K. Tel: (0753) 73273. Building materials (83 percent of revenue), paper and packaging (17 percent). 1989 revenue: 961 million pounds (US$1.6 billion).

BSG International, Burgess House, 1270 Coventry Road, Yardley, Birmingham B25 8BB, U.K. Tel: (021) 706-6155. Vehicle distributor and automotive business. 1988 revenue: 559 million pounds (US$1 billion).

William Baird, George House, 50 George Square, Glasgow G2 IRR, U.K. Tel: 01 409-1785. Textiles producer. 1988 revenue: 371 million pounds (US$671 million).

Bass PLC, 66 Chiltern St., London W1M 1LPR, U.K. Tel: 01-486-4440. Beer, hotels, restaurants. 1989 revenue: 4 billion pounds.

Bunzl PLC, Stoke House, Stoke Green, Stoke Poges, Slough SL2 2 4 JN, U.K. Tel: 0753 693693. Paper and plastics, industrial products, filters. 1988 revenue: 1.7 billion pounds (US$3.2 billion).

Cable & Wireless PLC, Mercury House, Theobalds Road, London WC1X 8RX, U.K. Tel: 01 242-4433. Telecommunication services, including telephone, telex, facsimile and data transmission. 1988 revenue: 932 million pounds (US$1.8 billion).

Dalgety PLC, 19 Hanover Square, London W1R 9DA, U.K. Tel: 01-499 7712. Food production. 1989 revenue: 4.8 billion pounds.

Delta PLC, 1 Kingsway, London WC2B 6XF, U.K. Tel: 01 836 3535. Electrical equipment, engineering, industrial services. 1988 revenue: 656 million pounds (US$1.2 billion).

Dowty Group PLC, Arle Court, Cheltenham, Gloucestershire GL51 OTP, England. Tel: (0242) 221133. Electronics and aerospace technology. 1989 revenue: 684 million pounds.

English China Clays PLC, John Keay House, St. Austell, Cornwall PL25-4DJ, U.K. Tel: (0726) 74482. China clays, ball clays, quarry materials, housing, drilling muds. 1988 revenue: 937 million pounds (US$1.6 billion).

Granada Group PLC, 36 Golden Square, London W1R 4AH, U.K. Tel: 01 734-8080. Rental and retail, television, leisure and business services. 1988 revenue: 1.5 billion pounds (US$2.5 billion).

Grand Metropolitan PLC, 11-12 Hanover Square, London W1A 1DP, U.K. Tel: 01 629-7448. Wines, spirits and beer, food, retailing, hotels; owns Pillsbury Foods. 1988 revenue: 6 billion pounds (US$10 billion).

Guiness PLC, 39 Portman Square, London W1H 9HB, U.K. Tel: 01 486 0288. Brewery and distillers. 1988 revenue: 2.7 billion pounds.

Imperial Chemical Industries, Imperial Chemical House, Millbank, London SW1P 3JF, U.K. Tel: 01 834 4444. Consumer and specialty chemicals, industrial products, agricultural products. 1988 revenue: 12 billion pounds (US$21 billion).

Laporte PLC, 3 Bedford Square, London WC1B 3RA, U.K. Tel: 01 629-6603. Peroxygen products, inorganic and organic specialties, building and timber products. 1988 revenue: 357 million pounds (US$647 million).

Lonrho PLC, Cheapside House, 138 Cheapside, London EC2V 6BL, U.K. Tel: 01-606-9898. Motor equipment, leisure, mineral refining, agriculture and other products. 1988 revenue: 3.3 billion pounds (US$5.5 billion).

Marks & Spencer, Michael House, 37-67 Baker Street, London W1A 1DN, U.K. Tel: 01-935-4422. Sells clothing, household goods and foods under the St. Michael label in the U.K., France, Belgium and Ireland. 1988 revenue: 4.6 billion pounds (US$8.6 billion).

Morgan Crucible Co., Chariott House, 6-12 Victoria St., Windsor, Berkshire SL 4 1 EP, U.K. Tel: 075 355 0331. Thermal ceramics, carbon, technical ceramics, specialty chemicals, electronics. 1988 revenue: 454 million pounds (US$821 million).

Pearson PLC, Millbank Tower, 16th Floor, Millbank, London SW1P 4QZ, U.K. Tel: 01-828 9020. Information services and publishing *(Financial Times),* entertainment, fine china, oil and oil services. 1988 revenue: 1.2 billion pounds (US$2.2 billion).

RMC House, Coldharbour Lane, Thorpe, Egham Surrey TW20 8TD, U.K. Construction material, concrete. 1988 revenue: 2.1 billion pounds.

Scapa Group, Oakfield House, 52 Preston New Road, Blackurn, Lancashire BB2 6AH, U.K. Tel: 0254 580123. Industrial textiles, stainless steel wire and cloth, industrial tapes, cable insulation and polystyrene packaging. 1988 revenue: 242 million pounds (US$457 million).

Smith Industries, 765 Finchley Road, London NW11 8DS, U.K. Tel: 01 458 3232. Aerospace, defense, medical systems and other diversified operations. 1988 revenue: 666 million pounds (US$1.1 billion).

Smith & Nephew, 2 Temple Place, London WC2R 3BP, U.K. Tel: 01 836-7922. Health care, consumer and medical products, textiles, plastics. 1988 revenue: 597 million pounds (US$1.1 billion).

Wagon Industrial, Haldane House, Halesfield, Telford Shropshire TF7 4PB, U.K. Tel: (0952) 680111. Material handling, storage, office equipment, engineering and automotive products. 1989 revenue: 197 million pounds.

Ward Shite Group, Hargrave Hall, Hargrave, Wellingborough, Northamptonshire NN9 6BU, U.K. Tel: 0933 624151. Retail auto parts and accessories. Fiscal 1989 revenue: 734 million pounds.

Williams Holdings, Pentagon House, Sir Frank Whittle Road, Derby DE2 4EE, U.K. Tel: (0332) 364257. Paints, consumer building products, vehicle distribution. 1988 revenue: 826 million pounds (US$1.5 billion).

UNITED STATES

Banc One Corp., 100 E. Broad St., Columbus, OH 43271. Tel: 614-248-5944. Midwestern banking organization, with branches in Ohio, Indiana, Michigan, Wisconsin and Kentucky. 1989 revenue: $3.2 billion.

Carter-Wallace, Inc., 767 Fifth Ave., New York, NY 10153. Tel: 212-758-4500. Produces health care products—both prescription and over-the-counter. 1989 revenue: $515 million.

Chemical Waste Management, Inc., 3001 Butterfield Road, Oak Brook, IL 60521. Tel: 708-572-8800. Specializes in treating hazardous wastes. 1989 revenue: $891 million.

Compaq Computer Corp., 20555 FM 149, Houston, TX 77070. Tel: 713-370-0670. Manufactures portable and desktop computers. 1989 revenue: $2.9 billion.

Food Lion, Inc., P.O. Box 1330, Salisbury, NC 28145. Tel: 704-633-8250. Grocery store chain in the Southeast. 1989 revenue: $4.7 billion.

Giant Food, Inc., P.O. Box 1804, Washington, DC 20013. Tel: 301-341-4100. Operates a chain of 150 supermarkets in the Washington area. 1989 revenue: $3 billion.

H.J. Heinz Co., P.O. Box 57, Pittsburgh, PA 15230. Tel: 412-456-5700. Produces ketchup, tuna, pet foods and other food products. 1989 revenue: $5.8 billion.

International Dairy Queen, 5701 Green Valley Drive, Minneapolis, MN 55437. Tel: 612-830-0200. Services a network of more than 5,000 franchised Dairy Queen stores in the United States, Canada and several foreign mar-

Walgreen Co., 200 Wilmot Road, Deerfield, IL 60015. Tel: 708-940-2500. Operates the largest drugstore chain in the United States, with 1,500 stores. 1989 revenue: $5.4 billion.

kets. Also operating under its umbrella is a network of more than 650 Orange Julius franchises, 160 Karmelkorn Shoppes and 70 Golden Skillet restaurants. 1989 revenue: $255 million.

Kellogg Company, Battle Creek, MI 49016. Tel: 616-961-2000. Major producer of breakfast cereals and other food products. 1989 revenue: $4.7 billion.

Eli Lilly and Co., Lilly Corporate Center, Indianapolis, IN 46285. Tel: 317-276-3219. Develops and produces a wide range of pharmaceuticals, medical instruments, diagnostic products and animal health products. 1989 revenue: $4.2 billion.

The Limited, Inc., 2 Limited Parkway, P.O. Box 16000, Columbus, OH 43216. Tel: 614-479-7000. Operates 3,200 apparel stores throughout the United States. 1989 revenue: $4.6 billion.

Loews Corp., 667 Madison Ave., New York, NY 10021. Tel: 212-545-2000. Major producer of cigarettes, including Kent and Newport. Also owns Bulova watches and a 25 percent share of CBS-TV. 1989 revenue: $11.4 billion.

Medtronic, Inc., 7000 Central Ave., NE, Minneapolis, MN 55432. Tel: 612-547-4000. The world's leading heart pacemaker manufacturer. It also produces a wide range of other heart-related medical products. 1989 revenue: $837 million.

National Medical Enterprises, 2700 Colorado Ave., P.O. Box 4070, Santa Monica, CA 90404. Tel: 213-479-5526. Owns 500 medical care facilities, including hospitals, rehabilitation centers, drug treatment centers and long-term care facilities. 1989 revenue: $3.7 billion.

Oracle Corp., 20 Davis Dr., Belmont, CA 94002. Tel: 415-598-8000. Produces a variety of computer software products. 1989 revenue: $584 million.

Quaker Oats Co., P.O. Box 9001, Chicago, IL 60604. Tel: 312-222-7111. Produces a variety of foods for distribution worldwide. 1989 revenue: $5.7 billion.

Safety-Kleen Corp., 777 Big Timber Road, Elgin, IL 60123. Tel: 815-697-8460. Cleans auto parts and recycles cleaning solutions and similar types of hazardous waste fluids. 1989 revenue: $478 million.

Sherwin-Williams Co., 101 Prospect Ave., NW, Cleveland, OH 44115. Tel: 216-566-2000. Manufactures paints and finishes and operates 1,900 paint and wall covering stores in 48 states. 1989 revenue: $2.1 billion.

Tyson Foods, Inc., 2210 W. Oaklawn Dr., Springdale, AR 72764. Tel: 501-756-4000. World's largest producer of poultry-based food products. 1989 revenue: $2.5 billion.

UST, 100 W. Putnam Ave., Greenwich, CT 06830. Tel: 203-661-1100. World's leading producer of smokeless (chewing) tobacco. 1989 revenue: $682 million.

VF Corp., 1047 North Park Road, Wyomissing, PA 19610. Tel: 215-378-1151. Manufacturer of clothing, including Lee, Wrangler and Rustler jeans and Jantzen sportswear. 1989 revenue: $2.5 billion.

THE 100 BEST BY INDUSTRY GROUP

Alcoholic Beverages

LVMH Moët Hennessy (France)
Anheuser-Busch (U.S.)

Automotive

Volvo (Sweden)

Building Materials

Lafarge Coppée (France)
Glynwed International (U.K.)
Ibstock Johnsen (U.K.)
Redland (U.K.)
Steetley (U.K.)
Wolseley (U.K.)

Chemicals, Coatings, Plastics and Rubber

BTR Nylex (Australia)
Pacific Dunlop (Australia)
BASF (Germany)
Bayer (Germany)
Continental (Germany)
RPM (U.S.)

Construction and Development

Boral (Australia)
Lend Lease (Australia)
Hang Lung Development (Hong Kong)
Daiwa House Industry (Japan)
National House Industrial (Japan)
Higgs and Hill (U.K.)
Tarmac (U.K.)

Consumer Products

Unilever (The Netherlands)
Reckitt & Colman (U.K.)

Corporate Services

Kelly Services (U.S.)

Cosmetics

L'Oréal (France)

Diversified Industrial

Adelaide Steamship (Australia)

Electronics

Email (Australia)
LeGrand (France)
Merlin Gerin (France)
Nintendo (Japan)

Entertainment and Accommodations

Accor (France)
Carlton Communications (U.K.)
Ladbroke Group (U.K.)
Walt Disney (U.S.)

Financial and Insurance

Dai-Ichi Kangyo Bank (Japan)
Kyowa Bank (Japan)
Nomura Securities (Japan)
Sumitomo Bank (Japan)
Banco Popular Español (Spain)
Torchmark (U.S.)

Food and Beverage Production

BSN (France)
Irvin & Johnson (South Africa)
Booker (U.K.)
Polly Peck (U.K.)
Ranks Hovis McDougall (U.K.)
ConAgra (U.S.)
Sara Lee (U.S.)
Wrigley (U.S.)

Food and Drug Retail

Coles Myer (Australia)
Delhaize "Le Lion" (Belgium)
Oshawa (Canada)
Seven-Eleven Japan (Japan)
Sainsbury (U.K.)
Tesco (U.K.)
Albertson's (U.S.)
McDonald's (U.S.)

Gas and Oil

L'Air Liquide (France)

Health and Medical

Hoescht (Germany)
Ono Pharmaceutical (Japan)
Yamanouchi Pharmaceutical (Japan)
Astra (Sweden)
AAH Holdings (U.K.)
Glaxo Holdings (U.K.)
Abbott Laboratories (U.S.)
Merck (U.S.)

Household and Commercial Furnishings

Toto (Japan)
Hunter Douglas (The Netherlands)
Newell (U.S.)
Rubbermaid (U.S.)
Shaw Industries (U.S.)

Industrial Equipment

Linde (Germany)
Atlas Copco (Sweden)

Metals and Mining

Metallgesellschaft (Germany)
Mitsui (Japan)
Trelleborg (Sweden)
IMI (U.K.)

Paper Products and Packaging

Arjomari (France)
CMB Packaging (France)
Toyo Seikan Kaisha (Japan)
Bührmann-Tetterode (The Netherlands)
KNP (The Netherlands)
Fletcher Challenge (New Zealand)

Publishing

Elsevier (The Netherlands)
VNU (The Netherlands)
Reuters (U.K.)

Retail

Ito-Yokado (Japan)
Wal-Mart Stores (U.S.)

Tobacco

Rothmans Holdings (Australia)
Philip Morris (U.S.)

Trading (Marketing and Merchandising)

Jardine Matheson (Hong Kong)

Transportation and Shipping

Brambles Industries (Australia)
Mayne Nickless (Australia)
Swire Pacific (Hong Kong)
Singapore Airlines (Singapore)

Utilities

China Light & Power (Hong Kong)
Hong Kong & China Gas (Hong Kong)

Waste Handling

Laidlaw (Canada)
Browning-Ferris (U.S.)
Waste Management (U.S.)

INDEX